Light on Sant Mat

MAHARAJ CHARAN SINGH

Light
on
Sant Mat

MAHARAJ CHARAN SINGH

RADHA SOAMI SATSANG BEAS
PUNJAB, INDIA

Published by
S. L. Sondhi, Secretary
Radha Soami Satsang Beas
P.O. Dera Baba Jaimal Singh
Distt. Amritsar 143204
Punjab, India

First edition	1958	1,000 copies
Second edition	1960	1,000 copies
(revised and enlarged with index and glossary)		
Third edition	1964	3,000 copies
Fourth edition	1971	3,000 copies
Fifth edition	1974	3,000 copies
Sixth edition	1977	5,000 copies
Seventh edition	1985	7,000 copies
(with new index and glossary)		

Photocomposed by Taj Services Ltd., Noida, U.P.
Printed by Indraprastha Press (CBT), Nehru House, 4 Bahadur Shah Zafar Marg, New Delhi–110002

CONTENTS

PART TWO
Excerpts from letters in reply
to seekers and disciples, 1952–1958   107

PREFACE

Light on Sant Mat, as its name would imply, deals with the basic concept of the Radha Soami faith, popularly known as Sant Mat, and its various aspects. The teachings are presented in the form of discourses by Maharaj Charan Singh Ji, the present Satguru at Beas, and by means of letters addressed by him to different persons. With his kind permission, these discourses and letters have now been compiled for the benefit of seekers and satsangis. The book is divided into two parts:

Part One contains a condensed translation into English of discourses (*satsangs*) delivered by Maharaj Ji in Punjabi. The original *shabds,* or hymns, of the respective Saints, have also been rendered into English verse for the benefit of the readers.

Professors Jagmohan Lal and Janak Raj Puri, and Diwan Daryai Lal, retired judge, have taken great pains in collecting these discourses and putting them into their present form and language. The Society is highly indebted to these satsangi brothers for their labor of love.

Part Two contains excerpts of letters concerning Sant Mat, written by Maharaj Charan Singh Ji in reply to satsangis and seekers from abroad. The selection was made by Maharaj Ji himself; personal matters discussed in some of these letters have been deleted by him, as he took care to ensure that only subject matter dealing with Sant Mat, and of interest to all readers, should appear in these letters.

Miss Louise Hilger, a satsangi from the United States of America, is solely responsible for typing and compiling the manuscript and giving it the shape of a book—a laborious task, but carried out willingly during her periodical visit to the Colony last winter. We are grateful to her for giving the book its present shape.

It is hoped that *Light on Sant Mat* will be read with interest and profit by persons interested in spiritual science, including seekers and satsangi brothers and sisters in India and abroad.

R. D. Ahluwalia
Secretary

Radha Soami Satsang Beas
1958

PART ONE

DISCOURSES
ON THE TEACHINGS
OF THE SAINTS

The following discourses have been taken from
Maharaj Charan Singh's Punjabi satsangs,
abbreviated and freely translated into English.

1

TEACHINGS OF THE SAINTS

WHAT IS SANT MAT or the teachings of the Saints? What is the Saints' mission in this world?

Saints are men of God who come here on a mission of mercy, to lead suffering humanity back to the feet of God. That is their only mission in life. They come not to divide but to unite, and are above the narrow distinctions of caste, color, nationality and creed. They do not wish to create new sects or castes; though, when they pass away, their followers lose sight of their real teachings, and take to various types of ritualism and narrow down the teachings—meant for all humanity—to particular sects and schools. This gives rise to castes and creeds, and even to bigotry and fanaticism; but there are no such differences in Saints.

Saints of all ages and countries have the same message to give, the same Truth to teach. They tell us that the soul is a spark of the Divine Flame, but its light here has been dimmed by mind and maya. They teach us how to pierce these veils and get united again with our Source or Origin.

People give God different names, according to their liking, but He who is known by all these is One without a second. They call Him 'Ram', 'Allah', 'Vah Guru', 'Radha Soami' or 'God', but He is one and the same. He is the one God of us all. There are no differences or limitations of caste, creed, color or country for Him. He is eternal and for all times and ages. He alone is eternal, permanent; all else is mortal, transient. In the beginning—before time—He alone was and created the whole universe out of *Nam*, which is also called the Word, Logos or *Shabd*. Man is the epitome of the universe and is also the real temple of God, where He can be realized. It is for teaching this technique that Saints come into the world.

The soul, in its descent into the physical body, had to be associated with the mind; but it was not intended that it should be dominated by the mind. The mind and soul are, as it were, coupled together and, wherever the mind goes, the soul has to go also. The mind receives and retains most of the impressions of the world. These impressions cause desires and hankerings, all of which cannot be fulfilled. Thus starts an unending chain of reactions which keeps it entangled in this or other forms of creation, according to its desires and tendencies.

The soul has been caught for ages in this world of births and deaths. The eighty-four *lakhs*[1] of species of creation are virtually the prison cells of the soul, with one exception, and that is the human body. Liberation from that huge prison can be achieved only in the human form, with the help of a Saint or *Satguru*, if we have the good luck to meet one and follow his instructions implicitly. Hence the importance of the human life. It is not without reason that the human body has been called *nar-narayani deh*, 'the human body divine', and man himself is believed to be the top of creation.

Since the soul and the mind are knotted together, as it were, the soul has perforce to follow the mind and lend its support and, as a result, has to be born again and again to suffer the consequences of karmas—the longings of the mind. To escape these dire consequences, the mind must be prevented from going out and running about after plea-

1. 8,400,000.

sures. It should be withdrawn gradually and kept more steady at its center, known as tisra til or the third eye, so that it may contact the Shabd, the Audible Life Stream, and rise above the world of phenomena. That is the only way to get permanent release from this prisonhouse. Saints and Mystics have compared the human body to a house with ten doors. The nine openings—organs—lead us outward and involve us in the world. The tenth leads us within, to our True Home, and brings our wanderings to an end. The secret of this door is known only to Saints and Mystics, though it has been referred to in the sacred books of almost every religion.

The pleasures of the world are not only transient but turn into bitterness and disappointment in course of time. No situation here is free from pain and grief. Disease, poverty, disharmony in the family, national jealousies and wars, are the lot of man here and make him miserable and wretched.

We are kept bound to this world by our karmas, both good and bad, as to a grindstone. The karmas that we perform lead to other karmas which fetter our life and conditions, our existence—now as well as in subsequent births. Saints, therefore, exhort us to turn within, knock at this tenth door and attach ourselves to Shabd, where alone we can find permanent peace and unalloyed happiness. But our desires and attachments stand in our way. Our egoism and desire for possession make us return to this world again and again. Egoism makes us claim and appropriate everything including our bodies, to such an extent that they occupy our minds even at the time of death. The result is that instead of possessing those things which we want to own, according to the well-known rule we are born again in the surroundings which so fascinated us.

The Saints take us out of this predicament by teaching us *Nam bhakti*, 'devotion to Nam, Word or Shabd', thus turning inward—and Godward—the tides which are now flowing outward. It is the nature of the mind to run after pleasure, but no pleasure in the world has the power to captivate it forever, so it flits from one object to another. When, however, it takes to Nam bhakti and, 'going in', tastes the bliss of Shabd, its fickleness is gone and it becomes steady. Guru bhakti and Nam bhakti are the means by which the mind is weaned from sensual pleasures and is attached to the Shabd, the Audible Life Stream, which ultimately takes us back to our origin—God.

Nam is of two kinds: *varnatmak* and *dhunatmak*. Any name that can be uttered by word of mouth, or that can be written, is varnatmak. Names of God like Ram, Hari, Vah Guru, Allah, and other names current in other languages and in other countries, are all varnatmak. They lead to the real dhunatmak Nam, the glories of which have been sung by Saints and Sages of all times. It is this Nam which created the universe and to which Christ refers as the Word which was with God and which was God. It is God still and, under appropriate conditions and correct guidance, can be contacted within ourselves.

Varnatmak nam is the means. Dhunatmak Nam is the end. There are many varnatmak names, but the dhunatmak Nam is one and the same for all ages and climes. It is the same for all religions—Hindu, Muslim, Christian, Jew, or any other. Huzur Maharaj Ji[1] used to refer to it as "the Unspoken Language" or "the Unwritten Word." Devotion to varnatmak names keeps our attention concentrated at the center between the two eyes, whence our inward and upward spiritual journey begins. People

1. The Master refers here to his own Master, Maharaj Sawan Singh.

forget this distinction and mistake the varnatmak nam for the dhunatmak Nam—the means for the end. Dhunatmak Nam transcends time and space; yet it has a local habitat within us, and it is there that it can be contacted. Devotion to varnatmak nam alone, to the exclusion of dhunatmak Nam, can lead to bigotry or fanaticism; whereas devotion to dhunatmak Nam makes us rise above castes and creeds, wars and strife, for then we see the Divine in all.

How is this dhunatmak Nam to be found? As said before, it is within us and resounds in the part of the body above the eyes. There it resounds in all of us, Saints and sinners. The first thing is to draw our consciousness up to the center between the two eyes, the seat of the mind and the soul. When our attention currents are concentrated here, we are ready to be connected to Nam by the Saints. Varnatmak nam is of use in the physical world. Saints teach us to draw up our mental currents with the help of varnatmak nam, and then connect us with the universal dhunatmak Nam.

Only Saints can teach us this secret. It cannot be learned from books or scriptures, however sacred, for it is a practical problem. Saints are themselves Shabd incarnate, an embodiment of Nam. The have been called incarnations of God. They are related to God as the sea is to its waves. Like waves, they emerge from that Divine Sea and, after doing their allotted work, go back and merge into the Sea. They alone can lead us on the true path and make reunion possible.

Once started on the path, we go on at our own pace according to our zeal for God-realization and the debts of karma which we still have to discharge. We are helped by being in the company of Saints and by attending their *satsangs*, or discourses; but we are not required to renounce

home or family. On the contrary, we are required to live
in the world and discharge our duties, but in an unattached spirit, with the idea of doing our duty and without caring for the result, leaving it to the Master. The
highest among men, like Kabir Sahib, Guru Nanak
Sahib, Raidas Ji and others, earned their own living.

We should live unsullied in the world, as the duck
lives in water and yet remains dry. This again is made
possible by Shabd practice. *Gurmukhs* and *manmukhs*
both live in this world and both are God's creatures; but
manmukhs are fond of the creation while the hearts of
Gurmukhs are set upon the Creator himself. As a married woman, staying in the house of her parents, has her
mind on her loving husband even while attending to all
duties in the parental home, similarly Gurmukhs, though
living in the world, keep the memory of the Lord every
moment in their heart.

How and where to find such Saints? This is in the
hands of the Lord, and with His grace and one's great
good fortune only can one come across such Saints.
When we do come across such a one, we should get the
secret of Nam from him, give him all our love and devotion, and implicitly follow his directions. First comes the
grace of God, then the company of Saints and then the
acquisition of the secret of Nam. Then, by constant application and unceasing devotion, comes the actual realization of Nam. That is the order.

The satsang of Saints is very helpful. It cleans the rust
off the soul and the mind, and changes the trend of the
mind. People give up bad habits and cultivate devotion,
in satsang. But it should be true satsang, that is, a dis-
sertation upon Truth, the way of achieving it, and instruction on how to combat the evil tendencies of the mind
which is the real obstacle between man and God—and

not mere interesting anecdotes and stories. Nor should we neglect our energy or our own mind. True, it is mind that stands between us and God, but mind can also be trained to be a good and useful servant. This is what the Saints aim at.

Another very great factor is our karma, which molds our mind too. Saints advise us to be careful; to avoid creating new karmas, by following the principle of non-violence and devoting as much time as possible to Shabd practice so that the slate may be cleaned and remain clean. The *pralabdh* or fate karmas are, however, irrevocable and should be gone through in a resigned spirit, as the will of God. The *sinchit* karmas—the store or leftover karmas from numerous previous births—are destroyed by Guru bhakti and Nam bhakti. Thus do the Saints remove all binding influences and, making us free from karma, take us to Sat Desh, the region beyond mind and maya, where love alone reigns supreme.

* * *

2

HARKEN, SURAT!

Surat sun bat ri tera dhani base akash
by Swami Ji

Harken, surat![1]
Your Lord dwells in heaven.
Discard the company of the mind
And behold His resplendent glory.
Follow the commands of the Master
And reach the immortal Abode.
Take refuge in Him[2]
And dwell in the mansion of Nam.
Body, the design of Kal,[3]
Is a cage for the soul.
Why pin your hopes on it?
The noose of sensual pleasures
Is around your neck.
Tied to the nine apertures,
You know no peace nor rest.
Open the tenth door
And enjoy the bliss.
So says the perfect Master,
Put faith in his words.
Practice Radha Soami Nam[4]
And destroy all karmas.

Sar Bachan Poetry, p.145, 19:6

---

1. Soul.
2. The Master.
3. The negative power.
4. Listening to the Sound.

This satsang is based on a poem by Swami Ji, which might be called an exhortation to the soul.

The soul is the essence of God, and the relationship between God and soul is one of love. Some compare it to the love between father and son, and call Him 'the Divine Father'. Others, like Shri Ramakrishna, compare it to the love between mother and child, and conceive of the Deity as the divine and universal Mother. Guru Nanak Sahib, Kabir Sahib, Swami Ji and others compare it to the love that exists between the lover and the beloved. The one thing common to all these relationships is the bond of love between soul and God; though, owing to the evil of maya, or illusion, and our attachment to the pleasures of the senses, we have forgotten what our relationship with God is.

The soul, in the course of its descent to *pind*, the physical body and the material plane, came to be associated with the mind and acquired a downward and outward trend. The pleasure-loving nature of the mind and its dependence on senses accentuated these tendencies to such an extent that the soul has forgotten its Divine Home, its Divine Origin, and is quite caught up in the net of desires and hankerings after the world of phenomena.

Thus entangled with the mind, it has to be born again and again in one or another of the eighty-four lakhs of species in this world, to work out its karma. In doing so, however, it acquires fresh karmas and fresh associations. The bonds thus get tighter and tighter, and the load of karmas becomes heavier and heavier with each birth. The soul has lost its way and does not know how to get out of this vast prison of eighty-four lakhs of species.

Seeing our plight and moved by our sufferings, Saints come to this mortal world on a mission of mercy, to show the way out and to help those who accept their lead. They reawaken the bond of love between the soul and its Creator, and pave the way for the happy reunion.

Where is this Lord of the soul, and how can we find Him? He is within us. Of course, He is everywhere and pervades every particle of the universe; but we can realize this only when we have first realized Him within ourselves. It is within that we must seek Him. The body is the temple of God, and it is in this shrine that we must worship, and not run to forests or hills.

Again, if we are to carry out spiritual research, the human body is the laboratory wherein we must work and make spiritual discoveries. Neither in scriptures, churches, mosques or temples, nor in forests, mountains or pilgrimages, but in this *nar-narayani deh*, 'the human body divine', can He be found. All faiths are agreed upon this point. Bulleh Shah says, "God is very near *shah rug*."[1] Hindus look upon the body as the abode of the Deity and all other gods and goddesses. Guru Nanak refers to this body as *Har Mandir*, 'the temple of God', and boldly declares that those who seek God outside, simply waste their time and energy. Christ likewise proclaimed that we are the temple of the living God, and that the kingdom of heaven is within us. The Jews also look upon the body as the tabernacle of God.

If we are to escape the wheel of birth and death, and get out of this prisonhouse, we can do it only while in human form. This form is the topmost rung of the ladder of life. If we slip down, we may again have to go through the maze of eighty-four lakhs, and who knows when we may be born again as human beings?

One may reasonably ask: "If the Lord is within us, why can't we see Him? Why do we suffer?" Mind is the

---

1. Literally, 'royal vein'; refers to the central current beyond the ey center, which is located and traversed by spiritual practice.

obstacle which screens God from our view and does not let us behold His glory. Mind and soul go together in this world of phenomena. The soul has perforce to lend its support to the activities of the mind and is dragged down along with it. Real spiritual progress is possible only when the connection between the two is severed. The soul is then ready to fly to its Original Home and unite with the Divine Source. It is in order to learn this technique that we go to Saints and Masters. They give us practical instructions to free the soul from the domination of the mind and lead us on the way, rendering help and support wherever we are likely to stumble.

We contact the outside world through the mind and the senses, but the tragedy is that the mind itself has been enslaved by the senses and has thus acquired a downward tendency. By nature fond of pleasure, it flits from one object to another. Yet no object in the world can hold it forever, or even for any length of time. If we can withdraw it from the outside world and make it 'go in', it will catch the Divine Melody which is echoing within all of us. This is so wonderfully attractive that after coming in contact with it, the mind does not go out again, and becomes still.

There is no other unfailing method of stilling the mind and making it steady. Austere discipline, rituals, penance, hard life and other such measures have only a temporary effect. The fire is only covered with ashes and will flare up again when the wind of the five passions blows. It is different when it has contacted the Divine Melody within. Then it loses its fickleness, becomes quiet and steady, and acquires an upward trend; because originally it, too, was a denizen of a higher plane—Trikuti—in the region of Brahmand, and would fain regain its place. It is after this that the hold on the soul is relaxed and the freed

soul rushes on to the feet of God. This is the rationale of
Shabd Yoga, or devotion to Nam.

Now, what is Nam and how to attach the mind to it?
Nam is of two kinds: *varnatmak* and *dhunatmak*. The first
can be uttered by mouth and can be written. It can be
traced to a definite period of time or origin in this world.
Several Saints have given names to God, according to
their liking and out of their great devotion to Him. These
are all varnatmak names. Some of them have fallen out of
use and have been forgotten in the course of time. Likewise, many others also may fall out of use in the future,
while Saints of the future may give new names to God.
All names that can be spoken or written, like God, Ram,
Hari, Vah Guru and Allah, are varnatmak names. On
the other hand, the dhunatmak Name is not limited by
time or space. Everything that we see in the universe, including time and space, has been created out of dhunatmak Nam. How then can it be limited in time and space?

Varnatmak names are different in different times,
places and countries, but the dhunatmak Name is one
and the same for all. In it there are no differences of
caste, creed, country or religion. Huzur Maharaj Ji[1] used
to call it the Unwritten Law and the Unspoken Language. It has also been called Shabd, Word, Bang-i-
Asmani and the Audible Life Stream. This dhunatmak
Nam is not a word. It is a Power, an Energy, and we have
to attain it by means of the varnatmak name. The latter is
the means; the former, the end. But people forget this
difference, ignore the dhunatmak Nam which is the end,
and confuse it with varnatmak nam which is the means.
They take the latter to be the end and become fanatic
over it. Hindus are keen on 'Ram' or 'Hari', Muslims on

---

1. Maharaj Sawan Singh Ji.

'Allah', and Sikhs on 'Vah Guru'. They forget the end and quarrel over the means. The result is discord and strife, which makes it difficult for men from different religions even to meet each other. The main duty of man, namely, returning Home and reaching God, is altogether lost sight of.

There is only one God, one Supreme Being, for all time, for all ages. If there are no differences in God, how can there be differences in the soul, which is a spark of the Divine Flame? No differences of caste, creed, country and time exist in the soul either. All apparent differences are the result of ignorance and egoism.

We should try to realize the dhunatmak Nam by means of the varnatmak nam, and not quarrel among ourselves. All Saints emphasize the importance of Shabd. They teach us to live amicably and peacefully, and not to fight among ourselves; but when they pass out of the world, their followers forget their real teachings and begin to carry out propaganda based on ritualism and sectarianism.

Where is this Energy or Power which we call Shabd? It cannot be found in scriptures. Holy books are only recordings of the experiences of Saints, Masters, Prophets and Mystics, who realized Nam under the guidance and with the grace of their Masters. They have left this record for the benefit and guidance of other people. From these books we can get information about God and Shabd, or the Audible Life Stream, and some knowledge of the path, including difficulties encountered. It is not possible, however, to contact Nam or to get over those difficulties unless we translate their teachings into practice. Who can ever get rid of disease by reading a prescription, even though he may go on reading it for hours? If we want to be cured, we should have the prescription properly dis-

pensed and then use it. Can we satisfy hunger by simply
repeating the names of our favorite dishes? Hunger is re-
lieved only when we prepare the food and eat it. Likewise, when we *act* upon the teachings in the Holy Scriptures, we shall contact dhunatmak Nam and be able to
enjoy the bliss of Shabd. We cannot reach Calcutta from
Sangli merely by reading timetables.

Scriptures contain teachings and experiences about
the realization of Nam and its bliss. Reading them inspires us and creates love for Nam in our minds. But Nam
itself can be acquired only by acting on the advice of the
scriptures and following the teachings. The reading of
scriptures is not to be condemned—rather encouraged—
for it purifies the mind and creates a desire for Nam.
However, that is not everything. It is like cleaning a vessel; but something must be put in it also. The mind should
be purified by reading religious books and by *Satguru
seva*, 'service to the Master',[1] before it can be filled with
Nam. If, however, the entire life is spent in reading scriptures, when will it be filled with the Nectar of Nam? The
latter is the most important thing.

We do not have to go far to find Nam. It is within us.
That part of the body from the eyes upwards is the seat of
Nam. There are nine openings or doors in the body from
the eyes downward; it is through these that the mind
spreads out into the world, and it should not be permitted
to roam about there. It must be withdrawn from the
world and the nine openings, brought back to the eye
center—which is the seat of mind and soul in the human
body—and held there.

From here we have to go upward. The mind will be
connected with the Shabd in the eye center and will there

---

1. The greatest service we can render to the Master is to do our spiritual practice
regularly, with love and devotion.

be able to hear the sweet, melodious Sound. The Shabd exists in all human beings, good and bad, rich and poor, Saints and sinners; men, women and children. There are no differences of caste, creed and country. Everyone has Shabd within him and can contact it at the eye center.

From where is this Shabd derived? From where does it come? It comes from the region of Sach Khand, also called Sat Desh. When the mind is connected to Shabd, the soul will also go up, reach Sat Desh by stages, and be liberated forever from the cycle of births and deaths. The mind, too, will be settled in its home—Trikuti—and will enjoy the bliss of Shabd there. Then it will no longer crave sense pleasures. Who would care for rupees and paisas when he has found pearls and diamonds? Who would eat tasteless food when delicious dishes are available? The attachment of the mind to the sense pleasures cannot be rooted out totally by hard discipline or penance. It can be destroyed only by giving it a taste of the bliss of Shabd.

Although Nam is within us, we cannot attain it by our own unaided efforts. The Creator has placed Nam in us, but the key is with the Saints and Masters who alone can connect our mind to Shabd. The way cannot be found by reading books. No science can be learned properly through books alone. A teacher is necessary. You cannot become a doctor by merely reading books on medicine. Correct medical knowledge can be acquired not by reading books alone but also by making experiments under the direction of an expert teacher for quite a long time.

Saints and Masters are professors of Shabd. They awaken our undeveloped intellect and understanding. They alone can teach us to fix our mind in the proper center and connect it with Shabd. Their guidance is absolutely necessary, but they do not put anything in us from the outside. They only show us the way to find the Shabd which already exists within us. We have to develop close and intimate contact with the Shabd by our own persistent efforts under the guidance of the Master, who awakens and stimulates our undeveloped spiritual powers.

Nam, as I have said, exists within everyone. We have to withdraw our mind from sense pleasures and connect it to Nam, which is already there. To live the worldly life successfully should not be our only aim. We should not be entangled in worldly life to the extent of forgetting God. Our supreme duty is to attach our mind to Nam and secure liberation. Then we shall be happy in this life and also attain release from the prison of eighty-four lakhs of species.

Swami Ji Maharaj points out how we are caught in the snare of sense pleasures, which is a veritable noose round our neck. If we wish to see the light of the Beloved, we have to withdraw our mind from worldly pleasures and direct it to Shabd. We should make the mind move in the bliss of Shabd. "Withdraw your mind, which is infatuated with worldly relations and possessions, and bring it back to the eye center; then fix it there so that your return to the Divine Home may be possible."

Simran, the repetition of the Names of God with attention fixed at the thinking center, is the method recommended by the Saints for withdrawing the mind from the sense pleasures. We have scattered our attention into the world by repeatedly thinking of worldly objects and faces; and we can withdraw and focus it in a similar way by thinking of God, thus replacing our worldly simran with simran of the Names. This simran should be almost constant, even automatic, and the more devotedly it is carried out, the easier it becomes for us to contact the realities of the Spirit. Fixing the mind at the third eye is to mount the lowest rung of the ladder of salvation. Thence it will rise up and up by means of Shabd.

Besides, there is only the illusion of pleasure in this world, for even what looks like pleasure here results in great suffering. We are happy to have children but if they are taken away, how sad we feel. Pleasure is sweet but its reaction is bitter. It is by untiring efforts that we accumulate wealth but how heartbroken we feel when it is lost. However, there is one joy, one bliss, that involves no reaction, and that is the bliss of Shabd.

Devotion to Shabd means devotion to our beloved Father, and after that there is no suffering. In order to be happy the soul can—and must—return to Sach Khand, whence it came. The eye center above and behind the two eyes is the door which leads to the passage Home. We can enter this door only when we withdraw our attention from the nine doors. All the Saints have assured us of these truths. We should have faith in their words and follow their advice. All great Masters, like Kabir Sahib, Guru Nanak Sahib, Dadu Sahib and others, have taught this same Truth, and we should benefit by their experience. Humanity would never have progressed as it has, if each person made every experiment for himself right from the beginning. We have to learn from the experience of those who have preceded us, in order to make progress possible.

Everyone wears the fetters of karma, be he prince or beggar, rich or poor, man or woman. Everyone without exception will have to clear the account and pay the debt of his karma. It is karma, the results of our past actions, that keeps us in the prison of the body. If we do good deeds we may be born as princes or rich men, but this does not bring about liberation from the wheel of birth and death. Instead of being 'C' class prisoners, we merely become 'A' class prisoners, but we are still in the jail. It is very difficult to be karmaless in practice.

Shabd practice, however, is the one infallible method of nullifying all karmas. Shabd comes from beyond the region of mind and maya. It eradicates all karmas and frees the soul from all downward influences. If we submit ourselves to it we shall be able to reach its source and origin, which is God. Swami Ji says, "Devote yourself to Radha Soami so that your karmas may be destroyed." *Radha* means 'soul', and *Soami* means 'Lord'; therefore, devote yourself to the Supreme Being, 'the Lord of the soul', and attain union of the soul with God.

* * *

3

HOW SHALL I MEET THE LORD, O MASTER?

Kin bidh mile Gusain, mere Ram Rai
by Guru Arjan Dev

How shall I meet the Lord, O Master?
Only a Saint who has attained sahaj[1]
Can show the path.
The Unseen is within,
And remains invisible
Because of the veil of ego.
Infatuated by maya,[2]
The whole creation is asleep.
How shall I wake from this delusion?
Dwelling in the same house,[3] living together,
We know not each other.
For lack of the One,[4] the five[5] torment us;
But that One is not easily reached.
Having built the house,
He has locked himself within,
And has entrusted the key to the Guru;
Try as one may,
Never shall this treasure be obtained

---

1. "*Sahaj*" means easy, natural, real; esoterically, the transition from the state of 'becoming' into that of 'being' one with the Supreme Lord.
2. "*Maya*" means illusion and delusion, unreality. All of the manifested universe is maya because it has no real, lasting existence. This veil conceals the vision of God from our sight.
3. "House" refers to the physical body, within which dwell the soul and the Lord Himself.
4. "One" refers to Nam, Shabd, the Word or the Sound Current within.
5. "The five"—lust, anger, greed, attachment, and pride or egotism.

Without taking refuge in Him.[1]
When the Lord wishes to cut the shackles,
The love and the company of Saints He grants.
When in their company,
One sings the praises of Nam.[2]
Thenceforth is one united with the Lord,
And no difference remains
Between the two, says Nanak.[3]
Thus is the Lord met,
Sahaj is achieved, delusion dispelled,
And the flame merges in the Light.[4]

Adi Granth, p.204, M.5

Man seeks the Lord because He is his origin. Having separated from Him, the soul has been entangled by illusion, or maya, in the snare of attachment, and it has taken to the company of the mind. Further, the mind itself is not independent, but has been enslaved by the senses and the worldly desires. It thus gets still more entangled and the soul has to bear the consequences of whatever thoughts and acts emanate from the mind, whether good or evil, because the mind and the soul are tied together in a knot. The soul has to suffer pain—sometimes of one birth, sometimes of another—and remains imprisoned in the jail of 'eighty-four'—*chaurasi*, the cycle of 8,400,000 births or species.

To whichever birth we go, we find pain and suffering. We can get deliverance from this cycle of birth and death

---

1. The Guru or Master.
2. "Singing the praises of Nam" means the spiritual practice; *simran* and *bhajan*; repeating the five Holy Names and listening to the Sound within until one becomes completely absorbed in it.
3. Hymns appearing in the Adi Granth which are composed by any of the Gurus in the line of Guru Nanak are attributed to him, and end with the phrase "says Nanak."
4. This means the same as 'the drop merges in the Ocean' or 'the soul merges in the Lord'.

only when our soul returns to its Origin. The only outlet from this jail is through the human form. In other words, of all the forms, it is only in the human form that the soul has the privilege of uniting with the Lord. The Hindus call it the house of God, the Muslims refer to man as the highest form of creation, and the Jews and the Christians hold the belief that the body is the temple of the living God. It is for this reason that in the human form man seeks the Lord, according to his limited understanding. He employs various ways and means to find Him, but all this proves in vain.

A seeker would like to be enlightened as to how and where he can find the Lord. If the seeker could meet a Saint who has attained the stage of *sahaj*, and if the Saint would disclose the secret and the path of meeting the Lord, and if the seeker would follow the path, only then could he unite with the Lord. What is meant is that if ever we succeed in being reunited with the Lord, it is through the Saints. The stage of sahaj can be attained only when we transcend the limitations of mind and maya. The Saints say that the Lord whom man seeks is not hidden in forests and mountains, nor does He dwell in temples and mosques, in gurdwaras and churches, nor is He asleep somewhere in the skies. He dwells within man himself. Whenever He is found, He is found within us; and whosoever has found Him, has found Him within himself. But when we close our eyes, we find nothing but darkness. Why can we not behold Him? This is because we have the veil of our own ego between Him and us.

What is the ego? It is 'I', 'me' and 'mine'. It is the self. It is what we day in and day out express by saying, "This is my son, my family, my wealth, my property, my achievement, my high position, my religion, my country, my race, my nation. . . ." All that exists belongs to the

Lord, but we think ourselves to be separate from the
Lord. We desire to possess things and try to make them
our own, but they never become ours nor have they ever
become anyone else's. Having become attached to them,
we exist only for them, and we continue to be born and
die here. It is not family, relatives and wealth, but our
own attitude of attachment and possessiveness which is
the obstacle.

The soul is within us and so is the Lord, and this has
been so for thousands of ages; yet, how strange it is that
those who live together, dwelling in the same house, never meet each other. This is because of the veil of ego.

How can this veil be lifted when we are fast asleep? In
the hypnotic trance of attachment, no one ever thinks of
Him. Taking the world to be real, they have become
attached to it. They are wasting days and nights in the
pursuit of pleasures. So long as we do not have a longing
for the Lord, we cannot come out of this delusion. In the
first place, we do not feel devotion to the Lord. Even if
we sometimes think of Him, it is for our own comfort and
happiness. We pray for some high position or honor, or
to be saved from sorrow and pain. So long as we do not
seek the Lord for His own sake, we cannot have love for
Him. True longing, true reverence, true devotion, are
necessary preludes to true love for the Lord.

Nam or Shabd is the link between man and God.
Without that 'One', we are being pursued by five enemies, and we suffer various kinds of pain and sorrow at
the hands of these enemies. Who are these enemies?
They are lust, anger, greed, attachment, egotism. What is
the 'One'? It is Nam. We are entrapped by these five
thieves because there is no practice of Nam. For example, when the owner of a house is asleep, thieves may
take away anything they like, but when the owner is

awake the thieves dare not come near. In the same way, when we practice Nam we wake up from this hypnotic state of a ceaseless chain of births and deaths.

The Lord who created us has placed the treasure of Nam within us and has entrusted the key and the secret to the Master. So long as he does not impart to us the method of the practice of Nam, we cannot obtain the treasure. The Master will not prepare something and put it within you, but will enable you to unlock the hidden treasure. The treasure is yours and it is within you. The Master will show you the path by traversing which you can obtain it. Similarly, the power or capacity to know is within all of us but is dormant; when we go to schools and colleges, work diligently, burn the midnight oil and follow the instructions of the teachers, then the dormant faculty is awakened and we become graduates and scholars. Those who do not go to the teachers and do not work hard remain uneducated. Thus, whatever devices or means we may use to get the treasure of Nam, they will be of no avail unless we unconditionally surrender ourselves to the Master and travel the path shown by him.

Now an important question arises: What do the Saints mean by Nam? Where does Nam reside? And by what means can that treasure be obtained? We have called the Lord by thousands and thousands of names. We have many countries, and in each country there are many languages, and in each language we remember the Lord by various names. Some call Him 'Vah Guru', some call Him 'Allah', some call Him 'Jehovah', some call Him 'Radha Soami', and some call Him 'God'. All these names are varnatmak; that is, they come within the scope of writing, reading and speaking. But the Name which is described and praised by the Saints is dhunatmak, that is, it can neither be written nor read, nor can it be seen.

Huzur Maharaj Ji used to describe it as Unwritten Law, Unspoken Language.

All varnatmak names have a history behind them and an origin in time. They may be hundreds of years old or thousands of years old. We have given many names to the Lord and many have been forgotten, and many more names there will be by which we shall call Him. But the Nam of which Guru Nanak[1] is singing praises here, has no time limit. In the beginning was Nam, and everything else emanated from Nam. According to the Adi Granth, "All creation has come out of Nam." And the Bible refers to it as Word: "In the beginning was the Word, and the Word was with God. . . ." All the stars, planets and the entire universe was created by it. Again, in the Adi Granth we find, "The creation has come out of Shabd." In various languages this Power has been described by different names. In the Adi Granth it is called Gurbani, Sachi Bani, Nam and Hukam—'the Guru's Word', 'the True Word', 'the Name', 'the Divine Command'. The Hindus have called it Akash Bani and Anahad Shabd —'the Sound from the sky', 'the Unstruck Sound'. The Muslims have called it Kalma—'Word'; Bang-i-Asmani —'Sound that comes from the skies'; Kalam-i-Ilahi— 'Voice of God'; and Isme-i-Azam—'the Greatest Name'. Christ has described it as Logos or Word.

It is through the varnatmak or the spoken and written word that we have to retrace our attention inside and connect it with the dhunatmak Nam. We should not attach ourselves to these words and become tied with the strings of ceremonies of various religions nor get embroiled in religious feuds between various creeds and

1. In the Adi Granth, all the hymns composed by the Gurus in the line of Guru Nanak end with "says Nanak." Wherever the Master mentions Guru Nanak in a discourse, he is referring to the "house" of Guru Nanak, or the line of Guru Nanak.

nations. The very nature of mind is that it must attach itself to something. If we practice devotion to dhunatmak
Nam we shall be freed from the bonds of nationality,
race, creed and ceremonies. We shall perform our duties
to the best of our ability but without attachment to anything but Nam. And so, automatically, we become better
citizens, better husbands, better wives. It is for such Nam
that we go to Saints.

Now a second question arises: Where can we get that
Nam? In religious books and Holy Scriptures we find the
praises of Name or Nam, and perhaps even a description
of the method of its practice. There is talk about the Holy
Name or Nam in the temples, mosques, gurdwaras,
churches, tabernacles, and in satsang; when we go there,
the desire to attain it is aroused. But that true and great
treasure of Nam is within us. When we are to realize it,
we shall do so only within ourselves.

There are prescriptions in doctors' books, but the
medicine itself lies on the shelves. The account books of
moneylenders contain accounts of credits and debits, but
the money itself lies in the vault. Likewise, Holy Scriptures contain only a description of Nam, but not Nam itself. Just as a disease cannot be cured by reading or recit-
ing prescriptions, just as money cannot be obtained from
the moneylenders' account books, so also Nam cannot be
obtained by merely reading or studying holy books.
Huzur Maharaj Ji used to say, "If a person goes on repeating 'laddoo'[1] all his life, he will not be able to taste it
nor satisfy his appetite. However, if he prepares the lad-
doos according to the instructions in a cookbook, he will
not only be able to satisfy his appetite, but will also be
able to relish the taste."

---

1. An Indian sweet.

This does not mean that we should give up the reading of sacred books. Rather, reading with understanding is very beneficial. Reading of the sacred writings will generate a longing for union with the Lord. It also enlightens us as to the method by which we can find Him. But if we think we can obtain Him by mere reading or studying, then we are mistaken. Reading is like cleaning a utensil. The cleaning of a utensil is necessary only if you wish to put something in it. We have to cleanse the mind in order to fill it with the nectar of Nam.

What are the sacred books? Rishis, Munis, Gurus, Saints, all holy men worked hard and attained God-realization. Whatever sights they experienced within, whatever obstacles they encountered on the way, they have set them down in writing for our benefit and guidance. Now, by mere reading of these books, neither can the obstacles be removed from the way nor can the sights be seen. The essence of this matter is practice.

The treasure of Nam is within us as fire is in wood, but we cannot see it nor is it of any use to us in its present dormant state. If we rub one piece of wood with another in the proper way, fire will be produced and we can make use of it. In the same way, the treasure of Nam is within us but we can obtain it only when we give up the path of the mind and take to the path of the Master. It is then that we shall be able to derive benefit from it.

Now this treasure is no doubt within us, but where exactly can we find it? There are two parts of the body—one below the eyes, the other above the eyes. Below the eyes are only the nine apertures and the sensual pleasures. Our center of thinking is above the eyes. Whenever we think deeply, we usually place our hands or fingers on the forehead. The more we concentrate, the better we think. Daily our attention descends from here to the nine apertures, and through them becomes scattered in the outside world. Saints tell us that we have to stop our attention from going out, and that which has already spread out has to be brought back to the eye center. So long as our attention is not concentrated between the eyes, from where the Shabd takes it behind the eyes and up, we cannot return Home. When our attention has been concentrated behind the eyes, we find the sweetest and most melodious Sound reverberating, attracting and pulling us toward itself. There is no question there of nationality, race, creed, wealth, authority or possession. This Sound is what the Saints call Shabd or Nam. When our attention is fixed on it, we will reach the place from where it comes—Sach Khand, where the Lord Himself resides.

Withdrawing our attention from the nine apertures and connecting it with the Shabd within leads us to the door of liberation. For when we have reached the first rung of the ladder, there is hope of reaching the top as well. The secret of withdrawing the attention from the nine apertures, and the technique of connecting it with the Shabd is imparted to us only by the Saints.

Those souls whom the Saints wish to liberate from the ocean of this world and unite with the Lord are first brought by them into their company and satsang. When we attend their satsang, various doubts and difficulties disappear. We come to know our Origin, our Home, and then a longing for union with the Lord is awakened in us. Satsang and good company are necessary preludes for devotion to the Lord. The mind is easily influenced by the company it keeps. If we keep bad company, we become wicked; and if we keep the company of Saints and devotees, we follow their example and, like them, we become devoted to the Lord. If perchance we are kept away

from the satsang of Saints, then we should continue to
read their writings so that the mind may remain detached
from worldly objects and free from all desire to dominate
anyone or to obtain power, position, wealth, etc. We
should also continue with regular and daily practice of
Nam. When we get the company of Saints and practice
Nam, we attain union with the Lord. Then there is no distance or difference left between us and the Lord.

This, then, is the method by which we can find the
Lord. Having realized Him, we shall attain the stage of
sahaj. We shall get deliverance from all our delusions, the
drop will merge into the Ocean and will become the
Ocean itself. The soul will merge with the supreme Soul,
'God', and will become one with Him.

* * *

4

BEHOLD, ALL THE WORLD IS GOING ADRIFT!

Dekho sab jag jat baha
by Swami Ji

Behold, all the world is going adrift!
Seeing the miserable plight of the world,
Repeatedly I spoke out thus:
"Through cycles of ages have you suffered
Countless births and countless deaths.
You have undergone intense pain,
You have even remained in hell.
Life after life you have gone through agony,
And you knew not a moment of peace.
Deeds—good and bad—became your fetters,[1]
You did not contact the Satguru's feet.[2]
Now you have the gift of this human body;
By devotion, burn karmas away.
Failure now will deserve no remission;
You must suffer a thousand ills.
Give up sloth, forget the world;
Apply yourself and ceaselessly drink the wine of Nam.[3]
Dread the mind,[4] serve the Master;
Heed this warning by Radha Swami."

Sar Bachan Poetry, p.119, 15:10

---

1. Both good and bad deeds bind us to the creation because we have to reap rewards or punishments for them.
2. An expression signifying devotion to the Master.
3. Listen to the Sound and drink the Divine Nectar within.
4. Dread the temptation of the mind.

Huzur Swami Ji is moved to see the pitiable condition of the world, to see how all have forgotten God and are rushing to their ruin through addiction to sense enjoyment. Nobody thinks of God or of practicing devotion to Him. We are all absorbed in sense pleasures. In the glamor and allurement of enjoyment, some even go so far as to say, "This world is sweet—who has seen the next?" Who knows for certain as to what the future will be, or whether there is any hereafter at all? Why should we deprive ourselves of enjoyment in this world, in the uncertain hope of achieving happiness in the next world?"

Man has been so completely enslaved by sense enjoyment that he even forgets his inevitable death. It does not occur to him that he too must die one day. He sees death and misery around him, but fondly fancies that these are for others and he is immune. Is it not strange that, though we see our friends and relatives die, and take them to the cemetery or the cremation ground, we never think of our own end? Swami Ji tries to arouse us from this apathy. He tells us, feelingly, "Brother, everyone must die, and a day will come when our friends and relatives will likewise take us to the cremation ground. This body, the support of our egoism and pride, will be consigned to flames or earth, and we shall have to stand before Yama to answer for our karma, our good and bad actions. We will have to take birth again in the form in which we can best pay off our karma, including unfulfilled desires. Our relatives and friends, our wealth and fame, will be of no use to us when we have to appear before Yama to answer for our karmas. All these worldly things will be left here. Only our love of God and service to Him will help us then."

Swami Ji points out that our soul is a spark of the Divine Fire but, owing to its association with the mind, it has forgotten God. The soul and mind are tied together, in a knot as it were. So the soul also is enslaved by the longings and hankerings of the mind and by karmas done under its influence. The soul has forgotten its divine origin and is caught in illusion. It has to take birth again and again, to suffer the consequences of the hankerings and karmas of the mind, to which it is chained. The soul thus has to incarnate into various forms of life and has been enduring this suffering for ages. That was because we forgot God and our divine nature. If we had devoted ourselves to Nam, we would not have had to take birth in this world of misery. We deserted God and are therefore suffering here. There is nothing but misery in this prison-house. Worldly happiness is only an illusion, for what seems to be happiness is momentary and brings suffering in its wake.

There is no happiness here, wherever we might be born. There is only misery and suffering everywhere. Just look around. In this world, who is happy? How hard is the horse whipped to make it go faster! The overworked bullock drops down fatigued and exhausted but, pierced with the goad, is forced to get up to work again. And the goats, cattle and fowl—how they are mercilessly slaughtered to fill our bellies! Do we ever think how we would feel if we were to change places with them and suffer similar tortures? Let us not forget that the law of karma is inexorable and we will have to reap what we have sown. Those whom we slaughter now will slaughter us one day.

Turning now to human life, has man peace and happiness? Human life is glorified by terms like *nar-narayan* life, the life or form in which the soul can realize God, or 'the top of creation'. But here too we find only suffering and misery. Poverty, disease, want, barrenness and other problems fall to the lot of man, and fill him with sorrow and anxiety. Unemployment, widowhood, murders, riots and wars play havoc with man's life. There is no end to this catalog of calamities. Swami Ji warns us that there is no happiness or peace in the human or any other life. There is no happiness except in God-realization and in loving devotion to Him.

The soul is caught in the wheel of births and deaths as a result of both good and bad karmas. This world is a mixture of good and bad, sin and virtue. Sin brings suffering, virtue brings happiness. Unmixed sin throws the soul in hell, unalloyed virtue takes us to heaven. Human life is the result of a combination of sin and virtue. Being a mixture of sin and virtue, it is a mixture of suffering and happiness too. Virtue will bring some happiness but will not enable one to attain eternal salvation. One may be reborn as a prince or a rich man as the result of austerities or devoted recitation of scriptures or performing charity, but liberation cannot be secured thereby. You are still in the prison, though you are now an 'A' class prisoner. You have to be born again to enjoy the fruits of your meritorious actions, and then again to reap the fruits of actions done as a prince or a rich man, and so on ad infinitum. The only way to attain liberation is to surrender oneself to Saints—God-realized souls—become worthy of their grace, learn the secret of Nam from them, and realize Nam by following their teachings. True devotion consists in realizing Nam.

It is possible to practice devotion and realize Nam in human life only. The human body is bestowed on us, as the highest gift and blessing, after passing through chaurasi—the eighty-four lakh forms of life. We get it by God's grace, and He bestows this favor so that we may have the opportunity to practice bhakti and thus put an end to all our sufferings by realizing God and achieving salvation. Human life is the only exit from this prison.

Swami Ji points out that all of us—kings and subjects, rich and poor, man, woman and child—are bound by the fetters of karma, and have to clear our accounts. Till all karma, good and bad, is destroyed, God-realization is not possible. It is necessary, therefore, to practice bhakti, which will destroy all good and bad karma. Counting beads, practicing austerities, and reading scriptures or giving alms do not constitute bhakti.

Karma is of three kinds: *sinchit*—the store or accumulated karmas of past births; *pralabdh*—fate or destiny karma, which is responsible for this form of life, and which we have to undergo; the *kriyaman*—the new karma that we are now creating, which will bear fruit in future lives.

Saints and Masters explain that of these, pralabdh or fate karma can be destroyed only by going through it. Therefore, we should accept it cheerfully, as a matter of duty, as something sent by God's will. If it brings happiness, it should not elate us, and if it brings misery, it should not depress us, nor should we resent it. Karma does not contaminate and bind us if we bear it with equanimity, without attachment or resentment, but with the attitude, "Thy Will be done." In this way it will not bear fruit again and we will not have to be reborn in order to reap its fruit.

What was kriyaman, 'new seeds', in past lives has become pralabdh for this life, and what is kriyaman in this life will become pralabdh in the next. How then to destroy kriyaman?—for actions must necessarily be performed as long as life lasts. Saints give us a hint on how to nullify kriyaman. They say that no bad actions should be done at all, as consequences of bad actions cannot be evaded and will have to be suffered; and good actions should be performed disinterestedly, without any desire to secure and enjoy their fruit. If actions are done in this way, they will bear no fruit, even as roasted seeds do not sprout. If good actions are performed with longing for their fruit, rebirth is inevitable, to enjoy the fruit of such karma.

As for sinchit, our store of unpaid karmas, they are destroyed by bhakti, devotion to Nam. In this way, all the three kinds of karmas can be cleared and the cycle of births and deaths comes to an end. Kabir says, "As a whole pile of wood is reduced to ashes by a spark of fire, so all karma is destroyed by a single atom of Nam." The practice of Shabd liberates us from the round of births and deaths.

In this poem, Swami Ji tells us, "Our present plight is due to our pralabdh. If, in this precious human life, we fail to devote ourselves to Nam but go on performing good and bad actions, we shall again be caught in the cycle of births and deaths, and shall suffer again. The only way out of this prison of eighty-four lakh forms of existence is through the human form. We, however, overlook this truth and waste the precious human life—bestowed on us for practicing Nam bhakti—in doing good and bad actions under the dictates of mind and senses. No attention is paid to the real duty of realizing Nam and reuniting ourselves with God."

This point is illustrated by a beautiful parable: A blind man is thrown into a large prison, which has only one door. He begins groping his way, feeling the walls with his hands—hoping in this way to find the door and get out. But when he comes fairly close to the door he feels like scratching his head, which he does and thus misses the door. He has to go around the four walls again to find the door, but misses it again for the same reason. Because of pleasure and sense enjoyment, we similarly miss the only door that leads out of this prison of existence, and again have to go through the whole cycle of births and deaths.

Swami Ji Maharaj advises us, in all earnestness, to ponder over this aspect of the problem and set to the task of realizing Nam in this life. Do not procrastinate. Do not postpone till tomorrow. Begin the effort here and now.

Some people think, "We shall turn to God when we become old. Let us enjoy life now, attend to our wife and children and make proper provision for them. There will be time enough for devotion to God." This is false reasoning. In old age the body becomes diseased and worn out, and the mind weak, and we get deeply attached to the world. And then, who knows when death will overtake us? The body may succumb to death in a minute, without notice. It is therefore wise to begin now, when both mind and body are strong, and not postpone any more. Do what you can as best you can, even if it is not deep and one-pointed. If you cannot find much time, if concentration is not attained and the mind wanders, do not be discouraged. The effort counts.

Saints do not ask you to renounce the family or to be a burden on society. You must earn your bread and do your duty, but keep your attention in Nam. All Saints have done so. Kabir Sahib followed the profession of a weaver. Ravidas Ji worked as a cobbler. Guru Nanak Sahib lived on the produce of his lands, and thus maintained himself and his family. And they all practiced Nam bhakti also.

You should live in the world, but disinterestedly, without attachment or hankering after enjoyment. Attachment should be for Nam, and its realization should be the only goal. Other things should be done as a matter of duty only and to the extent to which it is necessary to support oneself and the family. With this attitude towards family, all efforts should be directed to practicing Nam, which is our only provision for the other world. All temporal things—wealth, friends, relatives, good name, the body itself—for which we care so much, will be left behind when we start on our journey to the other world. Only Nam will befriend us; nothing else can or will. By accumulation of the wealth of Nam, man attains happiness and peace in this world and is united with God after death. Nam alone has the power to bestow these blessings on man. It behooves us, therefore, not to cling to worldly life, but to make strenuous and devoted efforts to realize Nam. As human beings, that is our real duty in life.

Mind is the obstruction between God and soul, so it must be subjugated. Mad after sense enjoyment, it runs after worldly pleasures. The soul, which is chained to it, is also dragged along and has to pass through births and deaths, and suffers the consequences of bad actions and hankerings. Only when the mind is brought under control will the soul be free to go up.

People try to conquer the mind by various disciplines—by counting beads, by doing penances, by worship or by reading scriptures. But all these methods are inadequate. They are halfway measures. Mind cannot really be controlled in this way. A serpent will be quiet as long as it is secured in a basket, but it will bite as soon as the basket is thrown open. It will be rendered completely harmless only when its sac of venom has been removed. Similarly, by adopting these methods, the mind may become quiet temporarily but will assert itself when it gets an opportunity. The practice of Nam or Shabd alone makes it powerless.

Mind is fond of pleasure, but no enjoyment in the

world can hold it permanently. It flits from pleasure to pleasure, being tired of each after a short time. It will be steady only when it gets some enjoyment which is greater than that found in worldly pleasures. Such happiness, or rather bliss, can be found only in Shabd, in Nam. When the mind gets a taste of this bliss, it will be weaned from sensual pleasures. Then it will be possible for it to go back to Trikuti, its original home. There it will lose its fickle nature and will stay, while enjoying the bliss of Shabd.

Then the soul, freed from the control of the mind, will be able to rise up to God and be united with Him.

* * *

5

MOMENT AFTER MOMENT
THE MIND WANDERS

Man khin khin bharam bharam baho dhave
by Guru Ram Das

Moment after moment the mind wanders;
Away from its center, it ever flounders.
The grace of the Master brings it round,
And draws it home by the Anahad Sound.[1]
Give me, O Lord, the company of Saints,
To find Thee and escape from this world's taints.
Thus will ego's disease be cured,
And so everlasting peace assured.
In sahaj samadhi the soul will find delight,
And jewels within are brought to sight.
As the water diviner finds hidden springs
And wells long buried to surface brings,
So does the Master reveal the treasure
Of Light and Truth beyond all measure.
Most unfortunate is the poor blind soul
Who does not knock at the Satguru's door.
This human life, so dearly bought,
He throws away without a thought.
O merciful Lord, to Thee we pray,
To the Master's feet please show the way.
O Nanak! Those alone true liberation attain

---

1. The inner spiritual Sound, the Shabd.

Who with Sadhus sing His praises
Again and again.[1]

Adi Granth, p.1179, M.4

This hymn is by Guru Ram Das, the fourth Guru in the line of Guru Nanak, and deals especially with the role of the mind on the path to God-realization. All Saints and Mystics, in the past as well as the present time, are agreed that God is within us and before we can realize His immanence we must realize Him within ourselves. And it is here that the mind comes in. It is actually a link between soul and God, but in its present condition it stands as a huge impenetrable barrier between the soul and God-realization. It is a force to be reckoned with, though it depends on the soul for its power and sustenance.

Mind and soul form one working unit, and wherever the mind goes, the soul has to go along with it. The mind is the instrument by means of which we make our contacts with the outside world and gather experience. Owing to its outward tendencies it keeps us away from God, but if it is turned inward and directed to the inner centers it enables us to contact the Divinity within ourselves. We are therefore anxious to reorient the mind on its inward course and bring it back to tisra til or the eye center, which is its headquarters in the physical body. Then, instead of being the cause of bondage to the world, it becomes the means of liberation.

This, however, is not easy. In this hymn Guru Sahib voices our difficulties forcefully when he says, "The mind continually goes out and does not stay even for a second

---

1. By "singing His praises" is meant the spiritual practice (*simran* and *bhajan*), repeating the five Holy Names with the mind concentrated at the eye center and then listening to the Sound within until one becomes completely absorbed in it.

at the third eye." Thus the mind involves us in a chain of actions and reactions, the cause of our birth and death over and over again in this world of phenomena. As long as the mind does not come back to the eye center, it is not possible for it to go back and reach its home, which is known as Trikuti. We adopt various methods to achieve this object and try to bring it back to its center. In fact, all spiritual disciplines aim at bringing back the mind. Some of us try to force it back under intellectual and moral discipline, and some try by means of various other practices, but without permanent success.

Mind is, by nature, fond of pleasures and will not be controlled till we can offer it something better and more pleasant than it gets in the outside world. It is powerful and unruly, but like an elephant—when the driver sits on its neck with goad in hand—even this powerful beast is easily controlled. Similarly, for the mind, Master is the goad and Shabd is the driver. When, through the help and grace of the Master, the mind is brought in touch with Shabd, it is easily controlled. By Shabd, of course, we mean the inner spiritual Sound which is technically known as dhunatmak Shabd. It cannot be written nor can it be expressed in words. Until we are in contact with that inner Sound, the mind does not go up from the eye center or tisra til.

The mind goes out and flits from one object to another in search of pleasure, but no pleasure is able to hold it for long. The bliss of Shabd, however, is so captivating that once the mind begins to enjoy this bliss, it does not go out. It finds the Shabd so blissful, so entrancing, that it automatically ceases its wanderings. The Nectar or Ambrosia which is to fill the mind with happiness and make it turn upward, can be drunk only when the mind goes in. We look for it outside, but it is within us.

We shall taste it when we are able to withdraw our attention from the nine apertures and fix it in the tenth.

This Nectar is being showered on all of us, irrespective of caste, creed or color, but the vessel in which it is to be received is turned upside down; our attention, instead of being inside, is outside. If we put a cup outside in the rain, but upside down, it will never be filled no matter how long it rains. But if we turn the cup right side up, it will soon become filled—if not in the first rainfall, then in the second or the third. The same is the case with our mind. The Shabd is contacted by means of simran, according to the instructions of the Master.

Having explained why we are not in touch with God and how the mind can be brought under control, the question arises, how are we to accomplish this? Are we to renounce this life and live in forests and lonely places, or in temples, mosques and monasteries, to achieve our goal? "No," says Guru Sahib, "we need not go anywhere, for it is within all of us." All that we require is satsang, that is, the society of a Gurmukh or Saint, so that we may have around us that atmosphere which will facilitate our concentration on Shabd and going in. The company we keep affects us considerably. We tend to become good and virtuous in the company of good and virtuous people, and are likely to go astray in the society of the bad and vicious. When we are in the society of holy men who work on the path of Shabd, we are inspired to labor on the path and our efforts will be more successful.

Going to forests or to solitary, lonely places does not necessarily make for greater concentration. We still have to care for our food and shelter, and in one way or another have to depend upon other people. Besides, eating only what has been earned honestly by one's own efforts is a great help in spiritual progress. Sant Mat does not teach us to be idle nor to be a burden on society but to work for our own living. In this respect also, Saints set an example by devoting part of their time to working and earning their own livelihood.

It is the nature of the mind to be open to all sorts of doubts, but if one keeps in satsang and reads Sant Mat literature, those doubts or difficulties are automatically cleared and one feels impelled to work on the spiritual path. Huzur Maharaj Ji used to compare satsang to the fence around the crops—the crop of bhajan and simran. By satsang is meant a discussion and explanation of Nam. In satsang there is no distinction between high and low, nor any distinction of class, color or creed; and all meet in a loving, friendly atmosphere. We should, therefore, pray to the Lord to give us the company of holy people so that we will always think of God.

By following the path of Shabd, 'egoism' or 'I-ness' is driven out of us, and peace and happiness take its place. All our difficulties and all our unhappiness are due to egoism or attachment. By working on the path of Shabd and getting ourselves attached to It, we automatically detach ourselves from other things. Thus the source of misery and unhappiness is cut off.

Our real home, that is, our inner home, is full of inestimable treasures, but the mind roams outside. How can it obtain these precious gems unless it enters the house? Like the musk deer which, intoxicated by the perfume of its own musk, keeps running in all directions but never suspects that the fragrance is within it, we also look for happiness everywhere except within ourselves. We are like the beggar who has a treasure hidden within his house but, not knowing it, goes about begging alms from place to place. Gurmukhs enlighten us on this point and give us the key also. They tell us that the treasure is within us and also instruct us how to get it.

Saints or Gurmukhs do not supply anything from the outside but make our own treasure available to us from within ourselves, just as water diviners—by means of their special gift—are able to locate buried wells at various places. Quite often wells lie buried under the debris of old and ruined cities. These are not known to the people living there, but the diviners are able to locate them and make the water available to the people.

What a pity for those people who have not been able to contact such a Satguru or Saint. Human life is the only form in which one can realize God and secure liberation from birth and death. If one does not find a Master who can give him the key to Shabd and turn him back to his Home, his life has been of no use.

We should turn our attention away from the body. Our object is not merely to seek comforts and pleasures but to seek and contact the most precious thing in the body—the Shabd Dhun. Then only do we fulfill the purpose of our human existence. We should not think lightly of our human life. It is only as a result of virtuous and meritorious deeds that we are born as human beings. We should not waste this life in useless pursuits.

Guru Sahib then prays to God on our behalf, to shower His grace upon us; for it is only by the grace of God that we come across a Master. Without a Master, we cannot catch the Shabd or Nam, and without Nam there is no salvation. Those who sing the praises of God in the company of holy men, that is, those who are in harmony with the inner Shabd, says Nanak, cross beyond the bounds of maya and reach the stage of *nirvan* or true liberation.

* * *

6

CLEANSE YOUR HEART'S CHAMBER FOR THE BELOVED TO COME

Dil ka hujra saf kar janan ke ane ke liye
by Tulsi Sahib

Cleanse your heart's chamber
For the Beloved to come;
Erase the false impressions,
To seat the Mighty One.
Look with the mind's eye
At the spectacle of life:
What enchanting scenes are there
To captivate your heart!
One little heart,
Teeming with desires ever increasing;
Where then is room at all
For your Lord's seating?
A thousand pities
That to artificial temples and mosques
You repair,
Though dwelling in the natural mosque,
Untold miseries you bear.
Listen with attention
In the real Ka'aba's arch, [1]
A voice from the Highest
Beckons you to march.

---

1. In the arch of the forehead, i.e., the eye center.

The Lord is sought in vain
In the wilderness afar—
The path to the Beloved
Lies through the Sushmana.[1]
Seek the perfect Master
With faith, love and patience;
He will give you Light
To find the hidden entrance.[2]
If with constant effort
You attune the inner ear,
The way to Allah opens
And the path will be clear.
"Put your heart to practice,"
This is Tulsi's call;
'Kun' refers to Allah, the High,
The All in All.[3]

This poem is by Tulsi Sahib Maharaj, a Mystic of a very high order who lived during the latter part of the eighteenth and the first part of the nineteenth century (1764–1845). He was born in the princely family of the Peshwas and was heir to the throne of the kingdom of Poona and Satara. At a very early age he began to show signs of a devotional trend of mind and had no attachment for worldly pursuits and pleasures. A few days before his coronation was to take place, he left his home and fled towards the north in the garb of a sadhu. After traveling a distance of about a thousand miles, he settled at Hathras, near Aligarh, in Uttar Pradesh, where he came to be known as "Dakkhini Baba" (the Sage from the South). Hathras is about twenty miles from Agra, the

---

1. The central current in the finer body, above the eyes, which is traversed by spiritual practice according to the instructions of the Master.
2. At the third eye.
3. *Kun* means the Shabd.

home of Swami Ji, and Swami Ji Maharaj came in close contact with him.

The poem represents a part of Tulsi Sahib's discourse with Sheikh Taqqi, a Muslim holy man who, on his way back from a pilgrimage to Mecca, had pitched his tent near Tulsi Sahib's hut, to rest there for a day. He heard about Tulsi Sahib and went to see him. As Sheikh Taqqi was a Muslim theologian, most of the terms used in this poem by Tulsi Sahib are common figures of speech in the religious works of the Muslim writers.

Tulsi Sahib says that all of us have a keen desire to see God and wish that He may make our hearts the seat of His throne. But where should He sit, when our hearts are so full of worldly desires and impure cravings that practically no room is left for the Deity? Unless the heart, the place which we want Him to grace with His presence, is thoroughly cleansed, and all the dirt and filth is absolutely removed from the inside, how can He care to occupy it? Even a dog does not sit in a dirty place. God's light penetrates only a pure and holy heart.

We know from our daily experience that the image of one whom we love deeply remains constantly hovering before our mind's eye, even when we are engaged in other pursuits. The forms that become the center of our love and attraction during our lifetime, and the figures to which our mind becomes fondly attached by long association, begin to move before our eyes at the time of death, like a cinema film on a screen. And after death we have to assume that form and are born in that place to which our mind is attracted at the time of death. This attraction is due to our long and deep association, and pulls us back like a magnet. It is our attachments to the world and worldly objects, our attraction to faces and forms, sons, daughters and other relatives, love of wealth, property, worldly pleasures, countries, religions and nations, that bring us back again and again to this prisonhouse of birth and death.

Since it is our love and attraction for this world and its objects which causes us to be born again and again into this world, Tulsi Sahib exhorts us to empty our minds of the world and its ephemeral pleasures, and to fill the mind with Divine Love and an intense longing to see God. We love worldly objects and at the same time want to be one with God. This is sheer madness, an utter impossibility. The Bible also states, "Ye cannot serve God and mammon."

At the death of a relative or on separation from a dear friend, how bitterly we weep and how piteously we cry! What restless nights of grief we pass at the departure of our dear ones from this world, and how keenly we miss them! But have we ever thought of our long, long separation from the Creator, the most beloved of all relatives? Have we ever shed a tear or heaved a sigh on not finding Him near and not being able to behold Him? Have we ever pined for Him? Have we ever passed a single sleepless hour in grief over this great separation?

So long as a true and burning love for God does not awaken within us, the grace and Light of God cannot enter the dark and dismal cavern of our heart. In the first place, we seldom do any act of devotion to God and we seldom worship Him. If we do, we do it not to earn God's grace but to achieve worldly objects or for some material gain. There are some people who worship snakes. They do not do so because they love the snakes but for fear of their venomous sting and to escape their bite. We should not worship God out of fear lest He may bring disaster on us, or that our business may not suffer, or that our children may not die, or that He may not fulfill our other worldly desires. We should create pure, true and earnest love for Him in our heart, for His sake alone, in order to meet Him, to be one with Him, to merge in Him. The basis of worship should be love and not fear.

Tulsi Sahib then explains to us the deceptive nature of the objects of the world. He says that if we look with a discerning eye at what we deem the objects of pleasure and delight—all the things in which we try to find happiness and pleasure—we will realize that ultimately they end in misery, suffering and sorrow. The reaction to them is always unhappiness.

Our sweetest songs give voice to saddest thoughts, and our greatest pleasures bring agony and grief in their wake. A thin partition divides the bounds between pleasure and pain. Even the little pleasure that we sometimes feel in the objects and forms of the world loses its charm in the course of time and ends in satiety. Then those dear faces and fair forms, for which at one time we were ready to sacrifice even our lives, become the object of indifference and aversion to us. Yet there remains a longing for something, but we know not what. Our soul is a spark of the Divine, a drop from the great Ocean of bliss. It will find peace and rest only after it merges into its Origin, the True Home from which it has descended so long ago, losing its way in the maze of this world. Guru Nanak says, "Brothers, happy alone are they who attain their Eternal Home."

Next Tulsi Sahib depicts the working of our mind, how this tiny mind of ours is full of thousands of desires and millions of cravings. And daily they go on increasing. There is no end to them. In this state of mind, how can one find peace and rest? Unless the mind withdraws its attention from the nine doors (the two eyes, two ears, two nostrils, the mouth and the two lower apertures), and peacefully settles down in the thinking center or eye center, it cannot reach its true home which is Trikuti, the region of Brahm, from where it came down into this world. And so long as the mind does not return to its home, the soul also, which is so firmly knotted to it in this world, cannot reach its destination, far beyond that of mind.

Where do we try to seek God, the Fountainhead of the soul and the Source of all energy? We seek Him in the stone mosques and earthen temples which we build with our own hands. How absurd it is that instead of searching for God in the temple that He Himself made for His residence in this world, we try to find Him in the houses which we build with bricks and stones. The human body is the temple of God, and He dwells within it. Christ, Guru Nanak, Mohammed and the founders of all religions agree on this point. But, ignoring their clear dictum—"The kingdom of God is within you"—we try to find it in churches, mosques and temples.

Yet the facts of history make us hang our heads in shame. When we read that if by mistake or folly a single brick or stone is knocked off a temple which we built with our own hands at the cost of a few coins, we rush out, armed with swords and daggers, to destroy in thousands the "living temples of God" that He made and in which He resides. Then we call ourselves martyrs and defenders of the faith. Can any folly be greater than this, that a man should hate God's creation for the love of bricks and stones?

Those who love God, love His creatures also. When the great God is the Creator of us all and gave each one of us hands, feet, eyes, ears and human form, and Himself dwells within us, whom should we hate and despise? If a person despises any of his fellow beings, I say that he despises the Creator Himself, who is within him. Christ calls the human body "the temple of the living God," and Guru Nanak calls it *"Har mandir"*—*Har* meaning 'God', *mandir* meaning 'temple'.

Tulsi Sahib says to Taqqi, referring to Taqqi's visit to Mecca, that the real Ka'aba is within us and this forehead of ours is its arch. Concentrate your thoughts between your eyebrows and listen intently in the center of this arch. You will hear a sweet Melody which flows from the highest heaven. This Celestial Music is resounding within the body of every human being, to whatever race, religion or country he may belong. This Voice of God constantly calls us towards itself.

Those who attend to this call of the Lord by concentrating their minds and attaching their souls to this sweet Music, reach the place from where it issues. This Sound emanates from Sat Lok, the region of eternal Truth and Reality, the everlasting abode of our Beloved Lord, the immortal, the indestructible, the *Sat* or 'True'. Christ calls this Sound the Word, the Logos. Guru Nanak, Kabir, Paltu and Swami Ji call it Nam, Shabd or Bani. Hindu Mystics call it Nad, Anahad or Ram Nam. Muslim Saints call it Kalma, Isme-i-Azam or Bang-i-Asmani. Various Prophets in different ages and in different climes have tried to explain the same underlying Truth—the Shabd, the Word—though in different words and languages.

Rituals and rites (the *shar'a* and *karm kand*), the ceremonial parts of every religion, differ according to the customs of the age and climates and conditions of the countries, but the real essence of Truth, the spirituality at the foundation of all religions, is the same. They all lead us to the Holy Sound, the Word, the Logos, by hearing which we attain salvation.

This great Saint further advises us that in our quest for

the Lord we need not leave our homes and go to the jungles, hills or mountains. The Lord is within us. None ever found Him anywhere outside. But the question arises, how to enter our body? How to search within ourselves? What is the path, by treading which we can reach Him? Tulsi Sahib says that the way is straight through the shah rug—'the royal vein' or central path beyond the eye center, referred to as *Sushmana* by the Hindu Mystics.

With love and faith in your heart, go to some perfect Master. He will impart to you the knowledge of the hidden entrance to this inner path. God is within you, but the secret of the way to approach Him and to realize Him within yourself is known only to the perfect Masters, from whom alone it can be had. The key to open the gate has been entrusted to their care.

When we act according to the advice of the Master and perform the spiritual exercises as directed by him, our internal ear is opened and we begin to hear the Heavenly Sound. By catching and holding onto this Sound, the Shabd, we eventually reach the place from where it emanates. The first station on the way is Allah or Sahansdal Kanwal.

The Bible states: "In the beginning was the Word, and the Word was with God, and the Word was God. . . . All things were made by him; and without him was not any thing made that was made." Guru Nanak says that Shabd, the Word, created the earth, the sky, the sun, the moon and all the world. According to the Holy Quran also, the world was created by the Word, *Kun*.

All the great realized souls have referred to the same Word or Sound as the Creator. Tulsi Sahib says that if we go on doing our spiritual exercises according to the directions of the Master and take advantage of his experience

by following his teachings, our mind will be connected
with the Word; we will ultimately become one with the
Word and will realize how the world was created by it.

* * *

7

IN CLEAR WORDS THE MASTER EXPLAINS

Guru kahen khol kar bhai
by Swami Ji

In clear words the Master explains:
Catch Anahad Shabd, which truly sustains.
There is no other way, save this Sound,
To get release from earthly bounds.
The key to the Five Tunes the Master knows,
Within this house, our True Home he shows.
With the Melody Divine link your soul;
Quit this prison and reach your goal.
Fathomless and limitless is that Abode,
Beyond the tenth[1] new worlds unfold.
Gained it is not without Master's grace;
Through Shabd alone can you reach that place.
Vacate your body and soar through the sky,
Follow the Shabd; it will take you high.
Your restless mind goes continually astray,
How shall it be curbed to faithfully obey?
Give all your heart and soul to Sound,
For no other way has yet been found.
Put all your faith in this true way,
And hang not back with feet of clay.
The essence of Sant Mat have I defined;
Surat Shabd Yoga,[2] bear always in mind.

---

1. 'Tenth door' is the same as tisra til or the eye center, the seat of the mind and the soul within the human body; the door that opens within.
2. Union with the Lord by attaching the soul to the Sound Current.

Radha Soami[1] the secret has imparted;
So without delay, let us all get started.

Sar Bachan Poetry, p.161, 20:10

Swami Ji reviews the methods we usually adopt and
the various disciplines to which we resort in order to realize God, and points out their inherent weaknesses. In the
hope of attaining liberation and realizing God we read
scriptures, go to temples and mosques or on pilgrimages
to holy places, give charity and do other pious deeds. We
forget the most important thing—that the kingdom of
heaven is within us; whereas all these things, laudable
though they are, turn our attention outward. We must
first realize God within ourselves before we can realize
His immanence in the outside world. We should, therefore, withdraw our attention from the outside world and
turn it inwards.

Our soul has been caught in the meshes of maya and
mind, and as a result of karmas done under the influence
of mind and sense impressions, we have to be born again
and again in this world. Our attachments and our unfulfilled desires, for which the mind continues to hanker, set
up an almost endless chain of reactions which keep us in
one or the other of the eighty-four lakh forms of creation,
and cause endless trouble and suffering. Even the most
happily circumstanced among us are far from happy. The
more thoughtful among us realize that happiness and bliss
are to found only in God; also that a return to God is
possible only in human life. But unfortunately they adopt
methods which are far from effective, and sometimes
even add to their egoism, and lead to self-righteousness
rather than liberation. Not only is the weight of karmas

---

1. 'Lord of the soul', a name for the Supreme Being.

still there but it also goes on growing into an unending chain.

Swami Ji tells us clearly and unequivocally that there is only one way of achieving our object. That consists in turning our mind inwards and connecting it with Nam or Shabd, the Audible Life Stream, the Divine Music which is reverberating in all of us—rich or poor, saint or sinner, high caste or low. In fact, Shabd was the foundation of the various mystic practices of religions, but with the lapse of time the key has been lost and the practices themselves have been smothered with ritualism. Shabd is the Creator and Sustainer of the world and is known as Word, Logos, Isme-i-Azam, Nam or Anahad Shabd.

We all talk of Nam but fail to distinguish between the spoken word—the varnatmak nam—and the Mystic Sound which is heard within by the mind—the dhunatmak Nam. It is this latter, the dhunatmak Nam, which is capable of detaching the mind from sensual pleasures and giving it spiritual bliss. This Nam, unlike all other names of God, like Ram, Raheem, Allah, Vah Guru and Radha Soami, cannot be spoken or written. We can trace the history of varnatmak names in time, but the dhunatmak Nam to which Swami Ji refers existed before time began. All this universe, including time and space, was created by Nam and out of Nam. Varnatmak nam is the means for the attainment of dhunatmak Nam. If we had not lost sight of this vital point, varnatmak nam would not have led to bigotry and intolerance, for the varnatmak nam is only a means and not an end. The moment we realize that varnatmak names are only pointers to indicate that inner Reality—the dhunatmak Nam—we would all agree that there is really only one way. Then fanaticism and dogmatism would come to an end, and man would not hate man.

The important point is to realize the difference between the name of a thing and the thing itself. We should
not confuse the doctor's prescription with the medicine.
There are no differences of caste, creed or color in Him
and there should be none in us, for soul is of the essence
of God. All these differences are the result of our narrow-
mindedness and our ignorance of the dhunatmak Nam.

Dhunatmak Nam or Shabd is not to be found in
books or scriptures; they only extol it, but Nam itself is
within us. Rishis and Sages who, in their time, realized
God, recorded their experiences and particulars of the
path for our guidance. We come to know the difficulties
of the path and obtain a clear conception of the ideal, but
we cannot realize God by merely reading books. We will
have to travel the path ourselves. The mere repetition of
the word *food* will not satisfy hunger. Mere reading of the
scriptures or listening to the teachings is not enough. You
must put the teachings into practice and travel the path
yourself.

How can we contact this Shabd within ourselves? The
entire mystery is in the part of the body above the eyes, in
the human brain. Between and above the eyes is the center called tisra til, the eye center, also the center of thinking, which is the seat of mind and soul in the human
body. This is the station for starting on our spiritual journey and contacting the higher spiritual regions, just as the
nine sense doors are our instruments of perception for
contacting the outer, material world. It is through these
sense doors that the mind goes out and spreads into the
world. Saints and Masters, therefore, exhort us to withdraw the mind from the nine doors and make it steady at
the eye center so that it may catch the Shabd, the Divine
Sound.

This Shabd is resounding within us day and night, and

its music continues even when we fall asleep. To connect the mind with this dhunatmak Nam or Shabd is to reach the door of liberation. The fickleness of the mind goes after it has tasted the bliss of Shabd. Then it turns away from sense pleasures and begins to look Godward.

The technique of joining the mind to Nam is to be learned from Saints and Masters, who are well versed in it. God has placed Nam within us and for us, but the key is in the hands of the Saints and Masters, who are Shabd incarnate. They have the knowledge of the spiritual science and teach us how to attain spiritual heights and realize God, just as the teachers of worldly science awaken and develop our intellectual faculties. This is the mission of Saints and Masters like Kabir Sahib, Guru Nanak Sahib, Swami Ji Maharaj and others.

Saints further tell us that there is no other sure method of getting permanent release from this cage of flesh—the body. It may sound dogmatic, but a little thought will make it clear. What brings us into this world? Our karmas, our desires, our attachments. We perform actions and entertain desires—good or bad—and have to take birth to reap the fruit of our actions and to satisfy the unfulfilled desires. Even good and pious actions cannot liberate us. They have their reward in this world or higher worlds; but when the merit of our pious deeds is exhausted, we have to come down again. That is not liberation from the wheel of birth and death. After every death there is stocktaking by Dharam Rai, the Lord of Justice, and the soul has to take on a new body. Death releases the soul from one body only to make it enter another, in accordance with its karmas and desires.

Can we really be without karma in practice? Even if we could, there is yet another factor, the sinchit karmas— the reserve or store of karmas which have not been able to bear fruit so far. They stand against our names in the astral records and are likely to come up at a very inconvenient time, perhaps just when we think we are free from attachment. This record can be wiped off by Shabd practice only.

The body in which we dwell is also the temple of God. It is the epitome of the universe. In it are all the spiritual regions right up to Sach Khand or Sat Desh, where the Lord dwells; but we know it not. Saints and Masters show us the way to this 'home within the home', and not only set us on the journey but guide and escort us to the 'Holy of Holies'.

Our spiritual journey really begins from the soles of our feet and ends at the top of the head. Our consciousness is scattered throughout the body and must be withdrawn gradually and concentrated at the eye center, where the Saints link it with Shabd or Nam, and then the upward journey begins.

This Divine Music issues from Sach Khand and, passing through the five spiritual regions, comes to the eye center from where it sustains and maintains our mental and spiritual faculties. Its origin is beyond mind and maya, and if we link our consciousness to it, it will carry us too beyond mind and maya. That is why Swami Ji exhorts us to attune ourselves to this Shabd Dhun, so that it may take us from this home to that Home.

This is the only way to escape from this vale of sorrow and reach the Divine Abode where all is happiness and bliss. Shabd is the means and the Master is the Guide, and the overall grace of God makes it possible for us to contact a Master. So first comes the grace of God, then the kindness and mercy of the Master who initiates us into the mysteries of Nam, and finally our own unceasing efforts to tread the path and follow the instructions.

To be in harmony with the Divine Symphony of Shabd and to hold fast to it is all that is needed. No other practice is necessary. The 'merit' of counting beads, doing penances, reading scriptures, performing worship, and much more, is all attained by Nam bhakti. "The elephant's foot includes all feet." Can there be a higher *jap*, 'recitation', than meditating on God and always having his Name in our mind? What greater *tap*, 'penance', can there be than surrendering ourselves unconditionally to His Will and accepting whatever comes—good or bad, pleasant or unpleasant—with cheerful resignation? What holier worship is there than to move about with the radiant form of Saints and Masters always with us? What nobler recitation of the scriptures can there be than keeping our inner attention day and night in Shabd? Can there be a more complete renunciation than the sublime non-attachment resulting from Shabd *abhyas*, the practice of Shabd?

But there is no rose without a thorn, and the thorn here is our mind with its fickleness and its cravings for pleasure. We cannot see our reflection clearly in muddy or shaky water, and we cannot see God till the mind is calm and steady. By moral and intellectual persuasion, by social or religious discipline, by reading scriptures and even by resorting to austerities, the mind is not completely purified nor is it made permanently strong against low and base desires. A serpent is quiet and harmless as long as it is shut up in a basket, but neither its fury nor its poison is destroyed. If at any time the lid is left open, it will come out and bite; but if the poison sac is removed, the serpent is rendered harmless. The practices referred to, bring mind under partial control, that is, its tendency to sensual pleasures is not really conquered. The snake is only suppressed, not killed.

Saints are able to solve this difficult problem by methods which are based upon the knowledge of the innate nature of mind. Its fickleness will be arrested when it is able to secure pleasure or bliss greater than any worldly pleasures; for the mind, too, has a high origin. In flitting from one object to another it seems to be seeking that old condition of bliss and happiness which it once enjoyed, before it lost its mastery and became the slave of the senses.

Where can this be secured? In the company of Saints who instruct us in the technique of catching the Shabd, the Divine Music. Hearing this Melody, the mind stands still, as does the running deer on hearing music. This is the keynote and the distinguishing characteristic of the teachings of Saints. Swami Ji advises us to hold onto it resolutely, and to guard against procrastination and sluggishness. "Make hay while the sun shines." As time passes, and we advance in years, we are likely to be less energetic and active in mind and body—and then, who knows when the angel of death may strike?

Swami Ji has placed before us the essentials of Sant Mat, and pointed out the unfailing and unmistakable way for reunion with God. It is now for us to accept and follow it. Finally, it may be pointed out that to go on making different experiments in this line is not a sound proposition. We should profit by the experience of others. The world would not have progressed so much if everyone had insisted on experimenting from the beginning in every science and ignored the proven results of their forerunners. It is not every time that one is born as a human being and that contact with a Saint or a perfect teacher becomes possible. Human birth and contact with the Guru are rewards for our good actions in past lives. Therefore we should make the fullest use of this oppor-

tunity by cultivating Nam bhakti, Surat Shabd Yoga—
merging the soul with Shabd—and thus achieve liberation
from the wheel of birth and death.

* * *

8

ATTUNE YOURSELF TO RAM, THE IMMANENT POWER

Rama Ram, Ramo sun man bheeje
by Guru Ram Das

Attune yourself to Ram, the Immanent Power,
Listen to Ram, the all-pervading Shabd,
And drench the mind with it.
Sweet is the Nectar of God's Name;
Drink it with the aid of Guru's grace.
As the fire is latent in wood,
And by friction properly directed
Is made manifest,
So is the Light of Ram Nam[1] in all of us.
Realize it by following the teaching of the Guru.
Nine outlets has the body,
All the nine insipid;
Real Nectar flows through the tenth.[2]
Thy mercy and grace I implore, Beloved,
That, through Guru's Shabd,
The Nectar of God[3] I may drink.
The human body is a city;
In this beautiful city, look for God's Love.
The rarest of gems and rubies there await you;
Acquire them by devotion and service to Satguru.

---

1. *Ram Nam*: 'the Lord's Name'.
2. The tenth outlet is the eye center.
3. God's Love is manifested by the inner bliss.

Infinite and inaccessible is the Lord,
Constant devotion alone can win His Love.
Like a chatrak that longs for rain,
I long for a drop of Nectar.
Scarlet red is the Satguru's vat;
Let us give him our minds to dye,
And quickly drink to our fill
This Nectar of God's Love.
The wealth of the seven continents,
The treasures of the seven seas,
Heaped in one place—
All this, the lovers of God would spurn.
They ask only for God
And a cupful of His Love.
Ever hungry are the sakats[1]
Who cry for more and more,
And constantly run after wealth—
Keep far away from them.
Holy and sublime is God;
Equally noble and sublime His devotees—
How can we describe their greatness?
They can be compared only to Ram Nam,
No other description would be right.
Their grace Nanak implores.

Adi Granth, p.1323, M.4

What is it that stands between soul and God, which does not permit us to see God—which does not permit the soul to see its Maker—though our soul is a spark of the Divine Source? That obstacle, that blinding screen, is our own mind.

---

1. *Sakats*: Worldly people completely dominated by mind and given over to sensual pleasures.

Owing to its association with mind, our soul, though a spark of the Divine Source, has been separated from its Maker and caught in the meshes of maya, and has come under the latter's influence and control. In fact, the mind and the soul have been tied together in a knot, as it were, and the soul—along with the mind—has to suffer the consequences of all actions. So long as it does not leave the company of the mind, it will not be qualified to return to its original state. This association with the mind will dissolve only when the mind returns to its origin, which is Trikuti.

Mind, too, has lost its original place and character, and is now dominated by the senses. The soul will not be liberated from the control of the mind till the mind goes back to its original place. Until then, we have to reap the consequences of our actions and have to move on the wheel of eighty-four lakhs of births and deaths. We cannot escape the results of our karmas as long as we are under the influence of the mind, which must therefore be brought under control. It must be made to retrace its steps upward and to withdraw from the world of phenomena. It must be brought back by the same way that it went out, and kept steady at its center.

What means do the Saints advocate to turn the mind back and take it to Trikuti? First, we have to consider the nature of the mind. Mind is fond of pleasure and runs after attractive things, but it does not remain attached for long to any one object. It is fickle, soon gets tired of every pleasure and begins to seek a new one. Thus it wanders from one object of pleasure to another. The only way to make the mind steady is to give it a taste of some delight higher than any worldly pleasure. Once it has tasted such joy, it will be attached to it forever and its fickleness will be gone. Then it will never again hanker after worldly pleasures nor run out through the nine doors. But until it enjoys this bliss, it cannot be withdrawn effectively from sense pleasures.

Where can such bliss be found? It is in Nam, Shabd, the Audible Life Stream, also called Ram, Akash Bani or the Word. *Ram* is one of the names of the Power that pervades everywhere, and that name has been used for the word *Shabd* in this hymn. It is the Power or the Divine Energy that has created the universe. It is the Creator and also the support of the universe. It is immanent in the universe and sustains it. It is also in everyone—rich and poor, good and bad, man, woman and child, irrespective of caste, creed, race or country. Guru Nanak Sahib says, "Meditate on this Ram, this Shabd. Let the mind taste its bliss and dwell on it. The mind will then lose its fickleness and come under your control."

This Nam, Guru Nanak Sahib tells us, is sweet beyond description. Veritably it is Nectar, for if we drink it, it will make us immortal. While pleasures of the world entangle us in the wheel of births and deaths, *Nam Ras*, 'the Elixir of Nam', liberates us from the wheel and bestows immortality. What is more, it is within us. To one who has tasted this Nectar, all pleasures of the world are insipid.

It may be asked, "Why then are people unhappy and full of misery in this world, and why are they caught in the wheel of birth and death, when the holy and sublime Nam is in every human being?" Guru Sahib explains the point by means of an illustration: There is fire in wood, but it cannot be seen nor put to any use until it is ignited. When we vigorously rub two pieces of wood together, or light the wood by other means, we are not only able to see the fire but also can use it. Likewise, though Nam exists in all of us, it is of no use to us nor can we enjoy its bliss unless we first attain it by our own efforts, according to the directions of the Satguru. Only then will it be possible to secure the benefits which Nam is capable of yielding.

This light of Nam is present in all of us, high or low, and God has placed it there for us, but it will not be of use to us unless we realize it within ourselves. This can be done only by following the practice recommended by the Masters. No amount of effort, no trick or thought or intelligence, will secure this treasure unless we unreservedly accept the guidance of the Master.

We must dive within our own selves in order to come in touch with Nam, for whatever is in the macrocosm is also in the microcosm. For this purpose the part of the body above the eyes corresponds to Brahmand and Par Brahm, and the lower part—from the eyes downward—corresponds to Pind. Nam is to be sought in the upper part. In the lower part are the sense organs—the nine openings—through which we establish contact with the world. The pleasures which we derive through them are evanescent, and bring grief and pain in their trail. Even the apparent charm in them is mere illusion. The momentary pleasures which they yield are sure to be followed by unpleasant and sometimes even painful reactions.

When shall we secure this Nectar, by drinking which we shall get eternal bliss and peace? We shall obtain that Nectar and the consequent bliss and peace when the mind withdraws from the nine doors and reaches the tenth. That Nectar is being showered within us day and night. But our mind is busy elsewhere, in quarrels, hatred, fascination for wife and children, and other temporal delights, and has no time to 'go in' and taste its bliss. Unless the mind is kept steady and in a receptive mood, at the center where God is showering this inestimable gift, we will not get it even though it is falling in showers within us. No water will be collected in a pitcher if it is put upside down, even in a heavy rain. It will flow off the sides. However, if the same pitcher is put right side up, it will be filled, if not by the first, then by the second or third shower.

Similarly, if we frequent the company of Saints, learn from them the technique of making the mind steady, and follow the practice assiduously, we shall be able to realize Nam, drink the Nectar and, one day, realize God. We will thus be liberated from the wheel of births and deaths. If the goal is not achieved in this life, it will be achieved in the next, or in the one after the next. Having once started on the path, to reach the goal does not take more than four lives at the most. The company of the Saints is very helpful in turning the mind away from the world, towards God. Salvation is achieved by means of Nam, and the secret of Nam can be learned only from Saints.

The question arises: "Why doesn't everyone approach Saints to learn the process and to accumulate Nam, when it is so great and holy?" The reason is that it is not possible to come into contact with Saints without the grace of God. Without this grace, even if a person does happen to meet them, faith in their teachings and in Nam will not arise in him. First God's grace, then contact with Saints and faith in their teachings, and then one's own efforts, as instructed by them. That is the order. Saints favor us by communicating the secret of Nam, then we turn towards God and begin our spiritual practice; but it is all in the hands of God, without whose grace nothing can be done. Hence, Guru Sahib implores God, on our behalf, "O Lord, shower grace upon us, so that we may have the good fortune of meeting Saints and acquiring Nam from them and, by working according to their teachings, we may be able to secure our release from birth and death and unite with God."

A blind person cannot catch hold of one who can see unless the latter calls him or puts himself within reach of the former. Grace is absolutely necessary because we are spiritually blind.

The human body has been likened to a city with beautiful shops where all sorts of things can be purchased. Nam can be bargained for in this city only. Hence it is that the human life is honored by names like 'the noblest of all created beings' or nar-narayan life—the life in which one can become God. It is possible to acquire liberation by realizing Nam, in the human body only. Strike the bargain of Nam and accumulate this treasure while God gives you the opportunity to live in this body. Do not waste this life, as it is not possible to attain salvation in any other form of life.

Guru Nanak Sahib sings the glories of Nam and calls it a priceless ruby, a jewel. Of course, these are not worthy of being compared with Nam, which is all-knowledge, all-bliss; and everything except Nam, or God, is trite and perishable. However, since pearls, rubies and diamonds are the most precious material objects, Nam is compared to them. Nam cannot be purchased with money, or it would have been monopolized by kings and rich people. It can be acquired only by serving the Satguru.

Now, what is the nature of this service? It consists in doing our meditation with devotion, acting according to the Satguru's teachings and, above all, unqualified surrender to him. It does not consist in rendering personal service, though this point cannot be ignored. How many people would a Master require for his personal service? Very few. Devotion and especially unqualified surrender constitute the highest service and lead to Nam.

God is infinite and cannot be approached easily in His

infinite and universal form, but He is localized, as it were, and centered in His Saints and devotees. Approach through them is easy and practical. For this reason, great importance is attached to devotion to the Master. It is only a living Master who can teach us the secret of Nam and give us guidance in realizing It. Nam can be learned only from a human teacher. Who then except a highly evolved person can teach us the secret of Nam?

Outwardly, Saints and Masters appear like ordinary human beings, but in their inner selves they are connected with Shabd, the Audible Life Stream—nay, they are Shabd incarnate. There is no difference between Saints and Shabd, or God. God is the sea, and Saints are its waves. Waves rise out of the sea, live on it and finally merge in it. Similarly, Saints are born out of Shabd, take up the body, teach the wisdom of Shabd to men, and finally go back and merge into Shabd. They unite us again to Shabd and so we love them. They make us like themselves and raise us to the same spiritual height which they have attained. If we bestow our love on the world, we will be caught in the wheel of births and deaths; if we love God, we shall be united with Him.

It is not enough, however, to know the secret of Nam. There must be an ardent fervor for its acquisition. We should cultivate one-pointed love and devotion to God, the most unselfish devotion, which asks for nothing but God. Think of the devotion of the chatrak, the rainbird, for the rain. The Ganges may be full, and flowing just in front of the chatrak, but it would rather die than drink water that does not come from the clouds. Its eyes are always imploringly directed towards the clouds. Our love for God or Nam should be just like that. But our devotion, alas, is often actuated by selfish motives. If we practice meditation for an hour or so, we entertain a thousand expectations and want God to fulfill them all, as a reward for our devotion.

Let our devotion spring out of love and not from fear or some selfish motive. Some people worship snakes. Do they love them? No. They worship snakes out of fear. Similarly, some worship God out of fear. That is not true worship or devotion. True devotion does not consist of selfish ends nor is it actuated by fear. It rises out of pure love. We feel unhappy, shed tears and pass sleepless nights if a friend or a relative passes away. Have we ever felt such strong emotions and shed such tears in our longing for God? If not, how can we hope to reach Him? Guru Sahib exhorts us to practice devotion, but not for worldly happiness or fame. Our devotion should be real, prompted only by pure love. Such pure, one-pointed love for God and real anguish for His grace is created in the company of Saints.

Satguru is a dyer, and a washerman too, and dyes our minds in love. Only when we surrender our mind unreservedly to him, will he dye it in the color of devotion, of divine love. But a piece of cloth does not take on color well unless it has been first washed and cleaned. We should therefore dedicate our mind to him, to be cleaned, and no matter how dirty it is he will wash it. A washerman does not refuse to wash clothes, however soiled and dirty they may be. He knows that originally they were clean, and can be washed white and clean again—perhaps only after repeated washings, in some cases, but finally they will become clean. Likewise Saints also do not avoid nor reject sinners. They say, "We shall not discard you. We know that every being is originally pure, is a spark of the Divine Source. Addiction to sense enjoyment has made you impure, but Nam will make you holy and pure again. It may not be achieved in one life, it may take two or three lives to do it; but it is certain that one day you will be one with God." That is why Saints ask us to surrender our mind with one-pointed love.

Those who are filled with the love of God drink their fill of Nectar, enjoy the bliss of God-intoxication, and care not for the riches and the glory of the world. If we were to heap in one place the gold and treasures of the seven continents and the treasures of the seven seas, and ask Gurmukhs and lovers of God to choose between Nam and this treasure, they would not look at the latter. They would ask of God only the realization of Nam and the nectar of Shabd. They care for nothing else.

Guru Nanak Sahib says, "As the chatrak asks only for rainwater, so do the lovers of God ask only for God and for nothing else." They pray to God, "O Lord, we want to see your divine face, we want to realize Nam, we care for nothing else." When you secure God, the greatest giver, will there be any dearth of gifts? On the other hand, persons who depend on their own strength are always hungry and needy in spite of all that may be given to them by God. They always hanker after more and more.

The devotees of God, who have received the grace of the Master, live a happy and contented life. Those, however, who have not been fortunate enough to receive such grace, but depend upon the powers of their own mind, are always hungry; their desires are never completely fulfilled. Even though God gives to them in abundance, they are not contented. By the time some of their longings are satisfied, as many more are born in their mind, demanding satisfaction. There is no end to their desires. They never get everything they want, and so they are always unhappy on account of some unfulfilled desires.

What should be our attitude towards people who love

things in the world and are attached to sense enjoyment? A devotee should put a safe distance between himself and such people, and avoid their company. Mind is quickly affected by company. One develops a craving for sense pleasures in the company of worldly people, and through this craving is caught in the wheel of eighty-four lakhs of species.

One should go to the Saints and Masters. In their company, vices are destroyed and good qualities blossom. Then love for the Lord, fervor to acquire Nam, and devotion develop. A stone will keep cool, at least protected from the sun's heat, as long as it remains in water. Similarly, a man in good company, even if he is not able to realize God, would at least be saved from vices and sins. The writings of Saints and Masters have only one aim: to create love for and devotion to God, and zeal and zest for acquiring Nam. Such devotion, love and zest will be more effectively created by actually living in their company.

How can we praise such devotees of God? With whom can these great and noble souls be compared? They are holy and sublime, like God Himself. In fact there is no difference between God and His Saints. They can be compared to God only. No other comparison would be adequate. "Devotees can be comparison to Ram only, and to nothing else," says Guru Nanak Sahib, and implores God to give us the company of Saints and Masters. That includes everything. In their company and by their grace everything will be achieved: we shall learn the secret of Nam, acquire the wealth of Nam, and thus finally secure real emancipation.

* * *

9

FORSAKE THIS DOMAIN
OF PLEASURE AND PAIN

Tajo man yeh dukh sukh ka dham
by Swami Ji

O mind!
Forsake this domain of pleasure and pain,
Rise to the skies and Sat Nam attain.
Short-lived is this human form,
Fleeting the pleasures which from dust are born.
Wealth and friends, so valued here,
Avail us naught when death draws near.
Your body is like a water bag,
At death it will be a shriveled rag.
A double stream of breath flows on
Till all is spent and life is gone.
But deep you sink in worldly love,
And fail to hear the Word above.
Why not abandon the bewitching wife,[1]
And, forsaking lust, live the true life?
Without Satguru's grace, there's no release;
In devotion to him, you will share His peace.
Fix Master's image in your heart,
And joy serene it will impart.
Guru is gracious and always guides;
Sustains us within when our faith subsides.

---

1. The "bewitching wife" refers to Maya, which means illusion in general and, in this case particularly, our own sensual desires.

Sensual pleasures breed disease;
Renounce them all—no peace in these.
Obey whatever Satguru ordains;
Peace and bliss are thus obtained.
All your sorrows shall he wash away,
And take you Home,[1] come what may.
Radha Swami does proclaim:
Search for that One True Name.

Sar Bachan Poetry, p.119, 15:9

Swami Ji, looking at people running after pleasures and worldly pursuits, and seeing that it is in these worldly things that we are trying to find happiness—sometimes in one thing and sometimes in another, sometimes in wealth, friends, politics, and sometimes in sensual pleasures; but all in vain—advises us to turn our back on this place of checkered joy and sorrow, and make for our true, eternal Home. He appeals to our mind because it is the mind which runs after these things and falls prey to the lure of the senses.

The mind and the soul are coupled together and tied in a knot, as it were. Therefore the soul cannot go up unless the mind also accompanies it. If the two pull in opposite directions we can never succeed. Hence this address to the mind. In fact, all satsangs are meant to turn the mind inward.

Mind too has known higher joys and hunts in vain for happiness in the world of phenomena. Its real abode is Trikuti. Satguru, therefore, exhorts the mind to cease running after fleeting pleasures and to seek abiding happiness in the place of its origin. In coming down and

---

1. Home: the highest region.

joining itself with the senses and the objects of senses, it goes out and continues running, seeking pleasures and satisfaction outside.

Mind also will find joy and happiness if it goes inward, though mind cannot go all the way along with the soul. When the mind and the soul together ascend to Trikuti, the mind merges into the essence of which it is a part, while the soul, freed from its limitations, goes up and reaches Sat Lok.

The various spiritual disciplines, the various practices advocated by religious and spiritual groups, are only attempts to take the mind up so that the mind may be freed from the grip of the senses and can go and rest in its origin. Thus only can the soul be free.

The Saints have compared this body to a cage. It is a cage designed by Kal, or the negative power, to keep the soul down in this world, and the force which keeps it down is its karma—good and bad—which it has done in the past.

Our relation with the world is based on our physical existence. As long as we continue to live in this body, we feel pleasure and pain, happiness and unhappiness. When we leave the body, all these states also cease to exist for it. The Master says that we should take advantage of the opportunity of being in the human form by putting our attention inside, so that the limited time which is granted to us may be utilized to the fullest extent to secure liberation. Then alone, coming into the human form will be fruitful.

This world is like a big hotel where people from all parts come and stay for various periods, after which they all go their different ways. Think of a number of logs floating in a river. One wave or current brings them together, another current comes along and parts them. In the same way do we meet and part. We come, meet and make friends or enemies, and then depart.

Friends, relatives, children and others for whose sake we often follow dubious ways, sacrifice our principles and have recourse to shady practices—what is their value? The relationship being of this world only, they are of no help to us when the soul leaves the body. When the time comes, the angel of death takes the soul away. We do not even know where the soul has gone or who has taken it away. How then can our friends and relatives help us at that time? Our relationship with them is really a business of balancing what we have to claim and what we have to give. Some are related to us as children, some as parents, some as other relatives, some as friends and some as enemies. When the account is cleared we part, and are judged by our karmas only.

Spectators see the actors on a stage behaving as if they were closely connected and actually lived the parts they were playing, but they know that they are only playing a part. As soon as the play is over, they get off the stage and are no more friends, brothers, enemies, husbands, wives, or whatever part they were playing. Similarly, on the stage of the world we play the various parts which have been allotted to us by our own karmas, and then make our exit.

This does not mean that we should give up our friends and relatives, or cut off connections with them; but while discharging our duties and obligations we are not to get entangled in these relationships, and should always keep an eye on our ultimate goal. We should be good and model husbands, wives, citizens. Sant Mat encourages the performance of our duties for the sake of duty and therefore improves the general relationship between human beings.

We have been allotted a definite number of breaths, and are breathing day and night through both nostrils. Just as a tank full of water, which has an outlet pipe through which the water is flowing, will one day be quite empty, in the same way our store of breaths will one day be finished and death will overtake us. But we are so engrossed in worldly pursuits that we have forgotten the all-important fact of death. Even when we see people dying, or accompany a corpse to the cemetery, we do not take heed. We seem to think that perhaps we are not to die. If we kept death or the end in view, then we would also try to find some means of facing it more easily and without dread.

This body is like an inflated skin, floating on water. As soon as the pumped air goes out, the skin sinks. So it is when our breaths are finished. As soon as we cease breathing, this body is either burned or buried. If we were to withdraw our attention from outside things and turn within ourselves, then we would be able to hear that Divine Sound which will release us from bondage.

That pristine Shabd, the Word, resounds in all of us but, our attention being outside, we cannot hear it. We cannot hear that Divine Sound because maya has cast a veil over us and under the influence of maya we have been lulled to sleep. Therefore we should go to a Gurmukh—a Master—who will teach us how to withdraw our attention and break this spell which maya has cast over us. Then it will be possible for us to go in and contact the Shabd. It is with the help of the Master that we take our attention from the things of the world and put it in Nam or Shabd.

Next, Swami Ji describes this process somewhat in detail. First we have to withdraw our consciousness or fix our conscious attention at the eye center by means of

simran—the repetition of the Holy Names. Whatever we
dwell upon, whatever thoughts and ideas we harbor, has
a very important effect on us and molds our mental self
accordingly. The repetition of the Holy Names will give
the mind a spiritual orientation and facilitate concentration. When we have in this way withdrawn our attention
from the nine doors to the eye center, we will behold the
form of the Master, who is Shabd incarnate. This inner
dhyan or 'contemplation' on the form of the Master is
necessary in order to keep the attention there. Our attention, even though brought up to that point, is likely to slip
down every now and then; but when it is fixed there by
contemplating on the form of the Master, it will learn to
stay there.

We contemplate on the form of the Master because
he is the embodiment of Shabd. Whatever we fix our
attention upon will attract us, so because of this dhyan,
we will also be with the Master. When the Master leaves
his body, he resides in Shabd. Therefore, if we love him,
we will also go and abide in Shabd along with him.

Realization of the help and protection which we receive from the Master comes only when we go in and see
his inner working. Then we realize how he guides, directs
and controls us. Of course, every satsangi receives the
Master's help and protection, but if one is not able to go
in he cannot actually see what is being done for him.
However, those who are able to go in, see his protective
hand every minute.

In the end Swami Ji exhorts us to give up the love of
sensual pleasures and worldly enjoyment. These are really not pleasures but a source of pain and unhappiness.
When we accept and follow the teachings of a Master,
contact the Shabd and go in, then do we realize the meaning of peace and happiness.

The Divine Shabd is the keynote. After explaining all this, Swami Ji again urges us to investigate the mystery of Shabd, work up to it and merge ourselves into it, so that we may reach our ultimate goal, Radha Soami.

* * *

10

AN INVERTED WELL IS THERE ABOVE

Ulta kuan gagan men
by Paltu Sahib

An inverted well is there above,
And therein burns a lamp;
A lamp burns therein
Without oil and without wick.
It burns night and day,
For the six seasons
And the twelve months 'tis lit.
He alone sees it
Who has the Satguru with him,
For without the Satguru
It ever remains unseen.
From within the lamp's flame
Comes a Melody,
He alone hears it
Who attains gyan samadhi.[1]
Whoever listens to it, O Paltu,
Is most fortunate indeed.
In the inverted well above
Burns a lamp that never dies.

Paltu Sahib ki Bani, I: Kundli 169

All of us are eager to realize God. This is the ideal
which every religion has set before it and has spared no

---

1. State of meditation in which the soul goes into the inner regions and attains spiritual knowledge (gyan).

pains in endeavoring to achieve. People have traveled far and wide, in most difficult places and to the distant corners of the earth, in pursuit of this goal. But have they succeeded?

God is within all of us. But so many people—of all countries and all religious organizations—are trying in their own way to find Him. God remains a mirage to all who seek Him by external means, not because He cannot be realized but because they are seeking Him in the wrong place and in the wrong manner. We are, in fact, no better than the man who searched on the roads for what was hidden in his own room. Whoever has realized God has done so within himself. It is only after realizing God within that we can be aware of His omniscience, omnipotence and omnipresence.

The way to God-realization is to seek him within oneself. All the Saints who are genuine Mystics have declared this from the housetops. The surest way to realize God is to contact that Divine Melody, Shabd, which is resounding in all of us. The key or the way is obtainable only from an Adept, a Master.

The hymn quoted above is from a well-known Saint, Paltu Sahib, who flourished in the eighteenth century and spoke from his own personal experience. He was a very bold and outspoken Saint, and explained everything fearlessly. The head, in which lies the secret and the key, has been compared by Paltu Sahib to an inverted well wherein the disciple sees the immortal, unextinguishable Light. From the mystic point of view, the body may be divided into two parts: one below the eyes and the other above the eyes. The highest mystic path, which leads to God-realization, is above the eyes. It is there that one can contact the Shabd, the Sound Current, by following the instructions given by a perfect Master.

Paltu Sahib says that within us is that great Light or Flame which goes on burning all the year round, without the need of oil or wick. This Light is in all of us and has always been there. But it can be seen only by someone who, having surrendered himself unconditionally to a perfect Master, faithfully and devotedly follows the path which has been chalked out for him by his Master. It is this spiritual Light which is the central part of the first region known as Sahansdal Kanwal, and it is from the rays or vibrations issuing from this Light that our entire universe is being sustained and managed.

It is not a small privilege to have a glimpse of this *Jot*; 'Light'. Rishis and munis of ancient times worked for thousands of years and subjected themselves to the hardest disciplines in order to reach this height, yet it is only the first stage of Sant Mat. But it cannot be reached without the help and the grace of the Satguru.

Out of the Light issues a heavenly Sound. That Sound can be heard only by the person who through the grace of the Master has completely withdrawn his consciousness from this house of nine doors—the body—and has gone up above the eye center. In order to accomplish this, it is first necessary to concentrate the attention at the eye center, as instructed by the Master.

Owing to the partial loss and misunderstanding of the mystic tradition, followers of most religions use the term *Bani*, 'Word', for their various sacred books. The books themselves, however sacred and to whichever religion they may belong, are only verbal descriptions of the real Bani within. Huzur Maharaj Ji used to emphasize this point: Our Scriptures and sacred books extol that Bani or Shabd which is within; the Bani itself is not in the books but it is within ourselves and it can be heard or contacted within ourselves by perfect discipleship and the grace of the Master.

In every temple of ours a light is lit, and at its entrance a bell is hung. The devotees ring this bell before they enter the temple. Likewise, in every gurdwara a lamp is lit and a conch shell is sounded. In Muslim shrines, too, lamps are placed on the graves. Similarly, in a church candles are lit and a bell is rung. The Saints employed all these devices to make us understand that an internal Light and an internal Sound reside within us. The external light and the external bells are mere imitations. The purpose behind all this was to arouse in us a keen desire to realize the original. Unfortunately we have forgotten the real and have become lost in the imitation.

It is only as a result of very good karmas that one is born as a human being and contacts a Master. And it is the height of good karmas to be able to get initiation from the Master, follow the path and contact that Sound Current within.

* * *

11

OUR SOUL IS IN GOD
AND GOD IS IN THE SOUL

Atam men Ram, Ram men Atam
by Guru Nanak

Our soul is in God and God is in the soul.
The Guru to his gurmukhs reveals the whole.
Immortal Shabd, the True Word sublime,
Kills the ego and cleanses the shrine.[1]
Nanak, the pernicious disease of ego
I find wherever I go.
To those that He wished to save,
The gift of Nam He always gave.
As a coin tester coins does test,
Cuts the false and stores the rest,
So the Lord selection makes,
And the pure He Homeward takes.
False are water, fire and air;
False is earth that looks so fair.
False are father, sister and mother,
False is body, false is brother.
False are the creator and the destroyer,
False the world and false the supplier.[2]
Of their falsehood only those were cured
Who heard the Word and in Love endured.

---

1. The human body.
2. The Hindu trinity of Brahma, Vishnu and Shiva—the creator, the nourisher and the destroyer.

False are all the seas and rivers as they stand,
False the lower regions and the netherlands.[1]
True only are His lovers,
On them His grace He ever showers.
False is philosophy with all its schools,
False the ascetics and all their rules.
In vain the books and Vedas claim;
They find not the Lord, though 'tis their aim.
Dainty dishes lead to disease;
Herbs and roots—no pleasure in these.
Who ignores the Word and its meaning forgets,
Suffers at death with dismay and regrets.
Not by pilgrimage is the malady cured,
Nor by learning is Truth secured.
Worship of gods and mammon vile
Makes us slaves of Maya's guile.
Master's gurmukhs are steeped in Sound,
And purified, are Homeward bound.
O Nanak, happy is the chosen son
On whom does glance the Beloved One.

Adi Granth, p.1153, M.1

"The soul is in God, and God is in the soul," says
Guru Nanak. But the realization that we are in God and
that God is in us, comes only when—through the grace of
the Master and by following his teachings—we are able to
develop this vision. The big banyan tree is potentially in
the tiny seed, and the seed of this large tree is very small.
If one did not know this fact, he would never believe it.
However, one has only to sow the seed in suitable soil,
water it and give it the proper care; then, in due course,
the sapling will develop. The trunk and the branches will

---

1. Everything that is not eternal is false; that is, all the regions below the fifth spiritual region as well as all the hells.

grow into such enormous size as to be able to shelter thousands of people beneath it. In the same way, God is within us and we are in Him, though we are not able to realize this truth owing to the veil of egotism in between.

Our soul is a drop from the ocean of Sach Khand. It is a drop from the Deity, but on account of association with the mind, we do things which involve us and keep us tied to this world of phenomena, through painful or pleasing experiences. Intrinsically the soul is divine, is pure, and has nothing to keep it down; but desires and association with the mind keep it in this world. The mind in turn is ruled by the senses, and the attachments and consequent desires pull us down and keep us away from our True Home.

The water in the clouds is pure, but when it falls on the ground it gets mixed with dust and becomes dirty. However, under the influence of the sun's heat, it goes up again as vapor. It is condensed in the clouds and, thus purged of the dirt and made pure as before, joins its origin—the place from which it came.

We seek God because it is only in Him that we can be really and permanently happy. All pleasures are temporary and evanescent. For a short time they please us, then they begin to cloy and, in the end, only make us even more miserable. We strive to gain wealth and position and to secure friends, but when we lose them, how miserable we feel! Friends, relatives, companions—all make us happy for the time being, but they cannot last forever, and then we feel the loss keenly. However, when we reach Sach Khand and attain union with God, there is nothing that can deprive us of happiness or bring us back here. Then we are eternally happy.

People have the wrong notion that God is to be found somewhere outside. We seek Him in temples, churches, forests, mountains, and other places. In reality, the Creator whom we seek is within us, and the human body is the real temple of God. Jesus refers to it in the Bible as "the temple of the living God."

Now the question arises, if God is within us as we say, then why can we not see Him? What are the obstacles and how can they be removed? The main obstacle to seeing God within ourselves is our own ego, I-ness, our sense of individuality. Individuality implies separation— separation from Love, from Truth. And this obstacle will be removed only when we merge ourselves into the divine Shabd or Nam. Then only our attachment to this world and to the things of the world will be loosened and discarded. We all try in our own way to get rid of the ego, but it is very difficult—actually, impossible—to succeed, until we drink the ambrosia of Nam. This we can drink only when through the grace of a competent Teacher, a Master, we get initiation into Shabd. That Nectar descends through the Shabd, and Shabd itself is that immortal Nectar.

What do we mean by Shabd? Shabd is a general term, but in this case we mean the dhunatmak or the spiritual Sound. Shabd or sound is of two kinds: varnatmak and dhunatmak; that which can be uttered, written or heard with the physical senses, and that which cannot be so described. The spiritual or the dhunatmak Sound is a spiritual melody, and we can only compare it, as nearly as possible, with the sounds with which we are familiar. When the Masters refer to Shabd they mean this internal, spiritual Sound which reverberates within all of us but which we cannot hear or get in touch with until we are given the key. The key is given by the Master at the time of initiation. This Shabd or Sound comes from the highest plane. If we catch it, then we ourselves will reach the place from where this Divine Melody issues.

Guru Nanak looks at the world and, seeing how people are engaged in this or that thing, all because of ego, exclaims, "Dreadful is the disease of egoism." If we cut the root of ego, we are one with God. But people are running after pleasure or acquisitions, and at the root of all this is the ego. So Guru Nanak continues, "No matter where I look, I find only one disease." How are we to get rid of this ego? We all try, but really it is in the hands of God himself. It is only when He showers His grace that we turn away from the things of the world and take to a life of devotion and Nam bhakti.

It is only in human life that liberation is possible, because in any other form we are not endowed with discrimination. It is only as a human being that we can follow a Teacher, understand the doctrine and practice it, and thus secure our liberation. This is an opportunity, a privilege which is granted to us, but the privilege also carries a responsibility. To what extent have we taken advantage of this great privilege offered to us?

At the end of every life there is a stocktaking, so to say. We are examined to see whether or not we have made good use of the opportunity that was given to us. If we have, then we will no more have to return to this vale of sorrows. Guru Nanak Sahib illustrates this by quoting the treasury practice then current in India: When a silver coin is presented to a treasurer, he checks to see whether it is a good coin or whether it contains base metal. If it is found to be a bad coin, he does not accept it but returns it with a punch mark. If it is found to be a good coin, it is deposited in the treasury and it no longer needs to come and go. Similarly, if we have made good use of our opportunity, God will unite us to Himself, just as the water in the mud and dirt becomes purified as vapor—by the heat of the sun—and joins the clouds again. Those who have not made good use of this opportunity will continue to remain here in the mud.

As said before, everything really depends upon His grace, but this does not absolve us from making effort and from shouldering our duty and responsibility. God showers His grace in this way: He brings about the meeting of the individual soul with a Master who gives him the key and initiates him, teaching him the practice of Shabd. He should then carry out the practice of Shabd Yoga while living contentedly with his lot, whatever it might be. Only by working along these lines can we get rid of our dross.

Bhana, or surrender to the Will of the Lord, is an important point. We have to carry on the spiritual discipline without grumbling about our lot in life. We should not be discouraged by disease, misfortune or calamity; nor should we be elated over any material gain, worldly pleasure, friends or relatives. We are to do everything according to the best of our knowledge, but the results are to be left entirely in the hands of God. Devotion to God should be only for the sake of the love of God, and not for acquiring any favors or possessions, or removing any ills or evils. "Thy Will be done." It is His pleasure to keep us as He likes, as He thinks fit, and always for our own good. It is not for us to appeal or pray that it should be like this or like that. We should acquiesce in His Will and try to merge ourselves into Shabd. Desires are born of the mind, and when we pray for our desires to be fulfilled we are placing the mind above God. We should surrender ourselves to God and accept cheerfully whatever comes from Him, confident that whatever He does will be for our own ultimate good.

Besides, our life in this world is ordained according to

our pralabdh or fate karma. It is our fate karma that determines where and in what environment we are to be
born, what our career will be and what course we are to
follow. All this is based on our own previous actions and
thoughts, both good and evil. If we had all good karmas
to our credit, we would be in heaven. If we had all bad
karmas, we would be in some lower region. This is a
mixed world, good and bad, wherein we have to face
some things which are pleasant and some which are unpleasant. Our life here cannot be all smooth sailing.

If we are discontented or unhappy when disease or
misfortune comes our way, or feel elated in success or
satisfaction of desires, when will the mind turn to devotion to God? Even in times of happiness, we are moving
along with the tendencies of the mind. The tendency of
the mind and the inclination of the spirit are different.
The inclination of soul is towards Shabd. So we should do
everything to keep the mind in its proper place and not
let it overcome or rule us.

The key to bhana, or 'surrender' to His Will: The eye
center, where we concentrate and fix our attention, is the
place where we should be and from which we should
function. This, of course, requires a lot of time and practice, but that is the key to surrender. On the other hand,
when we come down from this center we function
through this body of nine doors, the attention goes out
through the sense organs, and when it receives stimulus
from the outside it becomes involved in the world. Only
when the attention is withdrawn from the world and the
senses can we live in His Will.

This is the essence of spiritual practice: We should
submit to the Will of God, and do so joyfully and gracefully. In order to live according to the Will of God we have
to leave the senses and concentrate the attention at the

eye center with a feeling of love and devotion. Then it will be possible for us to merge ourselves into the Shabd, which is the real form of the Satguru, and reach our True Home.

Then Guru Nanak Sahib once again returns to the subject of egoism and says that all creation—men, animals, insects, plants, from the highest to the lowest—is infected with egoism. All are diseased. Nothing is wholesome or healthy. Whom then should we hold in reverence and worship?

All creation is made up of one or more of the five *tattwas* or elements. Plants consist mainly of only one element; the insects only two; the birds, three; animals, four; and man alone has all the five elements. The fifth element is *akash* or ether, which makes reason and intelligence possible. It is found in human beings only and therefore humanity is called the top of creation. A human being should not therefore hold in adoration any of the lower creation.

Then whom should man revere? The world and all that it gives rise to, is all diseased and transitory. Therefore we should not fix our attention upon any one of those things. We are greatly beholden to our parents and to our relatives; we owe them a duty. But even these are not permanent relationships, and love for them alone does not save us. We should fix our love and attachment on that which is imperishable. That only will help us in the end. However, this does not mean that we have no duty or responsibility towards our parents, friends and relatives. We should serve them, help them, discharge our obligations to them; but that alone should not be our ideal. Our real goal should be something else. This body is material and perishable, and therefore all human relations, which are based on it, are also perishable. True, we should love and serve our fellow men, but we should not be so absorbed in this love and attachment as to forget our destination.

Then there are the various gods—Brahma, Vishnu, Shiva, and others. They themselves are perishable, therefore worshipping any but the one true God is no good. The entire world is diseased and perishable. Only those escape these diseases who come to a Guru and follow the path of Shabd according to his instructions. They reach their Divine Source and become immortal.

This world is mortal and perishable, that is, all creation up to Sach Khand is perishable, though some regions may last for eons. Everything below Sach Khand—and that includes not only this but many vast universes—has always been governed by Kal, the negative power. Up to Brahm, the second spiritual stage, everything is managed by Kal. Those who worship Kal or those who worship the gods of the three worlds are all under the control of Kal. Those who go beyond Brahm come into the orbit of Sat Purush, 'the True Lord'.

Those who worship Kal or the gods are born and die again and again. If they have led good lives they are rewarded with long periods of enjoyment and happiness in various heavens; but everything comes to an end, and again they have to be born in this world. And who can say what will be their lot after that?

On the other hand, those who cross the region of Kal do so by means of Shabd and become eternally merged or united with the Lord. Such souls dwell in everlasting bliss. This is beyond the reach of Kal, who is the lord of Trikuti. Any person who merges himself into Shabd, automatically cuts his bonds and need not return again. Everything in this world, whether on land or in the sea, is perishable. Only the Supreme Lord is immortal and imperishable. Those who merge themselves into Him, through love and through Shabd, also become immortal.

So far this is a brief exposition of the philosophy of Sant Mat, why we are born again and again, and how we become immortal through Shabd. Now Guru Nanak Sahib compares Sant Mat with the various practices followed by other systems. The six systems of philosophy are inadequate because each one of them takes one aspect only of the universal Truth. It is incomplete and does not lead to the final goal. Likewise, those people who have renounced the world and go about begging, dressed in orange-colored robes, or those who lead an ascetic life, are also imperfect. Those, too, who perform austerities, undergo fasts and penances in order to control the mind, find in the end that the mind has gained control of them. It goes on accepting stress and then it suddenly rebounds like a rubber band. It is only by Shabd that one can overcome or control the mind effectively and permanently.

People talk of the Vedas or the Quran; but merely reading them cannot lead to salvation. What use can the reading of any book be to us if we have not put into practice what is stated therein? If you have not realized the One who pervades all, then it is no use reading the Vedas or the Quran. This is not meant to discourage the reading of scriptures or holy books. Guru Nanak Sahib means to emphasize that reading alone does not get us anywhere. Whatever knowledge or information we have gained from books must be transformed into experience. Then only can we benefit by reading books.

There are people who seclude themselves in mountains and in forests, and who live upon roots, herbs, berries and fruits. That also does not take us far. There are people who live in the cities, in luxury. That also does not help. Whether we live a life of luxury or a life of austerity, Nam alone leads to salvation. In fact there is only one method. All those who follow any other path except the path of Nam bhakti have to repent in the end.

The same is true of other practices. There are sixty-eight important places of pilgrimage in India. If we go on wandering all our life and visiting all the famous places of pilgrimage, that too will not bring about our release from mind and matter. Discussions only lead to useless hair-splitting. The soul is not liberated thereby. So if we over-look or ignore the method of Shabd and follow other practices we will find that we have unwittingly become in-volved in the subtler aspects of mind and maya, or illu-sion, and only wasted our time.

Whom shall we then revere and adore? The true Gur-mukh alone is the one whom we should love and revere. A Gurmukh is one who has merged himself in Shabd and has himself become part of that Divinity. Therefore it is but right and proper that we should adore him and love him.

Guru Sahib further emphasizes that the real Guru or Gurmukh is not the physical body but the Shabd. The current of Shabd comes from the throne of God and finds a place in every human heart, but we know it not nor do we know how to catch it and through it reach the throne of God. The Gurmukhs, by devotion to Shabd, have be-come a part of it, and when we love and worship them our contact with them awakens the Shabd in our hearts. We love the outward form or bodily form of the Master because he is the embodiment of the Shabd, which is the True Guru.

What is the result? If we love things of the world, we are drawn to the world. If we love the Master, who is the embodiment of Shabd, we are drawn towards the Shabd and our True Home.

"The servants of God, O Nanak, are always pure, are always good, for upon them is showered the grace of God."

* * *

12

LOVE ALONE COUNTS IN THE COURT OF THE LORD

Sahib ke darbar men kewal bhagti pyar
by Paltu Sahib

Love alone counts
In the court of the Lord,
Love and devotion
Are to Him most dear;
He shares not king's feast,
But poor peasant's fare.
Austerity and prayer
Are of little avail,
He prefers to eat Shivry's fruit
To the rich fare of rishis.
Hermits and sages
Grace the yag of the king,
But without the presence of Supach,
The bell does not ring.
Of his high caste, O Paltu,
Let none be proud;
For love, and love alone
Counts in the court of the Lord.

Paltu Sahib ki Bani, I: Kundli 218

All of us are in search of God, consciously or unconsciously, because there is no other way to obtain deliverance from the sufferings and sorrows of the endless cycle of birth and death except by being one with Him. We try to seek Him in various places and employ different methods in search of Him, each person according to his intellect and understanding. Some go to churches, some to mosques, some to temples and some make pilgrimages to holy places. Others seek Him in the solitude of jungles, mountains or caves—away from the din and noise of the world. There are those who believe that acts of charity, sacrifices and austerities will lead them to their goal. Still others resort to piety, celibacy and reading of holy books, thinking that this will bring them liberation. Different people apply different ways and means in their endeavor to attain God-realization.

Paltu Sahib says that of all ways, the way of Love is the only one that is efficacious and most pleasing to God. However, when we start on this path, we find that since God is invisible and cannot be perceived by the senses, it is very difficult to feel strong love for Him in our hearts. So the question naturally arises: Who is worthy of our love and devotion, and devotion to whom will lead us to love for God? In order to find a solution to this problem the Saints minutely scanned the whole visible creation. They found that the whole creation is made up of five *tattwas*, elements—namely, earth, water, fire, air and *akash*, or ether—and so can be divided into five main categories according to the quantity and quality of the elements active in their forms.

The first or highest class is that of human beings, within whom all the five elements are active. Next to them come the quadrupeds, like cows, horses and dogs. They lack the powers of reason and intellect because ether, the source of these faculties, is dormant in them. The third class is the bird kingdom, in which three of the elements predominate, namely, air, fire and water. Then we have the fourth group, which includes reptiles—snakes, lizards, worms and the like. They have only two active elements in them, fire and earth. The fifth class consists of vegetables and plants, in which the main element is water, and the other four elements exist in a dormant state only.

So it is obvious that man is the top of all creation, with all the five elements in an active state, and he either is or can be fully developed in every way, physically and mentally. Suppose a man worships a cow or a monkey, how could that improve his spiritual or even his mental and physical status in any way? In his next life he is sure to be degraded to the second class because according to the law of attraction we automatically go, after death, where our love and attachment are placed during our lifetime. Similarly, the worshippers of birds, snakes and trees—as the *tulsi* and *pipal* are worshipped by some in India—will be downgraded.

God is invisible. Heavenly beings and ethereal spirits we also cannot see with our physical eyes. Cows, birds and all creation below the status of human beings are unworthy of our worship. Then whom can we really love and worship with the ultimate object of attaining God-realization? If we say that man should be worshipped, then why should one man worship another who is just like him in every way, and more so in the present age of democracy when all human beings have equal rights and status? When some seekers reach this point in their quest, they are sometimes drawn towards atheism and deny the very existence of God. But they miss one important point. There is room for further research.

Huzur Maharaj Ji used to clarify the position by a very apt illustration. He used to say that suppose we place in a room a number of radio sets which are not connected with batteries or electric current. Would we be able to receive any news? Certainly not. The disconnected radios cannot receive messages unless their wires are attached to a battery or electric connection, and they are switched on to the wavelength of the station from which the messages are being broadcast. For this purpose we have to seek the service of an engineer who knows the radio mechanism.

Similarly, we each have within ourselves a radio—soul—that is capable of receiving messages from the Source; only we are disconnected. In order to reestablish this connection we need the help of the Saints, realized souls who are engineers in the art of connecting the radios, our souls, with the great electric current—the Shabd, the Word—which created and maintains everything. The radio is within us and so also is the battery. But we need the help and guidance of a perfect Master who can impart to us the knowledge of how to attach our own radio's wires to its battery so that we may hear the Voice of God within us. His message, the Heavenly Music, is constantly resounding within us but our internal ears are shut. They can be opened only by a perfect Master who has become one with God.

Saints, those elevated souls who have merged in the Ocean of Divinity, can wash us of our sins by imparting to us a drop of Nectar, or Shabd, from that great Ocean. So long as we do not see God, these realized souls, who are God-men on earth, are truly fit for our worship and worthy of our devotion. About them, Guru Nanak says, "Between His Saints and the Lord, there is no difference. A true devotee of God is just like God. Do not be mistaken because of his human form. . . ." He is like a wave that rises on the Ocean, and after some time again merges into it. As waves rise out of the material ocean and again merge and mix with the water of the ocean, in like manner the Gurmukhs, the Saints, are the waves from the Ocean of Sat Nam. They come out of Sat Nam, the Word, and show the path of the Word while here on earth. After fulfilling their mission here below, they return to the Shabd or Word.

In reality the Word is the Master. Guru Nanak says, "Word is the Master, and Master is the Word." The Word assumes the human form in order to give us the secret of Nam, that is, to bring us in contact with the Word. According to the Bible, "And the Word was made flesh, and dwelt among us." As we are human beings, and only a human being can impart knowledge to us, He has to assume human form in order to explain to us the secret of the Word. After performing his function here, the Master returns to his eternal Home from where he came. Drawn by the Master's love and our devotion to him, we are also attracted to the place from which he came, with which he is in constant communion even while on this earth, and to which he returns. Thus we also merge in the Shabd, the Word, and attain God-realization.

Separation from Shabd was the cause of our constantly roaming in the cycle of eighty-four lakhs of species. Only Master's grace can bring us in contact with Shabd; and Master's grace and mercy we can win only through love and devotion. Paltu Sahib explains this fact by illustrating from history how love succeeded over other means in pleasing the Masters, Sages and Prophets:

When Lord Krishna went to Hastnapur, the capital of Duryodhana's kingdom, the latter, in his kingly pride, expected that Lord Krishna would most certainly come to his palace and would love to have the honor of being a royal guest. But instead of coming to the royal palace, Lord Krishna went direct to the poverty-stricken dwelling of his devotee, Bidur, who was a very poor man of humble origin, the son of a maidservant. Forsaking all the royal comforts and dainties, Lord Krishna delighted in partaking of the single, unsavory vegetable offered by Bidur and to which he could not add even a little salt because of his extreme poverty. Krishna preferred the company of this son of a maidservant because, though very poor from the worldly point of view, his heart was full of sincere love and devotion.

The next example quoted by Paltu Sahib is that of Shri Ram Chandra and Shivri, the low-caste untouchable Bhilni woman. When Ram Chandra visited the Dandak Forest during his exile, each one of the rishis and munis living there thought that Lord Ram Chandra would come to him. Some were proud of their piety, others of their great austerities, still others of their learning, celibacy or sacrifices. The low-caste Bhilni woman also lived in the forest but was despised by the rishis and munis for her low caste and mean origin. She longed and prayed in her heart that the kind Lord Ram Chandra would grace her humble abode, but she had nothing in her hut to offer the Lord. Trees in the forest were laden with fruits of various kinds, but she knew that she was not allowed to pluck any fruit from the trees. All that she could contrive to get was a few dry *bers*, an inferior type of fruit, which she picked up from under the bushes. Thinking that perhaps some of them might be sour, she tasted each one in order to separate the sour ones from the sweet ones. In her simple but complete devotion, she forgot that by tasting the fruit she was polluting them and thus rendering them unfit for consumption by any other human being. Nevertheless, the Lord came direct to her hut, partook of the bers with great relish and repeatedly remarked how very sweet they were and that he had never tasted such delicious fruit before. Of course it was not the fruit but her great love and devotion that had attracted the Lord.

Another illustration is given by Paltu Sahib: At the end of the Mahabharat, when the Pandavas performed the Ashvamedh sacrifice to celebrate their victory, Shri Krishna told them that their sacrifice would be considered successful only if they heard the bell sound from the sky at the end of it. They had invited to this sacrificial feast all the holy men—rishis, munis and Brahmans—from far and wide; yet at the end of the feast, no bell sound was heard. They became very dejected when, even after Lord Krishna partook of the meal, the bell was not heard. On requesting Lord Krishna to see with his inner vision who and where the holy man was whose presence at the feast would successfully complete the sacrifice, the Lord informed them that not far away, there was a low-caste holy man, Supach, who had not joined the feast and whose absence was the cause of their failure to hear the bell sound. As their minds were still full of kingly pride, they thought that perhaps the poor holy man did not know that free food was being offered by them.

They sent for him through an officer, thinking that when informed of the free sacrificial feast, he would come running. But the Sage did not come. Then all the Pandavas themselves went to invite him. Still he refused, saying that he would not partake of their food unless they gave him the merit of one hundred and one Ashvamedh yagyas. The Pandavas returned in utter despair. How could they give him the merits of one hundred and one such yagyas when they had not been successful in performing even one single Ashvamedh yagya?

On seeing them so sad, Queen Draupadi, the wife of the five Pandavas, prepared many delicious dishes with her own hands. She then went barefooted to the hermitage of Supach and appealed to him with great humility and meekness to visit her home. He laid the same conditions before her as he had earlier done to the Pandavas. Draupadi replied that she had learned from Sages like him that when a person who has love and faith goes to see an advanced Sage, he obtains the merit of an Ashvamedh yagya for every step that he takes towards the Sage. So, she continued, out of the merit that she had earned by walking to his place, he might keep the merit of one hundred and one Ashvamedh yagyas for himself, leaving the rest to her. The Sage knew that her heart was sincere and filled with humility, so without raising any further objections he silently accompanied her to the palace. And the bell rang when this Sage joined the feast.

By these examples, Paltu Sahib wants to impress upon us that it is only through true love and humility that God's devotees, the Saints and Gurmukhs, can be pleased.

Thus Paltu Sahib explains that love is necessary for success in meditation, for God appreciates only love and devotion. He also tells us that where the reckoning of our life's account is to take place, nobody will ask us or care about our caste or to what religion we belonged. Nor would we be refused entry because we are not a Hindu, a Muslim, a Christian, or a follower of any other religion. We will have to account for the way we lived our life, that is, our thoughts and actions during our lifetime on earth.

God has no caste, color or creed; neither do our souls have such limitations. Our soul is a drop from the Ocean of Divinity. When God has no sect or caste or color, why should the soul have any, when both are of the same Essence? Paltu Sahib exhorts: "Let nobody be under the wrong impression that his high caste will take him to heaven, or because he belongs to a high-class family that he alone will see God." To whatever race, religion, country or station in life one may belong, if one worships God with true love and unalloyed devotion, he will reach Him without fail.

Our caste, color and creed are concerned with our bodies only and perish with them in fire or dust. Guru Nanak says, "Where reckoning takes place, there body and its caste do not go." Bulleh Shah says, "Your actions will decide your fate, and your caste will stand aside." Another Saint says, "In the court of the Lord, nobody inquires about castes or religion; he who loves God becomes His." The Saints and Sages come to take us out of the bonds of caste and creed, and to show us the true path of Love and Devotion.

* * *

PART TWO

EXCERPTS FROM LETTERS
IN REPLY TO
SEEKERS AND DISCIPLES,
1952–1958

1. Please try to understand Sant Mat thoroughly and make as much research as you can by a study of available Sant Mat literature and by contact with satsangis. When you have thoroughly grasped the principles and the spirit of Sant Mat and do not mind criticism, try to persuade and win over your wife by love. Great wonders can be worked by love. Point out the excellences of your system without criticizing her beliefs. Devotion to the Lord does not imply breakup of family life; rather, domestic life should be improved and made happier thereby.

* * *

2. Our aim is to achieve God-realization by going in and drawing our consciousness up, through mystic practice and discipline, to the center behind the two eyes, but without interrupting our daily duties. We are to live in the world, but in a detached manner. The Shabd, the Divine Melody, is the link between man and God, and the Guru or the Master simply gives you the technique and joins you to the Shabd.

* * *

3. Saints come from a region which is above maya and are love incarnate as well as Shabd or Word incarnate. Only by persuasion and love, and by kindling the inner spark in one way or another, do they bring the hungry soul into contact with that Shabd—the divine musical note within us—which comes directly from the highest sphere, the throne of God.

As the disciple follows the prescribed way of life, he pays off his karmic debts, works his way up steadily and experiences the highest ecstasy. Ecstatic experiences can be and are enjoyed at almost all spiritual centers, for ecstasy means giving one's self up or merging into something higher. Ecstatic experiences are also possible at various chakras. The effects and consequent elevation of the spirit are different at different centers.

Self-realization is a great thing. It is an essential step to God-realization, which comes later. We realize the self—that is, we *know* and not merely affirm theoretically that we are of divine origin and of the same essence—only when we have been able to shake off the three gunas, or rise above them.

Shabd or the Word is a projection of the Divine; and the Saints and Masters, by bringing the disciple in touch with Shabd, restore his or her link with the Divinity, and supervise his or her efforts. As you know, our main plank is the Surat Shabd Yoga, and bhakti is the line which we follow—bhakti of the Shabd and of the Masters who are devoted to the Shabd. Saints follow the middle path. They are not in favor of austerities. *Vairagya*, 'detachment', comes automatically as a result of devotion to Shabd or Nam and Guru.

* * *

4.   Sant Mat is the practical part of self-realization, and Shabd or the inner Shabd Current is the essential part of Sant Mat. Shabd detaches us from the outside world and turns our attention within, thus freeing the mind from worldly associations and pleasures.

It is the nature of mind to run after pleasure and enjoyment, which it seeks here and there. When it comes in contact with Shabd, it gets that supreme and lasting enjoyment which enthralls it for all time. Then it no longer runs after worldly pleasures.

Shabd or Sound Current is the *essence* of Sant Mat. One is put into contact with this Sound Current by a Master—a realized Soul—who is himself well versed in it. There are certain conditions to be followed by the disciples, not least important of which is a strict vegetarian diet—without meat, eggs, fish, or any alcoholic beverage.

* * *

5. Ultimately every one has to solve his own problems. Others can only help and guide.

As regards your interest in Sant Mat and your desire for initiation, I have to say that no compromise can be made as to a vegetarian diet. Renunciation of meat, fish, eggs and anything containing them, as well as alcoholic drinks, is a precondition. Vegetarian diet, so far as our experience goes, has been suitable and useful to our disciples in both East and West. In fact, it cleanses the body and the mind. In your particular case, if you are allergic to all sorts of vegetarian diet (fruits, vegetables, nuts, honey, cheese and all milk products included in variations and combinations to suit the individual) then you can follow some course of mental concentration which would be helpful to you. However, unless you can live on the prescribed diet, you cannot be accepted as a disciple on the path of Shabd.

* * *

6. I note your grief at the death of your only son. This is the way of all flesh. We come into this world with a fixed plan, finish our karmas—the springs of life—and then leave our field of activity, as ordained, some in one way and some in another. According to our merits, we either rest in some place—usually sub-astral—or are born again and again, till we come across a perfect Master who gives us the method of freeing ourselves from the bonds of karma, and of going back and resting in peace with our Heavenly Father in Sach Khand, whence we came. You must have read all this in *The Path of the Masters*.

Yes, it is possible to trace the departed soul, especially if it has not yet taken birth. But to do so is only a waste of energy and no kindness to the disconsolate survivor. It only serves to increase the attachment which is the bane of life and causes our return again and again to the earth life. You can help him though, wherever he might be, by prayer and meditation, and by doing bhajan and simran. On account of your close connection and your love for him, your meditation and prayer benefits him also. I would advise you to accept the facts of destiny and to do bhajan and simran so that *both* of you may be benefited. I shall be glad to help you on those lines and will willingly answer any questions that you may have to ask.

* * *

7.   The best way of ensuring the grant of initiation is to study Sant Mat books and to keep strictly on the vegetarian diet—free from meat, eggs, fish and fowl, or anything containing them, and from alcoholic drinks; but cheese and milk are permitted.

As for guaranteeing one's release after not more than four births, it is expected that a serious and earnest student would devote his time according to instructions, to the study and practice of Sant Mat, and therefore his next birth would surely be an improvement on this one. By the end of four births one should have finished one's karmas and be able to go to final rest whence there is no return. This does not mean that one has not to work nor that one should necessarily take four births in order to reach the place of Bliss. Our attempt should be to finish off as soon as possible our karmic obligations which keep us bound here, and to go back to the True Home whence we came.

Regarding your question, I can tell you this much: A Master is absolutely necessary but it is for you to accept whom you like. The initiation is not the spoken word but a touch of the soul—from the soul of the Master to the soul of the initiate.

* * *

8. A Master not only guides the student in this physical world, but also instructs, advises and helps the disciple on the inner planes when the disciple is able to go in.

Our aim should be to realize God or Truth within ourselves, but we must know the technique first as to how and where to go in. These instructions are imparted to the applicant either personally by the Master or through one of his representatives.

The real awakening which you are seeking comes not by sending the attention to the solar plexus but by concentrating it at the center between the two eyes. It is not the eyes which are to concentrate, but the attention of the mind which is to do work. It is from this center that our real spiritual journey begins. At present our soul and mind currents are scattered throughout the body. We have to learn to draw them up and to concentrate them at the eye center. This does not in any way interfere with the normal routine of one's life nor is it necessary or even advisable to give up one's profession or home. Our worldly duties and obligations are to be fulfilled along with the spiritual practice. But one has to take a vow to live on a vegetarian diet and to eschew alcoholic drinks. The prescribed diet includes all vegetables, fruits, cheese and milk.

You realize your own true form when you rise above mind and matter. The soul is encased in three bodies— the physical, the astral and the causal—and only when we have been able to detach ourselves from these three bodies can we realize our true form. All that is required is to work at the spiritual practice according to directions, for a minimum of two and a half hours daily. If you persist in this with faith and devotion, within a few months or even a few weeks you can feel that you are making progress. But the actual goal is reached after a very long time, depending upon the previous background and the amount of effort put forth in individual cases. The grace of the Master, which is very necessary, is of course there all the time.

You will be happy to know that in this science you do not need to study philosophy or to do any reading unless it be to satisfy your own mind. What is needed is all the *practice* you can put in. I may add that the first step for initiation is to go on a strictly vegetarian diet. Try this for a few months and see if you can conveniently follow it. I would also advise you to thoroughly study Sant Mat literature to enable you to make up your mind that this is really what you want, and thrash out any questions that you may have, before applying for initiation through the representative. You may write to me whenever you feel like it.

* * *

9. The sole object of the Radha Soami way of life and practice is to gradually withdraw the soul from the affairs and entanglements of the world and to unite it to God in this very life. It may not be possible to achieve the goal in this life, but if we are set on the path we feel the difference in this way of approach to Reality.

Devotion and practice bring about a change. The disciple soon feels how different he is from what he was before, and begins to get glimpses of Reality. The technique is imparted to a disciple at the time of initiation, in order to receive which there are certain conditions; and you may discuss all this with ———, who lent you the books. Before asking for initiation, one should make a thorough inquiry and satisfy oneself as to whether or not this is what one really wants. I might also add that it would be well to go on a vegetarian diet and to eschew alcoholic drinks for a period of six months before applying for initiation.

* * *

10.   Sant Mat is essentially a school of practical mysticism and aims at self-realization and God-realization *within* ourselves. The stress is on meditation while discharging one's obligations in the world. There are no ceremonies, rituals or priests. The inner spiritual progress sought is to be achieved with the help of the Guru or Master who keeps in touch with the disciples through the Shabd or the Divine Harmony within, also called the Word or Logos.

* * *

11.   About your views on religion, I perfectly agree with you that one should try to learn and understand with an open mind, that is, without any prejudices. If we thoroughly study these religions, perhaps we shall find the same essence in every one; only some have become more covered with ceremonies, rites, rituals and incorrect interpretations than others. However, I am sure that the founder of each religion had exactly the same thing in view, as Truth is the same, no matter where you find it.

The teachings of Radha Soami, known also as Sant
Mat, dwell entirely on the Truth which is the essence of
all religions, and thus enable each one to better understand and *put into practice* that which he has been taught
in religion, regardless of the nature of his creed. In other
words, Sant Mat is not a new religion nor does it interfere
with any, but simply enables the follower to *live up to* the
teachings of the founder of whatever religion he is following or chooses to follow. It is literally the science of the
soul. As God is one Supreme Being, so also are the
teachings of his Saints the same—whether in the East or
in the West—because they all point the way of God-
realization.

* * *

12.   It must have been quite a shock to you to learn of
the sudden death of your mother. Souls come and go.
This world is like a river and we are like logs floating in it.
A current in the river brings us together—some for a long
time and some for a brief meeting—and another current
in the same river parts us. Of course, the closer the association, the sadder the parting. But at its best it is only a
worldly relationship. The soul never dies. Please accept
my sympathy in your bereavement. I hope that God will
give you strength to bear it and to realize that all life in
this world is transitory. We come here for experience and
with a definite purpose, and when that is finished we go.

Your travels and experiences give you a good opportunity to study comparative religion first hand. I think
that all religions point to the same fact, namely, that everything is within and that we must search within ourselves. Every religion teaches that there is a God and that
we have a soul, and that the soul is a part of Him. The
very word *religion* means the relationship of the soul with

God. We have been born as human beings to know God,
to love Him and to serve Him. We know that God is om-
nipresent, yet we can find Him only within ourselves.
That each individual has to do for himself—of course,
under the guidance of one who has himself attained God-
realization.

* * *

13.   Your desire to be on the path is appreciated, but
merely reading books and trying to concentrate without
any guidance or instruction is neither sufficient nor does it
take one far. The inner Sound is the practical way to detachment and also brings about discrimination in its train.
Love for the inner Sound embraces *all* love and, in due
course, raises you above the phenomenal world and
brings you nearer to Reality.

It is possible, but not desirable, to know one's past
lives. It may make you even more miserable and create
difficulties on the path.

* * *

14.   Your religious life from early days, that is, the
reading of books, etc., has brought fruit in the shape of
an eager desire to find out the real spiritual path.

What you have read in the books is all right, but
books only create and stimulate an interest. The path itself is within you. The key to this path can be found with
a living Master, and you are right in thinking that it is
only by initiation or acceptance as a disciple by a living
Master or Teacher that the path inside can be traversed.

* * *

15.   I am glad you appreciate your initiation, and the
proper way is to devote as much time as you possibly can

to bhajan and simran. There is absolutely nothing to be afraid of. This is what you have been looking for, and now that you have obtained it, it is for you to make the best use of it. Going in is a delightful experience and there is nothing frightening about it. Besides, it happens only gradually and by degrees, not all at once. I hope by this time you have overcome the feeling of fear. At any rate, the repetition of the five Holy Names is to be done with a feeling of devotion and faith, with the *attention* fixed at the eye center. There is absolutely nothing that will suggest nervousness or fright.

* * *

16.   What you say is true. The world is full of misery, selfishness, cruelty and greed. Your Master used to say, and all the other Saints say so too, that if you want to find happiness and peace in this world, or anywhere below the two eyes, you will not succeed. In the same way, it would be equally impossible to find misery and cruelty above the eye center.

It is true that karmas play a great part, and all this drama is staged by our own karmas. The only way to get out of it and to find peace is to withdraw yourself by concentration at the eye center, repeating the five Holy Names with faith and devotion, and attaining shelter and peace in the Sound Current.

It is good to have sympathy, but unless we are in a position to render substantial help our sympathy is not very effective. It is no use trying to think with the animals or trying to go with them in their suffering, mentally or otherwise, because in that case you would be shouldering a burden which you would be unable to carry. You can, of course, ask the Satguru to help them. This would also have a chastening and purifying effect on you, because it intensifies the spirit of mercy, charity and kindness, which are divine qualities.

In the midst of all this, please manage to go on with your bhajan and simran. And whenever you feel very sorry about these things and they prey on your mind, repeat the Names intensively and try to go in.

* * *

17.   The law of karma is extremely complicated, even as nature is so varied, and it would not be a very profitable occupation to go on pursuing the inquiry which, after all, will end in that same formula: "As you sow, so shall you reap." What is more important is how to nullify this law of karma, or how to escape its clutches. The answer is to apply yourself to simran and bhajan. When you go up and get absorbed in Shabd, it is as if you had gone to the hills and escaped the heat of the plains.

What Sardar Bahadur wrote to you is correct, though you may not be able to grasp these things fully. It is much better to postpone these inquiries and to apply yourself to bhajan and simran, so that you may go in and find out these things for yourself.

Yes, spiritual healing is very popular these days, and people may be deriving benefit from it. I would not suggest your resorting to this type of healing, but if there is any physical malady, have recourse to a doctor and apply yourself to bhajan and simran. If by simran you can elevate your consciousness, the pain would not be felt or would be considerably reduced. It is the body which suffers, and when the consciousness is drawn up to the eye center we do not feel the pain. It is only when the attention goes down that we feel the pain.

* * *

18. I am glad that you are devoting proper time to bhajan and simran, and I assure you that, as a result of devoting full time to meditation, there is absolutely no difficulty in carrying on our ordinary daily work. Rather, it helps us in our daily work.

When you say that only infrequently does meditation bring you the peace of mind that you have been led to believe it should, and you ask for an explanation, that is quite right. In the first place, there is no peace of mind as long as there is worldly attachment of any kind, as all these things are perishable. The real and lasting peace of mind comes to us only when we have vacated the nine doors of the body and contacted the Shabd within. According to our progress, that is, to the degree of success we obtain in rising above the senses and concentrating our attention in the eye center, we get shorter or longer snatches of this peace of mind, as the case may be.

Please feel free to write to me any time and I shall always be glad to help you.

* * *

19. Your earnest desire for enlightenment brought you to satsang and got you initiated, but this is only pointing out the road or charting the map for your guidance. You have now to make arrangements for the journey and to start right ahead. As you know, our spiritual journey begins from the soles of the feet and ends at the top of the head, as man is the epitome of the universe and contains in himself all that is outside.

The first thing is to collect and draw up your consciousness, and bring it to the eye center. In Sant Mat this is done by the repetition of the five Holy Names—for at least two hours every day regularly—with attention fixed at the eye center. There should be no strain on the physical eyes, as it is the attention of the mind which is to be engaged in repetition at the point of concentration. This is much easier than the long and even risky processes recommended elsewhere. When the mind is concentrated at the eye center, we are able to hear the Divine Sound (Shabd) which is ultimately to draw us in and take us up.

It is the first part—the concentration of the mind— which is the most difficult and requires time and labor, for that means turning the mind within, at will. That is why regularity in meditation is essential. As you practice, you will feel certain sensations—first in the lower part of the body and then a bit higher up—which are only temporary and natural and need cause you no alarm. Patience and perseverance, coupled with faith, devotion and reliance on the Master, are the foundations of progress in bhajan and simran.

I shall always be glad to hear from you and to answer any questions which you may have about the course of your meditation.

* * *

20. Progress on the spiritual path depends, as you know, on several factors, not the least being the karmic background. It is also regulated from time to time, according to devotion and practice. The Master exercises overall supervision. The duty of the disciple is to carry on his bhajan and simran as instructed and to leave the rest to the Master. It is not necessary for that purpose to come here as meditation can be carried on anywhere.

* * *

21. By simran and bhajan we learn to put faith in a higher power; then the burden is shared, and that makes us feel lighter. Besides, regular simran and bhajan help you to rise above routinism and develop the quality of being impersonal. Life is fluctuating and we are changing, even though we know it not.

* * *

22.   Church service and other ceremonies may be a sort of aid to some extent in inducing a reverential attitude, but generally lose their force after some time. The important thing is to be able to worship at the inner sanctuary. "Knock and it shall be opened unto you." Simran is the key or the knock which makes the door open.

* * *

23.   I appreciate your desire to be awake and alive but, as you have correctly remarked, the journey is long and the waiting also is usually long. That should spur us on to more earnest effort rather than discourage us in any way. The key to success lies in *simran,* which should be done at the eye center, i.e., with the attention fixed at the eye center, in order to facilitate the withdrawal of consciousness. The nearer you come to the center and contact the Shabd, the more will you experience the joy and the cheerfulness of the spirit. Please go on with love and confidence, and if you feel any difficulty do not hesitate to write to me.

To be impersonal, you should fix your attention upon the center between the two eyebrows and not upon the heart. Incidentally, that is in fact the correct way of doing simran.

* * *

24.   Fear results from ignorance, from lack of confidence and self-realization. Self-realization of course takes time, but confidence in the Master and his all-protecting

power is sufficient. This confidence and love spring from meditation and inner experience. Repetition of the five Holy Names with love and regularity beget this confidence. These are Names of great power and spiritual import, and will protect you from all disturbances and obstructions.

The sense of uneasiness, or 'that unaccountable something', is the result of our own subconscious impressions which seem to slacken us at times, but can be combated effectively by simran—the repetition of the five Holy Names.

* * *

25. Regarding the question which you have asked: Opening the inner eye, and even meeting the radiant form of the Master within, does not necessarily imply that there would be no further karmas. You can contact the radiant form of the Master at the first stage. What happens after that is more important.

As to whether you are able to work out all karmas and cross Trikuti, or whether some remain which have to be accounted for, the Master may, in his mercy, so arrange that the remaining karmas be worked off by devotion at some inner stage, and one need not be born again into the physical world. This happens when there are no pronounced desires or attachments. Normally a person may be born again into this world but under much better circumstances and with improved facilities for bhajan and simran.

Meeting the radiant form of the Master within is a wonderful experience.

* * *

26.   Regularity in bhajan and simran is very important, and even punctuality has its own effect. It may not be possible always to be punctual under modern conditions, but regularity should be adhered to. Four hours a day is a good target. When you want to improve upon it, you should aim at *gradually* prolonging *the* sitting rather than increasing the total duration of several sittings.

The Sound is always there, has always been there and will not be lost as long as you live. It makes you live. So you need have no anxiety on that score. When people say that the Sound is lost, it is the attention that has been scattered and the inner concentration that has been lost. Sometimes, but rarely, the Sound may recede into the background under certain karmic conditions or when the mind is full of worries and anxieties, but it is not lost. This is a temporary phase and the situation is met by resorting to simran.

Shabd is the real essential form of the Satguru and it is in this essential form that the Satguru is present everywhere and looks after the disciples. Letters from the Satguru, or reading satsang books, are also links and remind one of the connection with the Master.

You should not repeat the Names when you are listening to the Sound—except when you have some doubt or fear—and should try to put all your attention in the Sound, so that it may pull you up in due course. The bell sound is good. You will in time get the big bell or the gong sound which has a pulling effect. But you must not expect or anticipate any sound, as that mars the concentration of the mind.

About lights too, you should not look for them, but observe what comes before you and do not miss them if they do not come. Keep your attention concentrated and put all of it in Shabd.

As for visualizing when you reach the proper center by simran and Shabd, it will of itself come before you. Do not talk to other people of what you see or hear. I am always glad to hear from faithful satsangis who strive earnestly on the path.

* * *

27.   I am happy that your wife feels that this is the right path and has voluntarily asked for Nam. Husband and wife are the two wheels of the chariot of domestic life, and it makes not only for domestic happiness but spiritual progress also when the two cooperate and move in the same direction. Moderation is a good rule. Sant Mat is the middle way and does not favor extremes. All debts are adjusted through the clearing house of the Master and Shabd.

* * *

28.   I am glad that you have found the instructions helpful and that you can hear the Shabd louder and clearer, and can also hold to it for a longer period. It is very encouraging to learn that you have extended the main sitting from two hours to three hours, and this should in due course of time bring good results. A good deal of the time is generally taken up in overcoming the initial resistance of the mind and fixing the attention in dhyan or Shabd, hence the desirability of extending the first period. This is also the reason why the more time is devoted, the easier it becomes. It is not imagination.

The fact that numbness of the extremities comes quicker in meditation is an encouraging sign and implies easier and quicker withdrawal of consciousness. As you get fixed in Shabd more and more, the consciousness will be more and more oriented inwards and you will begin to have the feeling of the Shabd form of the Master hovering over or around you almost at all times and not only on going to bed and rising. Everything in due course.

Persevere with love, faith and regularity, and leave the rest to the Master.

* * *

29.   Your happiness is perfectly justified. The domestic cart moves more smoothly and it makes for increased domestic and spiritual happiness when both husband and wife follow the same path. Your worldly and spiritual interests are now in common, and this will help you in your spiritual efforts.

The numbness of extremities results from withdrawal of consciousness and is a sign of progress. It is temporary and should cause no alarm.

* * *

30.   I appreciate your resolve to follow the path and be a good disciple. As your husband is already a satsangi, this will facilitate the spiritual progress of both, for now you will both pull in the same direction. Please remember that simran is the key. It enables us to withdraw and concentrate our attention at the eye center, after which the inner spiritual journey begins.

* * *

31.   It is the nature of the mind to be flitting from place to place, to create doubts and difficulties and then occasionally sit down to solve them, thus keeping you involved in a more or less useless activity. The proper thing is to draw up the mind by concentration and hold it at the eye center as long as possible. There alone is peace. Below that is only strife and discord.

We are accustomed to pick out faults in other people. But this is not the way of spiritually inclined people. A satsangi or anyone keen on spiritual progress should try to find out his own faults and endeavor to give them up, one after the other, rather than find faults in other people. It is only a sense of superiority and of being above others that induces this habit in us, which is the very opposite of humility.

As for free will, it is an old controversy. The best and most satisfactory solution, and the one which brings an element of certainty with it, comes when one goes in and sees the workings of karma. We seem to have a free will but it is hedged in by so many circumstances that there is really very little of it after all, and it is no exaggeration to say that we are puppets in the hands of the Power that rules the world, that is, as long as we have not come to the Satguru and Nam. It is also to be remembered that what we call fate or destiny is not something which has been imposed on us by some outside power against our will, but is the natural result of what we have done in the past. We must reap what we have sown.

As concentration improves and withdrawal is more complete, the ringing of the bells will become clearer. Laziness should be avoided at all costs, for it cuts at the root of meditation.

* * *

32. Ego, as you know, persists for a long time, sometimes in the background and sometimes openly exercising its tyranny. By practicing repetition and meditation, and listening to the internal Sound, we should gradually shake off its domination and rise above it, so that it becomes a willing and useful servant and not a master. By spiritual practice we develop power to face these situations, since the Sound and the Master are one.

* * *

33.   Our Great Master is always with his disciples, watching their progress and helping them. You may be sure that any loving effort is never in vain. One day you will see the radiant form. But please remember that when we were ushered into this world we also brought our pralabdh karma with us, and this has to be liquidated or gone through. A loving and faithful disciple goes through it all in the name of the Master, keeping the ego back. We should realize that when he thinks it is right and proper, he will call us to his abode.

* * *

34.   Criticism of somes sort or other is more or less bound to come, but criticism from true seekers and real inquirers should be welcome. True faith based upon reasoned understanding of the principles of Sant Mat is much more valuable than mere blind faith.

* * *

35.   I am sorry to find that you are still struggling with the problem of simran. It really has nothing to do with breathing. To do simran in rhythm with the breath is a wrong habit and, like all habits that need to be changed, it will gradually be overcome. You should not bother about it but do your simran in the right way, as you have been instructed. If by chance the attention sometimes drops down or turns to breathing, just ignore it and resume the correct practice.

Whatever makes the body less unsteady at the time of bhajan or simran is good and preferable, and this applies

to your use of the blanket roll also. As for sitting, whether you remember anything or not, or enjoy your bhajan
or not, your duty is to sit for two and one-half hours without fail. The Satguru will look to the rest. You may be
sure that he is not unmindful of those who are knocking
at his door. The idea of 'I' which has disturbed you, can
very easily be disposed of. After all, for best results the
disciple has to surrender himself to the Satguru. Why
should then the idea of 'I' creep in? Please do not worry
about it.

Every one of us has his shortcomings. If we were perfect, we would not be here. It is a blessing to be aware of
our shortcomings. Then the right thing to do is to try to
remove them and not moan over them. The longing for
darshan has a purifying and chastening effect, and when it
becomes too intense it is answered in one way or the
other. Bhajan and simran with devotion improves one's
worth and makes one better qualified for darshan.

As to marriage parties, etc., you cannot reasonably
avoid such social functions. We cannot improve matters
by being unsociable. We should go, but at the same time
try to do all that we can in the way of meditation, particularly simran. One can easily do simran, even when one
is in the company of others and not engaged in conversation.

Please do not worry about asking too many things or
having too many faults. Go on doing your best. I am
pleased with your efforts.

* * *

36.   It is good that you realize your mistake, but having once realized it, there should be no repetition of the
same thing when you know that it is something wrong.

This can be possible only if you sit every day, *and regularly*, in bhajan and simran.

The Master is always there to help if the disciple turns to him. The best way to turn to him is to sit every day for two and a half hours without fail, as you promised at the time of initiation. We keep our promises with worldly people even in spite of difficulties. Why should we not do the same with the Master? God helps those who help themselves. And the best way to help ourselves is to follow the Master's instructions.

* * *

37.   I note the struggle through which you are passing, but there is absolutely no need to be disgusted. We have to fight with the mind and vanquish it. Giving up bhajan and simran is like throwing down your weapons before a mortal enemy. A good warrior continues the struggle to the end.

Read Paltu Sahib, *Sar Bachan* and other Sant Mat literature. They all say that this is a lifelong struggle with the mind, until victory is gained. Think of the Satguru, draw your strength from him and carry on the fight. God helps only those who help themselves.

It does not matter if you are unable to come to Beas. The Satguru is within you and you can carry on your bhajan and simran anywhere you like. What is wanted is the determination to carry on the struggle, and if you do this with the grace of the Master in your heart, you should succeed.

Please concentrate on simran. If the thoughts go out while sitting, get up and walk while carrying on the simran, and do not stop until the full time is up. You cannot help but win the battle if you persevere like this every day.

38.   I understand your difficulty, but on the whole it would be better for you to pull on with your people as far as possible. As a satsangi, one should not mind what other people say if he himself is doing right. Try to act conscientiously according to the principles and teachings of satsang—Sant Mat, do your bhajan and simran regularly, and pray to the Satguru within.

* * *

39.   Regarding the problem which you have posed, there is no ban on associating or dining with friends who are not satsangis, although according to Sant Mat principles one should try to associate more with satsangis. It is almost impossible to cut off altogether associating or dining with friends who are not satsangis. However, we should not compromise our principles in any way. This might create occasional difficulties, but in the end they will appreciate our stand.

Spiritual progress depends on our mental attitude. So if we are not influenced in any way contrary to the Radha Soami principles, then there can be no harm in these associations. But there is another side to this and that is the point of your husband. Domestic felicity and agreement between husband and wife are even more important than association with friends. Besides, meditation and spiritual progress are appreciably affected if there is no harmony in the home. I would therefore ask you to lovingly talk the matter over with your husband and persuade him if you can; otherwise follow his advice. Please do not try to create any difficulty on any point on which your husband is keen.

* * *

40.   I appreciate your difficulties and am pleased that you have been trying nevertheless to follow my advice and fall in line with your husband. Your mental suffering is chiefly due to the fact that you accept the position with some reservation. Even though you may be right, it is best, in the interests of all concerned—and not the least in your own interest also—to be in harmony with your husband; and do not make him feel that you think differently. It may be a little difficult for you in the beginning, but in the end it will help you in both the worldly and the spiritual life.

You have to bring back your husband and win his approbation by love and gentle persuasion, and not by resentful acquiescence. This is bound to change his attitude and then all will be perfectly well. Whenever you are unable to accept a situation or feel worried or resentful, find time if possible to retire for a few minutes, at least, into silence, do your simran and meditation, and it will have a very calming effect.

I am glad that you are able to hear the bells occasionally—and so soon after initiation too. If you do a lot of simran and meditation with the attention fixed at the point between the two eyebrows, you will hear the bells more often and better. Then in due course you will also have darshan.

Please do not be discouraged by the waywardness and the tricks of the mind. It is like that. But knowing its nature we have to curb it and to modify it. With faith and devotion, always remember that the Master is ever with and helps the struggling disciples.

* * *

41.   I am glad you are putting in two and a half hours every day. The mind is like a restive horse, and it takes a long time and a lot of training before it is broken in and forms the habit of permitting the soul to be the leader, instead of the senses, by which it has been led for many ages. If we only follow the Master's directions faithfully, everything will be done.

The sound of the bells is very good, but because the mind feels disturbed and annoyed at outward circumstances it does not draw up. When by and by you learn to ignore or to think lightly of the outer things, the Sound will pull you up and make you very happy. Yes, Light is sometimes seen, but it is different with different people. Some see the Light first and hear the Sound long after; some hear the Sound first and see the Lights, etc., long after. This also should not worry you in the least. Make your *nirat* strong by fixing your attention between the two eyebrows, all the while repeating the five Holy Names with the attention of the mind; in fact, that is the way to do simran. Concentration and dhyan will also help you to hear the Sound better. Whenever you find that things outside are not to your liking, try to repeat the Names mentally for a few minutes, then the feeling of annoyance and frustration will either pass away completely or grow much less.

There is no harm in laughing and feeling happy. On the contrary, it is a virtue to be happy and think of our Guru under all circumstances, and to be content with our lot. It is he who sends us happiness and it is he who sends us pain, depending on what is best for us at the time. I may tell you, however, that when you will be in sufficiently long contact with Shabd, you will never feel lonely and will even prefer to be alone so that you may enjoy the blissful company of Shabd, which is the real form of the Master. When you are ill or have to remain in bed and get to feeling lonely, try to keep your mind busy either in simran or in some good, wholesome reading. It would also help to remove your loneliness and keep you interestingly busy if you could spend some time with and take an active interest in the children. That does not mean that you should be active with them, but rather to supervise and enjoy their activities only to such an extent that it is no strain on you.

* * *

42. Concentration comes only by and by, but the effort is never wasted. It was in the course of years—perhaps many centuries or even ages—that the mind became so scattered outside; therefore it will also take some time to concentrate it and draw it up. You should never become disheartened or think that nothing is being accomplished. If you get too tired, you might take a few minutes intermission and then start again.

As the concentration improves, the Sound will also improve. The feeling of disappointment or frustration will gradually disappear as you begin to draw up the consciousness and concentrate at the eye center, for then the thoughts will be turned more upwards than outwards. This is the only sure way of escape from the ills of the world.

* * *

43. Please do not mind the fact that you live so far from the Dera. The real Satguru is the Shabd, and when the surat goes into Shabd, we not only meet him but become one with him.

* * *

44. Whenever it is not possible to have privacy, it is best to retire and carry on the simran in bed; and occasionally, if you can do so, cover the right ear and listen to the Sound. "To walk is better than to sit still." Some distance is covered every time you make an effort.

* * *

45. Regarding bhajan and simran, one should go on doing his duty and leave the rest to the Master. The Power within is infallible and perfectly just also, always giving everyone his due reward. The time that you sit in bhajan, and your struggle, are all taken into account. What you should do is to go on devoting the usual time to bhajan and simran, as you are now doing, lovingly and without any strain. Reading a few pages or even one shabd from *Sar Bachan* or some other Sant Mat literature before sitting in bhajan is very helpful in concentrating the mind. If any thoughts disturb you at that time, say to yourself that you will attend to them after bhajan. Then ignore them until the period for bhajan is over. Please do not feel disturbed, but as is the rule in Sant Mat, resign yourself to the Master. Everything in proper time.

* * *

46. *Daya* and *mehr* come from within. The more you turn your attention inward and hear the Shabd, the more will daya and mehr, 'mercy and grace', flow.

As for *surat*, 'soul', having darshan when in contact with Shabd, it is only when it has merged itself and become one with the Shabd that the *sarup*, 'real form', comes and remains. Now that you are having darshan in sleep and also sometimes in bhajan, you should be happy. As for a continuation of this state, that is, constant darshan, etc., try to get it by the same means by which you got this darshan, namely, *prem, bireh* and *abhyas*, 'love, longing and spiritual practice'.

When the surat begins to go in and contact the Shabd, Kal and mind also become active and by various means try to prevent the attention from going up. In fact, this goes on more or less till one crosses the boundaries of mind. Swami Ji cautions that while carrying on our meditations we should be alert and avoid any possible attacks of mind and its agents. Constant simran, dhyan of Guru, and Shabd abhyas are our greatest protection.

* * *

47. I am sorry to hear of your trouble. Practically, I do not find any difference between you and your husband. It is just a way of looking at certain things. As you know, marriage means understanding and tolerance. We should not try to make very small things a big issue nor should we dwell on them. Look at everything from a practical point of view. Unless we have deep understanding with each other, it is difficult to pull through. You know how we are to live our lives from the Sant Mat point of view. You have to do your duty and should be quite dutiful and devoted, but attach yourself to the Holy Shabd as much as possible. That will help you to undergo your duty as a wife. Rather, it will make you an ideal one.

* * *

48. It is good if one really can leave everything to His Will, but one only *seems* to do so, and so many ideas crop up from time to time. Leaving everything to His Will means surrender to the Divine Will and accepting whatever comes.

* * *

49. One ought to cultivate the habit of doing simran at odd hours of the day; in fact, at any time when one is not particularly occupied. This would in due course develop into subconscious simran or what you call automatic simran at the back of the mind. On such occasions, however, you need not close the eyes nor adopt any position. But when sitting at the regular time, every attempt should be made to keep the attention between the two eyebrows while repeating the Holy Names. Likewise, whenever an unpleasant situation has to be faced in this world or some difficulty has to be overcome, one ought to repeat the Holy Names and think of the Master. If properly done, this will bring about relief.

* * *

50.   This practice of concentrating the attention is helpful, both physically as well as spiritually. But we do not adopt this practice for the sake of curing any ills or diseases. Nor is it suggested that the adoption of the Radha Soami course of mental concentration will remove any physical defects. It is meant for spiritual improvement and for raising the spiritual current—which now pervades throughout the body—to its center in the brain whence it receives the Divine Shabd.

51.   What you have said about the distractions of the mind is correct and is quite often the case with many satsangis, but by practice the mind can be brought under control. These distractions come from our interests in the outside world and our associations, likes and dislikes which, at a time when we want to still the mind, quietly come up and cause waves in the mental sea. The repetition of the Names, lovingly and steadily, with *attention* at the eye center, is very helpful. You should not get discouraged but try again and again. Then if thoughts and

distractions continue to disturb you during meditation,
you should quietly dismiss them and tell them to wait until your meditation period is over. The mind does not like
to be imprisoned or channeled. It is like training a wild
colt—but it *can* be trained.

* * *

52.   Liver extract is not to be used by satsangis; but a
chemist caters to all classes of people, and so long as a
satsangi chemist does not use them himself but only sells
them, there should be no objection. That is taking a
broad and practical view.

The monetary problems should be faced and solved in
the ordinary way as other people do, and should not be
mixed up with bhajan and simran. The effect of bhajan
and simran should be to make the disciple rise above
these fluctuations. You have had the good fortune of
being initiated by the late Sardar Bahadur Ji and you may
obtain help and advice from him when you go in, as you
say, to Sahansdal Kanwal.

The unfailing method of getting rid of all these troubles is to devote as much time as one can to simran and
bhajan, and vacate the body.

* * *

53.   I cannot send you a better message than to remind
you of what the Master told you at the time of initiation:
Life is precious and it is only after thousands of years that
you got your turn to be born as a human being. This opportunity should not be lost, and every minute that you
can spare from your duties should be devoted to simran
and bhajan so that you may soon go in and thus finish
your round of births and deaths.

* * *

54. You have done well in referring the facts of the case to the higher authorities and requesting the arrangement for your representation. You should endeavor to clear any misunderstanding that might have crept up, and not allow your case to go by default. Being upset or getting worried never helped anybody. You should take proper steps to clear your position, and pray to Satguru inside.

* * *

55. He knows what is best for us. That which is best for our spiritual progress may not always be pleasant in the material sense. However, we should not fail to make every effort to fulfill our duties and leave the results— whether success or failure—entirely in His hands.

* * *

56. I appreciate your desire to be present on the memorable occasion of your Master's anniversary, but one has to accommodate oneself in this world to so many pressing needs which cannot be put off. The Master understands our feelings and knows our thoughts, but the people of the world do not. Therefore, we have to be more particular in discharging our duties and obligations to them. The fact that you thought so strongly about that day and longed to be here is in itself sufficient, as you were here mentally.

As your Master must have told you, and as you must have heard in satsang and read in books, the most important thing for a satsangi to achieve is *detachment from* the world and *attachment to* Shabd, as well as poise by regular attention to simran and bhajan. Simran or the repetition of the five Holy Names is the basis of the entire discipline. And this can be carried on by any person, under all circumstances, whether he is moving about or is in bed. What is required is the turning of the attention from without to within. In the course of time it becomes a habit. Then you will find it will be so much easier to turn your attention inside, to stay in, and to catch the Shabd Dhun which is to take you across. The more you try to concentrate at the center between the eyebrows, the more your inner vision will be opened.

Swami Ji also has said that if it is not possible for one to attend satsang, one should spend that time in reading books, doing bhajan and simran, and keep his *attention* there. Whenever an opportunity occurs, you may come here. But please do not worry if you cannot come on any particular day.

* * *

57.   The very reason we are placed on this earth is to enable to realize God within ourselves. Whatever circumstances we find ourselves in are due to previous karmas, and so long as we try to act in accordance with His Will, whatever the results may be—whether pleasant or unpleasant—it helps us in our spiritual progress. To go back to our Father's House is the main purpose of our coming into this life. All other things we do simply to maintain ourselves in this world. But while doing so, we should not forget the Father who has given us all these things.

You are very lucky to have been given the way to realize the Master within yourself, so you should always devote as much time to bhajan and simran as possible, as that is the only way by which we can be cleansed so that we may be liberated. The more we attempt to do this, the more grace and blessings we receive from him within.

This Master is *within* us and so near, but the curtain of

the mind stands in between. If we cleanse and vacate the chamber of the mind, and wait lovingly and expectantly for him, surely he will permit us to see him within. The best way to cleanse the mind is to vacate the nine doors of the body through *repetition of the five Holy Names with love and devotion*. Faith and despair are two contradictory things. Happiness lies in surrender and resignation to the Master within. Therefore, please continue with your spiritual practice with increased faith and love, and the Master within will take care of everything else. The results are all in his hands and whatever happens will be for your spiritual benefit.

* * *

58. All existence is checkered with light and shade. Storms do come and blow away but they should not shake us. If we do our daily duty—the spiritual duty—as promised at the time of initiation, we will have strength and confidence, and the mind will be calm and undisturbed because of faith in the Satguru. The Satguru always helps and supports us, but if we are regular in bhajan and simran we can see and feel what the Master is doing for us. I am glad you have begun in right earnest and there is no reason why you should not make progress.

* * *

59. You are right, life is not only dry but one is really alone in life. One tries to feel that he has some company but there comes a time when one does realize that he came alone into the world, he is alone while here and he will have to go alone. There is really no enjoyment in the world that does not have its counterpart of grief in some form or other eventually. If there is any peace of mind, it is not in worldly achievements or in worldly affections. It is only in *Nam*. You are very lucky that you have been initiated by Maharaj Ji [Maharaj Sawan Singh Ji], and you should try to make the best use of it.

* * *

60.   I am glad to learn that you have been initiated by Huzur Maharaj Ji [Maharaj Sawan Singh Ji]. You should not forget that it is a rare privilege and you should try to devote as much time to bhajan and simran as possible. Even if you have been going astray, that is all the more reason to devote more time to the spiritual practice. He is within you, and you had better ask him for forgiveness.

There is hardly any pleasure in worldly surroundings—even under the best of circumstances—but you should work hard to look after your family and yourself and devote good time to bhajan and simran.

* * *

61.   Please do not try to force matters in any way, that is, either to change your job or to try to come to the Dera to settle before you are really independent. It may be a very good desire but you must let things take their course—all the while having full faith in the Satguru and being regular and punctual in your spiritual duties, with devotion.

What you have described is good but you must persevere and not let any thoughts disturb you at the time of meditation. It is good that the patches of white lights are making their appearance but you should not speculate over them; only gaze steadily and note what appears. In the course of time both the light and the sound will clear up. Generally people hear other inferior sounds before they catch the bell sound. It should not therefore worry you. Listen to whatever sound comes in the right ear and if you hear more than one sound, give up the coarser one and take to the finer one; then you will reach the bell sound.

* * *

62. The Master never dies. His power is the same as before and he still supervises over the destiny of those disciples whom he initiated. If we do not comprehend this, the fault is in us and it is because we do not try to do our duty and go in. In that case we do not contact him nor see what he is doing for us.

Instead of speculating whether the Master's power has left with his physical body, it would be much better to do your duty by doing your bhajan and simran with utmost faith and devotion for at least two and a half hours every day without fail—thus making an effort to wipe out the karmas which block your way—and go in. Help and guidance would come to you from within and the Master is always there waiting for you to contact him consciously.

A good satsangi, while cheerfully accepting his pralabdh or his destiny—realizing that he is himself responsible for all his troubles—puts his faith and confidence in his Guru and devotes not only the two and one-half hours every day, but all his spare time, to bhajan and simran. The object is God-realization and not worldly benefit, but if one lovingly performs his duty he gets both.

* * *

63. Generally we discourage the use of such medicines as contain a great deal of alcohol except in the case of homeopathic medicines, of which only a few drops are used. Regarding the tonic you are using, you may try to find a substitute if possible. But if no substitute is available, and the percentage of alcohol is small and the dose also is small, you may use it as long as it is absolutely necessary. Please also remember that tonics are to be used only when the body is weak and you cannot properly carry on your duties. In this case the main object should be to enable you to do your duty in the world *and* attend to your bhajan and simran regularly. I hope this answers your question.

* * *

64. I fully realize your difficulties and the situation through which you are passing but you know we cannot avoid the results of our karmas, whether they stem from this life or previous lives. Satsangis should cheerfully and patiently go through them, following the Satguru's instructions and relying on his mercy. He minimizes most of our troubles. We see only what we have to pass through but not what we have been spared. In the meantime you should go on trying to secure employment, relying on the grace of the Master. When the time comes your efforts will be rewarded. In all these difficulties, hard though it may seem, never, please, forget the Master nor omit your daily bhajan and simran.

* * *

65. There is no harm in attending any satsang delivered by anybody. The object of satsang for a non-satsangi is to understand Sant Mat and about himself, but for the satsangi the object is to enhance the desire to concentrate the mind and to devote as much time to bhajan and simran as possible.

Maharaj Ji [Maharaj Sawan Singh Ji] has been very kind to bestow Nam on you, and now the object of satsang is to create a desire to devote as much time to bhajan and simran as possible. Satsang only helps us in concentrating and reminds us of Maharaj Ji and our own drawbacks. And if it does not do all these things, then there is no use for that satsang.

It is very good for the whole family to collect for the satsang, but it is always useful to sit for bhajan for an hour or so after that. If your mind is not satisfied with your family satsang, you may attend satsang anywhere you like.

* * *

66. Sex is a powerful force, and the best way to deal with it is not to suppress it but to sublimate it. Huzur Maharaj Ji [Maharaj Sawan Singh Ji] also used to recommend reading aloud, but slowly, Kabir's verses on *kam*, 'lust'.

Keeping good company and reading good moral and spiritual books is also very helpful, but simran is the most effective method. Long and steady simran will turn the mind inwards and bring it in contact with Shabd. Shabd is *the* thing and as you begin to enjoy the Divine Harmony you will automatically forget the lower and sensual pleasures.

If lascivious thoughts disturb you at the time of simran, open your eyes and repeat the simran audibly till you find it necessary to close your eyes again. (Of course, the audible repetition is not to be done within the hearing of others.) Before sitting in bhajan, pray to Maharaj Ji.

* * *

67. You need not feel perturbed if some of the tenants are non-vegetarian. You cannot put restrictions on tenants after renting them the house.

* * *

68.   I am sorry that you have to face all these troubles in life. There is no lasting peace in anything that pertains to this world. If we do find peace, it is quite short-lived. The only real and lasting peace that we can get is when we have concentrated to such an extent that we vacate the nine doors and catch Shabd. You have received the instructions at initiation. Now the only thing for you to do is to give a fair trial to what you have learned and try to attain that peace.

There is no necessity for you to take such a long journey. Wherever you are, devote your time to bhajan and simran, because the very object of this human life is to afford us an opportunity to merge ourselves in Shabd. If you have any difficulty in doing that, I am always at your disposal and shall be glad to help you.

* * *

69.   I quite understand your position and would repeat to you what our Great Master used to advise satsangis:

It is not enough to be good and honest yourself. That helps you in the eyes of God and your Guru. But in dealing with the world and worldly situations, a little tact also is useful. While strictly following the rules ourselves, we should try to be on good terms with our subordinates as well as our superiors, and give no cause for offence to our superiors. This is not only good policy but also helps substantially in our bhajan and simran, for then we have no worries to distract our attention.

* * *

70.   How happy is the satsangi who can have visions of the Satguru—and feel his help. What else can he desire? But of course, pride is a bad thing. In all one's difficulties and in the face of temptation one should turn to the Satguru and rely on his help and protection. Then there is no pride, no *ahankar*.

The world is full of temptations, and a traveler on the higher path should expect them to cross his path and test him. Satsangis are warned to this effect. Not only is the path beset with temptations in this world but inside also. Maharaj Ji used to say that a person who succumbs to temptations here will not be able to stand the temptations inside. Temptations are tests and show where we really stand. Yet if a person fails once he should try again, for we fall but to rise. With faith and confidence strengthened by the memory of the fall, let him spur on and work with redoubled zeal and caution, and beware of the snares of the mind. The Master helps and guides and saves you at critical junctures if you turn to him.

The Shabd is within you. You can tune yourself to it by intensive simran and meditation. If you make it a practice to repeat the Names mentally while hiking or riding, or on other occasions, you will by and by develop the habit of raising the consciousness to the eye center, and Shabd also will be heard more easily.

* * *

71. I would advise you not to worry too much about coming to the Dera, but do your bhajan and simran where you are. After all, it is the attitude of the mind which is important.

As for falling asleep, there are two things:
(1) You must have good rest physically, and
(2) Try to keep the attention between the two eyebrows. As long as your *attention* is there, you will be free from sleep. And if you find that you have been asleep, it is because the attention has slipped from that center. Everything becomes easy by practice.

72.   I am glad that you appreciate the blessing of Nam. Everything is within us and therefore the great advantage in this system is that you need not go out anywhere. All that you have to do is gradually withdraw your attention and practice concentration at the eye center, then consciously contact the Shabd which pervades everywhere, and it will take you to your True Home. That is the real way to seek and meet the Satguru inside. This does not interfere with the performance of our daily duties. One can devote time according to his convenience and still discharge his obligations to society.

I hope you will devote as much time as possible to the spiritual practice.

* * *

73.   By means of simran we have to draw up our consciousness to the eye center, which is the place where the mind and the spirit normally reside together. For the purpose of carrying on our work in the world, the consciousness comes down and is scattered through the entire body. This is a natural arrangement.

In ordinary persons, except in times of deep thought or emotional stress or a great shock, this consciousness seldom goes up. But satsangis are taught to practice the withdrawal of the consciousness, gradually and daily, from the body to the center. When this is complete—that is, when all the consciousness has been drawn up and the body has been vacated—the body temporarily becomes the same as dead. But when the meditation period for that particular sitting is finished, the consciousness returns and there is no harm either to the body or to the intellectual faculties. Rather, they become stronger and keener.

It is at this point of complete withdrawal that we really catch the Shabd. Once this stage has been reached, then there is no break. Otherwise there are temporary breaks because the connection has not been thorough and complete.

Whenever you sit in bhajan and find it difficult to concentrate the attention, you may read a shabd from *Sar Bachan* or some other Sant Mat literature and then sit in bhajan. You will find this very helpful. The Master is always there—inside—but our attention is scattered and therefore we are not able to contact him.

* * *

74. Please do not dwell too much on what people may have told you regarding evil spirits, etc. Whatever be the case, if you keep your *attention* in simran with love and faith, no outside force can disturb or harm you. The Master is always there to protect and guide his disciples.

Yes, people can see the Master face to face in meditation, but only when they are able to reach the eye center or when the Satguru, out of his grace and mercy, sometimes gives darshan to satsangis in a vision or a dream. The normal time which a satsangi should devote to bhajan and simran—as is always emphasized at the time of initiation—is *two and one-half hours every day*. You should not expect darshan when you sit for only forty minutes as that time is barely sufficient to steady the mind. The Master is within us but we have to withdraw our mind from the outside things and from the body itself, by means of simran, in order to have darshan of the Master. If you go on working regularly and steadily, one day you will have his darshan. If bad pictures come before your mind's eye, dismiss them. If that is not possible, then open your eyes for a while and repeat the Names audibly until the bad thoughts have vanished. Then again continue your simran, by repeating the Names inaudibly, with eyes closed and attention between the two eyebrows.

You are right. Peace and consolation come from within. The Master is within us, is looking after us and is always ready to help us. All we have to do is to turn our attention inwards so that we may be conscious of the grace which he is showering on us, and receive his message. He certainly knows what is best for us. As long as we do not contact him within—and that is due to our being merged in worldly affairs and desires—we are not able to appreciate what he does for us.

* * *

75. The real independence or the real liberation comes when we cross the limits of Kal and maya. You have already been set on the path and should not find the goal too difficult to achieve with your love and your persistent efforts. I very much appreciate your loving sentiments, but would ask you to sublimate all thoughts and emotions in the inward direction, and this will provide a powerful leverage for going up.

As for your question, the real and the correct answer you will get when you go in. In fact, there the question is automatically answered without your having to ask. Outwardly, there may be a distinction without a difference. A good deal depends upon the interpretation of the word *self* and the life that overpasses one's own. Self-realization, as you undoubtedly know by this time, comes only when we have crossed the limits of maya and Kal, that is, at the third stage. And then, according to Sant Mat, the soul becomes fit for real bhakti to Sat Purush.

The 'mergence', according to Saints, is not a mere nothing but a fuller and a deeper and a higher life.

* * *

76.   I congratulate you on your success in bhajan. When there is both love and conscious effort, there is no reason why one should not succeed. Love, in fact, is the essence of Sant Mat. God is Love. Saints who are the essence of Sat Purush are also embodiments of Love, and can be easily contacted inside by loving devotion, but the love should be one-pointed and progressive.

* * *

77.   My advice is that you continue honestly and conscientiously with your work, and at the same time sit in bhajan and simran regularly, every day, and pray to Maharaj Ji [Maharaj Sawan Singh Ji] within. The Satguru is within and, even though we may not be aware of it, sees all our actions. It behooves us to live and act in such a way that we may not feel ashamed before him. You may be sure that he always extends more grace and blessings than we deserve.

Please do not worry about these ordinary worldly things which come and go and which should not affect the mind of a satsangi. A young man is naturally disappointed when, after receiving a good education, he does not get a good job. But that should not make him a useless neurotic. Let him work hard, put his faith in God and wait for opportunities. The Master always helps. We should conduct ourselves so that we may really deserve that help.

* * *

78. I am sorry to learn of your troubled mind, but you really should not allow the emotions to rule. The Master is within you, and distance does not matter. If only you go on meditating and keep your attention inside with a cheerful attitude, most of your trouble will disappear. It is when we think that we are in difficulties and dwell upon them, that our trouble increases. But if we leave all these things to the Guru and try to submit ourselves to his will, then both the body and the mind will gain thereby.

* * *

79. The Master or the Satguru who initiates a disciple, from the moment of initiation does always take charge of him and keeps on watching, but the disciple is aware of this only when he goes up and contacts the radiant form of the Master within. Besides, the Master's protection and help are more effective when the disciple's attention is directed toward him, which is the beginning of *gurmukhta*.

I am glad you are eager to contact the Light and to get the Shabd, but you know the way to do it is to take your consciousness up to the eye center—the tisra til. That which is to see and hear inside, now is night and day involved in worldly affairs outside. All that we have to do is to try to practice vacating the body, that is, to take our attention away from everything else and from the body, up to the eye center. Concentration of the attention at the center between the two eyebrows is achieved by means of simran. Then the attention is automatically taken in and up by Shabd.

Heavy work and heavy duties do not stand in the way of the performance of bhajan and simran. On the contrary, they cultivate in us the habit of concentration and hard work, which habit is actually helpful in meditation.

When we are tired, our attention naturally tends to go in, instead of going out and thinking of things and persons. Thus also the tiredness resulting from the performance of our duties proves helpful. You will find that as you develop good concentration and proceed *regularly* with your meditation, you will be able to attend to your outward duties also in a better and more efficient way.

Please do not worry about the literal meaning of the Names which were given to you for the repetition or simran. Literal meaning does not count. The real significance you will comprehend later on.

This is what commonly happens to disciples in the beginning, and sometimes even after a long time. The simran ceases because the attention slips down and the mind is off the track, so to speak. You should call the attention back and begin anew. If, while you are repeating the Names, you do the actual repeating *with the attention* of the mind and keep the attention fixed on the eye center, you will not fall asleep nor would the mind slip down. This will be achieved by constant practice.

Yes, one may hear that ringing, or even the distinct bell sound even when not in the position, when moving about in the house and doing other work, if the attention is concentrated. You should always hear it through the right ear only and never through the left ear. If sometimes it persists in the left ear, you should stop listening for the time being and begin again. The Sound is always there, but our attention is not. By simran we come close to the center where the Sound is audible. The right course in meditation is to devote the *entire attention* to repeating the Names during the time of simran, and pay no attention to the Sound at that time, even if it is audible. This will help you to listen to the Sound more clearly when you sit for it.

Yes, an advanced satsangi may hear the Sound or the Shabd constantly, irrespective of position, but in a subdued form. If the Sound were strong, it would become almost impossible for him to attend to his worldly duties.

* * *

80.   Sleep at the time of bhajan and simran may be due to a number of reasons. If the early hours of the morning do not suit you, by all means change the time. Do not think of your adverse *sanskaras,* but act in such a way as to nullify them. Sleep may also be due to heavy or unsuitable food, which cause can easily be corrected. If you feel very, very sleepy, get up and dash cold water in your face and then sit again. Sleep can be conquered by firm determination and perseverance.

Try to keep up your bhajan and simran as much as possible; if not in the morning time, then at any other time in the day or whenever you feel like it. And do not let your mind feel distressed at the idea of your failure, but keep your faith in the Satguru. Pray to him earnestly, and remain cheerful in the idea and faith that Satguru will help you if you turn to him.

The path of Sant Mat is very clear, and the "obstructor" is, unfortunately, your own mind. As you continue in satsang and go on doing your bit, by and by your karmas will be lessened, your *adhikar,* 'fitness', will gradually increase, and you will begin to see the protecting hand of the Satguru. If the student does not run away from the class, he will benefit and one day achieve his object. He may fail once or twice, but he will ultimately succeed. However, if he gives up his studies and runs away to play with the boys, what can be' expected? Saints do not use force. Persuasion is the only means which they favor. The Satguru does watch over his disciples, but the disciple can see it only when he is able to rise a little above the eye center or even comes up to the eye center.

* * *

81. All these trials that come to us in life, if taken in the proper spirit, as a satsangi should take them, will develop strength of character and make one throw himself absolutely at the feet of the Satguru within. On the other hand, they may also discourage us and make us unhappy, which reveals to us our own weakness.

I am sorry I do not appreciate your attitude of being fed up with life and having no interest in it. Life was given to us for a definite purpose and that, as a satsangi, you know well. It was given to us in order that, by complete surrender to the Satguru and daily spiritual exercises, we might be joined to Shabd and rise above this valley of tears. That is a privilege which nobody can take from you unless you yourself, in a fit of petulance or despondency, give it up or cease to make use of it. Even then, no satsangi's life is hopeless. But the road is much easier for us if we do our bit.

You have to take care of your worldly duties and give as much time to bhajan and simran as you possibly can, and then leave the other matters to the Satguru. When one has thus surrendered himself to the Satguru, why should he worry? For by heeding his advice, the adverse karmas which stand in the way will also be mitigated to a great extent, and their force will be lessened.

* * *

82. Only the Shabd from the right side should be heard. When you hear the sound from the left ear, please remove the thumb from the left ear and keep only the right ear closed. The cause of hearing the sound from the left ear is deficiency in simran. Give more time to the repetition of the five Holy Names, and you may totally give up listening to the sound till it sweetly resounds from the right side or the center.

While doing simran, please keep your attention fixed on the point in the center, between the two eyebrows. Give at least two hours daily to simran—every day without fail. Regularity in bhajan and simran is very necessary. It is a great thing. Also during your daily tasks, while eating, drinking or walking, etc., keep your mind in simran of the five Holy Names. Never forget it for a single moment. Thus you will find a great change in a few days.

About the "mystery of death," a satsangi has no fear or any trouble about death. Rather, he eagerly waits for it with love. Those who have been regularly attending to their bhajan and simran are instantly taken to higher regions when they leave their bodies. The Master himself comes at the time of their death and takes them with him.

But those satsangis who have still a very great inclination towards worldly desires are given birth in this world; however, in a much better position (for spiritual progress). Those who have no worldly desires but have not been able to do bhajan and simran properly are placed by the Master at some higher stage, and from there are taken to Sach Khand by and by.

In the case of non-satsangis, as their minds are strongly attached to the world and its objects, at the time of their death they feel great pain on separation from those objects and are afterwards naturally drawn towards them. This causes them to be born again and again amidst those objects. According to their karmas, they assume various forms which Nature automatically keeps ready for them as soon as they leave their former bodies. All this arrangement goes on mechanically.

* * *

83.   This means gaining control of the lower mind. But you know it never ceases playing pranks and we should always be ready to control and curb it if it shows any signs of revolt. The essence of Sant Mat is to control the mind and to put it under the discipline of the Satguru. The spirit is of the essence of God and does not need improvement or reformation. It is on account of its (the soul's) being coupled to the mind that it has to undergo this suffering and is kept back from its Home.

The natural inclination of the spirit is to join the Supreme Father, but the mind, which is scattered and fond of phenomena and sexual pleasures, keeps it back. By proper meditation and spiritual exercises the mind is brought under control, made introspective and then taken up till it reaches its own center, where the soul and the mind part, leaving the soul free to go up. As you can imagine, this is quite a job; in fact, it is more than a lifetime's work. We have first of all to collect our attention and hold it at the eye center. I would ask you to continue doing the meditation and trying to hold the attention at the eye center as long as possible for at least one regular period every day, and adhere strictly to the diet for a few months more. Then you will be initiated.

* * *

84.   It is gratifying to note that you understand the true significance of initiation. The Divine Sound is the true link between us and the Supreme Being, and if we develop and keep our connection with it, we shall one day reach our Home. As long as we are in the Shabd Dhun, we are, as it were, in a citadel and safe from the enemy's attack, but we are not to discard our professions or business, nor should we neglect our duties, as these are obligations which we have to perform. And unless we discharge all our obligations, we will not be accepted or absorbed by the Shabd Dhun except for short intervals. Therefore, we have to live in the world but not be of the world.

I am glad you find your meditations easier, and this spirit of meditation will make your path smoother. Please also remember that simran is the foundation and should be done with attention fixed at the eye center. It should even become subconscious in course of time.

* * *

85.   I am glad to learn that you are facing the situation very bravely. It is the body which feels and suffers, and our pain and suffering is due to our attachment to the body. The more we are able to dissociate ourselves from the body by keeping our attention up in the Shabd or in simran, the less do we feel through the physical senses.

One can do simran (repetition of the five Holy Names) while lying in bed. I am told you read *Spiritual Path* and such other books, so it would be easy and useful to start simran after the reading period. Please do not worry about anything, but put your faith and trust in the Master and in Shabd, and resign yourself to him. Also try to cultivate an intense longing to meet the Satguru within.

* * *

86.   I am pleased to hear of your inner experiences. It is really very creditable that you have accomplished so much within such a short time. Please be assured that you are definitely on the right path, and I am glad that you are on your way. After all, this is our real mission in life and for which we have been given this human birth. All else will be left behind as it is transitory and is of no use except for our experience in this world. The only thing which will accompany us is our internal experience, the real happiness beginning when we start to travel consciously with the Master within. Until that time, and according to the rate of our inner progress, we get such snatches of peace and bliss as you describe. The higher the soul goes, the greater and longer will this feeling last, until it is finally eternal bliss. The sooner we realize that and cover the distance, the better it is; for until that time there are always tendencies to slide back because of worldly attachments which pertain not only to the things of this world but also to family, friends, etc. This does not mean that we are not to love others, but it should be a love without the feeling of possession.

Your experiences prove that the Master is well pleased with your efforts, that they are sincere and you are really traveling in the right direction. Please bear in mind that the point of concentration should always be at the center between the eyebrows and *continue to repeat the five Holy Names,* no matter what you see. That which remains and speaks to you may be relied upon, as no negative force or beings can interfere as long as you repeat the five Holy Names.

* * *

87. Alas! We are all lonely in this world, even in the midst of friends and the pomp and show of the world. Only we do not realize it. When we meet with failures and disappointments, then we realize our loneliness. I think the sooner we realize it the better, for then we

would seek some other and better support. Worldly relations and friendships are temporary, and leave us moan-
ing and mourning. But if we turn within, and seek solace
and comfort and support within, we shall find that we can
be really happy. The Master within and the Shabd are in-
contestable Realities. They guide and protect you here,
and make you happy and guide you after death too—till
you reach your Home.

Unhappiness results from frustrated desires. When
things do not turn out as we wish, we feel unhappy. The
practice of Shabd abhyas is the best antidote against desire and unhappiness. Simran or the repetition of the five
Holy Names—regularly—will help a good deal in catching the Sound and holding onto it.

This does not mean that one should become a hermit
or a recluse. Rather, while living in the world and meeting
our social and other obligations we should find time regularly for bhajan and simran, and leave the rest to him.
This is the way to reconcile ourselves with fate and feel
happy while still in the ups and downs of life. Faith in the
Satguru, however, is essential. Then in moments of difficulty or despair, we turn automatically to the Satguru.

* * *

88. Grief at the passing away of the Master is natural,
and especially when he was such a great and unfailing
friend: but there is an infallible Power that rules our destinies and knows what is best for us all. His Will be done.
Besides, your Master is not very far. He is within you and
if you go in, you will be able to contact him and receive
consciously the waves of grace that flow from him. By in-
dulging in grief and despondency we create negative conditions which stand in the way of our receiving such
benefits. Please do not lose heart nor give way to grief

and despair, but with love and confidence continue with your meditations. Your love and devotion to the Master should provide an incentive for you to go in and see your Master once again, face to face. Please try to develop a subconscious attitude in which the loving remembrance of the Master may always be there.

Yes, the body should be vacated and the entire consciousness should be concentrated at the eye center, but it is not the work of a day. By steady and regular application of the mind to simran, over a period of time, it is possible to achieve this goal—not a small achievement by any means, for it means the completion of Guru bhakti. But even when we have been able to withdraw up to the navel or sometimes even lower, we can see flashes of light and experience a great feeling of peace. If we are able to vacate the body at will, it is a great thing, for then we have access to the astral form of the Master. But the Master is so kind that he occasionally contacts the struggling disciple even before that, especially when he or she happens to be a loving disciple.

Yes, your Master will come to take you at the time of death; but why not contact him during your lifetime and set all doubts at rest?

A satsangi should neither long for death nor fear it when it comes, but resign himself or herself entirely to the will of the Master. Death is no remedy—not even an escape—from the ills of life, and *only he who knows how to live, knows how to die*. In the case of a satsangi, life and death are in the hands of his Satguru.

With faith in your beloved Master and confidence in yourself, *apply yourself with a will* and complete the usual two and a half hours, even in two sittings if weak health stands in the way of your sitting so long at a stretch, and you will regain what you have lost. The Master is *within* you, and when you look up to him with faith and love, your prayer will be answered. It is our mind that becomes distracted and worried and loses its one-pointedness. He never forgets and is always willing and eager to welcome us back.

* * *

89.   In this vale of tears all of us have to taste of the bitter fruit of sickness and death due, no doubt, to our own past karmas. But those who are under the protecting and guiding influence of the Shabd form of the Master have nothing to fear or worry about.

The only way to escape suffering is to leave the body and go into Shabd. There death and pain and sickness have no place. That is what our late Master used to urge all of us to do. Vacate the body, die in life so that we may not have to be born and die again.

This suffering becomes necessary at times to balance the karmic budget and to chasten and purify us. The best thing is to have recourse outwardly to the usual treatment and inwardly withdraw ourselves into the Sound or at least concentrate upon listening for the Sound. Also, while in bed, please do as much simran as you can because that will ultimately lead you to the Sound. Listen to the Sound and internally pray to the Master who is all attention.

* * *

90.   We have to fulfill our destiny or karmas as already ordained, and your going to another place is part of that plan. The important thing is not to be disturbed by these changes but to rise above the circumstances.

We should aim at spiritual development or the raising of the spirit (soul)—which is now enmeshed in the body

—to the spirit center, namely, the center behind the two eyes. The closer we come to this goal, the more indifferent we are able to become towards outward surroundings.

Real spiritual development, however, has nothing to do with spiritualism or occultism as it is generally known. No harm has ever been known to occur to students who practice spiritual development according to the teachings of Sant Mat. In fact, when we do our spiritual practice regularly every day, it is the means of warding off these very dangers.

You must take all reasonable care of your family and make provision for their education and maintenance, for it is your duty. Please be assured that you not only can but should go on with your meditation, wherever you may be.

Thank you for your congratulations, but it is an awful responsibility. I am carrying it on because I was enjoined to do it by the late Master, whom I miss as much as everybody else does.

* * *

91. I appreciate your desire to be helpful to others and to do good, but before one can be really helpful to other people and render them substantial good, one must be in a position to do so. The more we are able to rise above the senses and keep the attention at the spirit center, the more are we able to help ourselves and others too.

* * *

92. I am sorry that I am late in answering, but I assure you that sincere inquiries are always welcome and are attended to.

God's laws are, as you say, immutable; however,

most of us do not understand the laws in their fullness and entirety. There was a time when people flouted the idea of a machine flying in the air, against the laws of gravity. But a fuller understanding of the law made it possible, even though the force of gravity works today as much as it did then. This is only by way of example.

Yes, we have to reap what we have sown and work out our karmas. The Guru enables us to pay off our karmic debts easily and in such a way that we do not have to pass through more than four births. What is more, if a disciple follows the Master's instructions to the best of his ability and has no attachments, that is, that nothing could possibly attract him to return to this earth at the time of death, then he need not come back even a second time, as the Master arranges that the remaining karma may be worked off on an intermediate plane and under more favorable circumstances.

For this purpose, karmas may be divided into three categories: (*a*) kriyaman—that which we are doing here and now in this life; (*b*) pralabdh—the so-called fate karmas, due to actions in previous lives and which have determined our present birth; (*c*) sinchit—or reserve karmas—those which have been stored and which we have yet to account for in subsequent lives.

As a rule, while we are reaping the results of previous karmas—whether the actions be good or bad—we create many more, and there is an unending series of births and deaths till we come across some Saint or Mahatma who can guide us out of this labyrinth.

The Saints prescribe for us a certain course of spiritual discipline and a certain way of life, which together cut down a good deal of seed formation of new karma. We are to live according to a certain pattern—not to kill, injure or harm others—and if we faithfully follow the rules and practice the spiritual discipline prescribed, we might finish up even earlier than four lives. It is like this:

What little karma we accumulate here is taken care of by the daily practice prescribed by the Master. The pralabdh or fate karma has to be gone through anyway. Then the Master helps the disciple to destroy the reserve or sinchit karmas by means of Shabd abhyas, the practice of the Sound Current. When the disciple reaches Trikuti—the causal region—which contains the seeds of these sinchit karmas, or we might say it contains these karmas in seed form, then with the help of the Master and by long practice of Shabd abhyas, these seeds are rendered incapable of germination. And this is not mere metaphor.

As previously stated, this may even be brought about in one life, but never more than four. The Master assumes responsibility, that is, he gives a personal guarantee to the Lord of Karma that the debt will be fully paid. It is for the Master to decide how to bring it about, how much of it to take upon himself and in what manner; but four lives are quite sufficient for any disciple. Even if he is not a good disciple in this incarnation, the next birth will be a better one from a spiritual standpoint, and the upward spiritual tendencies will already have been planted in his soul consciousness. He gets better opportunities for spiritual progress, meets a Master or Guru who helps and guides him, and a good deal more is accomplished. The cumulative effect is wonderful. Before being put on the path the student only occasionally thought of higher spiritual things; now his face is definitely turned in that direction and only occasionally does he lapse into error. I hope I have covered the point.

It is not difficult for the Saints to know in advance the souls who have to come to them, but it is seldom necessary. *Sanskari* souls, namely, those who have already had such contact in a previous life, are easily spotted and we had several such cases in the lifetime of our Great Master, Baba Sawan Singh Ji Maharaj. He would be in touch with all of us at the same time and would inwardly appear and talk to so many of us at the same time. However, everyone who is initiated is not meant to carry on the teachings, but everyone is expected to *live the life* and *practice* the teachings himself or herself. This is more important.

I think you should continue trying and as you listen to the teachings or read about them and come in frequent contact with good satsangis, you may be more firm. It is only our mind with its wishes and desires that stands between us and the Divinity. But once the better side of it has been appealed to, it is even sailing. That, of course, is not easy because the mind is our own worst enemy as long as it is ruled by the senses.

* * *

93.   You ask, "Who is a good initiate or satsangi?" The answer is very simple: He who keeps all his love and attention in the Divine Sound, and performs his worldly duties as a matter of routine. He is not affected by anything that comes in his life—good or bad—because he has perfectly submitted to the Master, who is "the Word made flesh." Of course this is a high ideal and very few achieve it. "Many are called but few are chosen." However, this is the aim of every good satsangi. Of course, he should abstain not only from eggs, flesh foods and alcoholic drinks, but also from doing harm to any living creature.

Sant Mat does not separate wife from husband or husband from wife, as you seem to think. On the other hand, by making them fellow travelers on the path, they develop a truer and stronger love and interest in each other. Our Great Master was always very pleased when both husband and wife entered the path, for that made the journey easier if they cooperated with each other and were a source of help and understanding to each other.

Yes, the mind is weak and erring but, then, the Master is always there to guide and help. If a satsangi does his spiritual practice as instructed at the time of initiation and thus develops contact with the Master within, he receives help and guidance at all times, wherever he may be. We are a part of him but we have to realize that fact, and unless that fact has been realized during the life of an individual it does not help him in any way, just as electricity is present in all things but cannot light or heat our rooms unless it has first been isolated properly and then connected.

I quite understand and appreciate the frank confession that you cannot love a Master whom you have never seen and about whom you know so little. But, when a person starts meditation after having been duly initiated and listens to the Sound within, the contact is established and the more devotedly he follows this course, the more is the love developed. Photographs or pictures of Masters and Saints who have left this world and with whom we have had no personal contact do not really mean much. Sant Mat insists on a living Guru and personal discipleship.

If I may say so, there are two separate and important forces: the mind and the soul. The mind is a very powerful factor. All the comforts and the wonders of civilization that we see today, we owe almost entirely to mind. But if we dwell within and take our cue from the mind only, the soul would never be free from the mind. Our object is to release the soul from the mind so that it may then go back to its Divine Home and be one with the Supreme Father.

* * *

94.   I like being frank and appreciate your attempt to study Sant Mat principles and philosophy from all angles. There is no comparison between mediumistic or spiritualistic phenomena and the teachings of Sant Mat, which represent the highest Truth. The aim of Sant Mat is the liberation of the soul from the trammels of mind and maya, and the ultimate union of the soul with God. That soul will have no more rebirths. On the other hand, mediumistic and seance room phenomena may even retard the progress of the aspirant by diverting his attention to unimportant matters.

However, it is not very easy to live fully up to the ideals of Sant Mat, so if we find people (including satsangis) here and there whose actions are contrary, we should not feel discouraged or disappointed but should try to follow the path ourselves, irrespective of what others may do or not do. Other people's experiences do not mean much to us. It is only that which we ourselves achieve by the grace of the Master which is of any real value to us.

I compliment you upon the advice you gave to the lady, "not to worry about personalities but to study and seek to appreciate Sant Mat for its own sake." Incidentally, you have answered your own problem too. Our late Master, Sardar Bahadur Jagat Singh Ji, had advised me not to look right or left, but to the Master only. In India, the oxen working the oil mills have to go round and round in the same circle, so leather goggle-shaped blinds are put on their eyes. Satsangis should similarly look up to the Master only. In the Western world you would probably say that it is like side blinders on a horse, so that he will look only straight ahead. Perhaps this advice may be useful to you too.

The radiant form of the Master is contacted only after one has *completely* withdrawn his consciousness from the body and, after having concentrated it between the eyes, has gone up and crossed the stars, sun, and moon. This radiant form will protect you in times of danger, advise you in times of difficulty; in fact, it will be with you always.

* * *

95. Let me tell you at once that instead of discouraging, we encourage a thorough study and investigation of the various spiritual disciplines, for it is only by impartial, comparative study and investigation of the various teachings that one comes to know the true value of any system. I am glad that you are investigating ——— also in the same spirit.

The claims which, according to you, are advanced by ——— are very big claims indeed. But you will find that in all these matters, the philosophy of Sant Mat is the final word. I do not wish to persuade you but would rather that you see things for yourself. The time which is spent in investigation is not time lost, for when one ultimately takes to the path, he follows it unswervingly and devotedly, and the results are therefore quicker.

I am glad to learn that you are again seriously trying to adhere to a strict vegetarian diet. In Sant Mat this is very necessary, and it is almost impossible to make any real progress unless we eliminate all flesh foods, including fish, poultry and eggs, owing to the burden of karmas involved. The desire for alcohol is likewise a great obstacle, but if you will exercise a little firmness, I am sure it can be

controlled and altogether given up. Hundreds have done
that here and elsewhere, and surely you can do it too.
The Master's grace is always there and perhaps even
more on the stragglers who are trying to line up. It is only
the will and a firm determination that are lacking.

* * *

96.   I am gratified to learn that you have given up alcoholic drinks. Even that weakness of desiring a cold beer
on a hot day would also vanish if only you definitely make
up your mind never again to indulge in this habit under
any circumstances whatsoever. There is no habit or weakness which a man cannot successfully overcome, provided
he has the grit and the right mental attitude. Habits are
not formed overnight and in most cases they cannot be
given up suddenly unless the man has a very strong will.
But now that you have seen both sides of the picture and
have realized how detrimental the drinking habit can be,
besides being an extra expense too, I have no doubt that
you will discard it absolutely. Many people delude themselves into thinking that they indulge in this vicious habit
for the sake of a 'pick-up' or cheering themselves up.

The only way to bring lasting peace and happiness
and a sense of real comfort is to go within and rely upon the inner Power. The best way to contact that inner
Power is through a real Master. A living Master can be approached outwardly as well as inwardly. Hence, the disciples have confidence and a sense of security, knowing that
they would not be left dangling in mid-air and they can always have their doubts or difficulties resolved. But as you
know, there is a time for everything. Our duty is only to
make continued and sincere efforts, and when the proper
time comes and the Lord so ordains, the great gift comes
to us.

"Unconditional surrender," to which you have referred, is a wonderful thing, but it is not an intellectual or a theoretical proposition. Before you can surrender yourself, you must be master of yourself; or how else can you surrender? You can make a gift only of what is your own and not what is claimed by others. In Sant Mat this is achieved by physical, mental and spiritual service to the Guru, and the spiritual service is no more than joining the spirit to Shabd.

* * *

97.   There should be no persuasion. The request must be the result of an understanding and a sincere desire. If the desire is sincere and the yearning is for spiritual progress, then the applicant will be shown the light, but he or she will have to work for it. The Masters give the instructions, put the soul in touch with Nam, which is Shabd or the Divine Sound, and also help and supervise the student on the path. But the *effort* must be made by the student himself, that is, he or she must withdraw the consciousness to the eye center so that this collected consciousness might be brought in full contact with the Shabd. The spiritual journey, as a matter of fact, begins from the toes and ends in the higher brain centers. So if the student has faith, perseverance and the requisite amount of time, nothing more is required.

All reading, clarifications, etc., are for satisfying and convincing our intellectual being that this is the right path. Once you are convinced about it and are on the path, you are only to apply yourself to the journey to be traversed within, and therefore outward help is not necessary except insofar that there be an encouraging and devotional atmosphere, and that there be no possible obstacles or distractions.

I am glad you have taken to the diet again and do not feel the least desire for alcohol now. The Master is always ready and willing to help, to guide and to show the way, but the initiative must come from the seeker. Persevere on and convince yourself, namely, persuade your mind to believe not only by hearsay but by careful study, analysis and association with satsangis that this is the right way and, once again, if there is any doubt, any difficulty, do not hesitate to refer the matter to me; but there should be no sliding back, no vain regrets. You should gradually turn your back upon the world and follow a life of the spirit if you really want to achieve anything in this lifetime. This does not mean that we are not to perform our duties and obligations, nor are we to run away into forests and mountain caves. In fact, we can make progress on the path only if we also perform our worldly duties. But living in the world, we should not be of the world.

* * *

98.   It is amusing to read what you have written about the path of love and devotion. Quite a number of people in India, too, think much on the same lines, but the contrast is between *bhakti* and *gyan,* 'devotion' and 'knowledge', and not between bhakti and occultism. Occultism has no place in any serious yogic discipline and is definitely discouraged as an obstacle on the path to realization. The essence of bhakti is loving surrender to a higher Power and there is nothing weak about it. In fact, it requires the greatest courage to fight the mind, resist the egotistical tendencies, and surrender to the Master. Most of us surrender to the mind.

Sant Mat has no quarrels with anybody or any system, but it assigns its proper place to all systems and disciplines. They go up to a certain point and have their value,

but Sant Mat goes much further. It represents the uncon-
ditioned and limitless self-existent Power.

I am glad that you are at ease with everybody. We
may or may not agree but there is no point in harboring
bad and wrong feelings. Needless criticisms, pointless discussions and arguments are only a waste of energy. Our
time is precious and it should be devoted to useful and
valuable activities. There is none more useful than trying
to get out of this round of birth and death and striving on
the path to the region of Truth.

* * *

99. A little introspection now and then is a very useful
thing and, in the case of a man of determination and
perseverance like yourself, should enable him to turn a
new leaf. There is no reason to be despondent or to feel
disappointed. Work cheerfully on and try to practice
those beautiful principles in your daily life. Everything in
good time.

* * *

100. It should be possible for you to arrange a good
vegetarian menu which would supply all the necessary
elements of nourishment, including especially the proteins, and at the same time be helpful to your liver.
"Plenty of raw liver," as the doctor gratuitously advised
you, would in India be considered a beastly suggestion by
most people. But of course, people do take all sorts of
things. Those who wish to follow a spiritual course know
the disadvantages and easily discard injurious habits and
foods. You might be interested to know that even Muslims, who are habitually a meat-eating people, abstain
from flesh diet completely when they follow an intensive
spiritual course. I am sure that, in spite of what you say,

you have plenty of strength of mind and will; and if you apply the same properly to this problem, you will be improving your health and save some needless expense.

* * *

101. Regarding the most important thing in life, the first thing for you to do is to make up your mind firmly and finally, and then follow the path so that you may realize the truth of it in your own lifetime. Christ could help those who came in personal contact with him during his own time. Now a study of his teachings can give you only some mental uplift, but cannot take you to the spiritual regions. The question is not whether the West wants the teachings, but whether *you* are in need of them. If you think like that, follow the path and solve your own problems first. The problems that present themselves to the mind from time to time cannot all be solved intellectually, although it is true that in the company of good and intelligent satsangis who sincerely travel the path, a number of things can be cleared up.

It is almost impossible to have all the problems solved before you have set your foot on the path. It is like the man who said that he would not step into the water unless he knew how to swim, lest he might be drowned. Obviously he could never learn to swim. The Masters are always ready to condone our shortcomings and show us the path, and give us the help to make progress, but we must be willing and ready to work and cooperate as much in this endeavor as we do in worldly pursuits. It is good that you are again following the diet. Whenever you have successfully stuck to it for six months, you may apply again.

* * *

102. Your longing for the Master is commendable. As long as the true longing is present, he furnishes the grace to enable us to make the necessary effort. Thus grace and effort go hand in hand until we reach our goal.

* * *

103. Life is such. Some people see through it and wish to know what is beyond it. Others continue to cling to it, to enjoy and to suffer till the last moment. We should not hate life but properly evaluate it and make the most of the opportunity which is offered to us here. Worldly scientists also tell us that we have evolved through endless centuries and myriads of lower lives into that of a human being. There must be some purpose in it. That purpose must be sought and fulfilled. (Of course they do not realize that originally man transmigrated from the Divine Source to the lower forms according to his own desires, actions and resulting effects.)

It is only as a human being that we can seek God and try to unite with Him. In Him alone is peace and security. He is the True and abiding One, and the nearer we get to Him the more happy and peaceful we become. Your desire to escape the world and all that it implies is in itself a qualification, but it must be maintained and the correct road followed. Please contact ——— who will make the Sant Mat literature available to you. In the meantime, while you practice meditation, try to keep your attention between the two eyebrows. Please write to me again after you have read a book or two on the subject.

* * *

104. You are so right in saying that the 'myself' factor is very important in all cases, for ultimately it is the disciple who has to tread the path. The Teacher guides and helps but the student must work. It is our own karmas—retributory karmas, so to say—which bar the path. They will be weakened by and by, and ultimately spent.

You do well to pray to the Master and harbor a longing for the path, for this too has a purifying effect. For the present you should read the Sant Mat literature and, with closed eyes, mentally repeat the words 'Radha Soami' for not more than half an hour every day, without any strain. Nothing could be more unfortunate and disastrous—not to talk of being sinful—than the idea of voluntarily quitting this life. Suffering is purificatory if intelligently submitted to, and hope there always is.

* * *

105.   I appreciate your doubts and difficulties, and the attitude which you have taken. It is perfectly correct for you to make sure that you really want to tread this path. We do not discourage inquiry but rather encourage it. Even if you spent half your life in investigating the truths and possibilities of Sant Mat, I would not be sorry. I would even add that you will get credit for any honest and sincere inquiry.

The path of Sant Mat *is* the inner path and not the outer path. Sant Mat discourages all formal and outward forms of worship, and teaches one to worship at the inner shrine. But before one can reach there, he should know how to get in. Instructions for doing so have necessarily to be outward. The path begins when you begin to follow these instructions and, in pursuance of these directions, try to gather up, day by day, your attention currents at the eye center, whence the real spiritual journey begins. Then the Shabd or Divine Sound is contacted.

It is necessary for the disciple to be a strict vegetarian—not even an occasional plate of soup containing eggs, fish, fowl or meat or meat broth so as not to create more adverse karma.

So-called spiritual or spirit-healing is not permitted because the aim of the disciple is to draw all his attention inward, hold it there by means of contemplation and proceed upward. In the aforementioned type of healing, etc., the attention goes outward or gets involved with the karmas of other people. It would be very much like painfully trying to roll a huge stone uphill and then letting it roll downward.

Nam is centered in our hearts (the upper part of the brain, the spiritual heart center), and though it is good to have devotion or praise for it, one can actually contact it only by going in. If a person keeps one leg in the room and one leg outside, sometimes looking inside and sometimes looking outside, he cannot have a seat in the room. We recommend outside activity only to the extent of earning a living, going through the karmic debts, etc., so that after death one may have no longings, no desires, and it may be easy for the disciple to be taken up by Shabd to the throne of God. Naturally, this is not very easy and requires some amount of self-denial also. That is why people do not always like Sant Mat. It is all right in their case. They are not yet fit for it.

* * *

106. I appreciate your earnestness and sincerity, and your desire to realize yourself is very laudable. Self-realization is but a step to God-realization. We can realize our true divine nature only when we can shake off the covers of maya (illusion) and matter, which in our present stage are very real to us.

Peace, perfection and happiness are to be found *within* us and not outside. God is also *within* you and can be realized with the aid of a Guru or Teacher and the practice of appropriate discipline. This will enable you to draw up and concentrate all your consciousness—which is now scattered throughout the body—at the spirit center behind the eyes.

This practice is to be done regularly till the withdrawal of the spirit or consciousness is complete or almost complete, when you will be joined to the Shabd or the Divine Melody which comes from the highest divine center—Sach Khand, the Everlasting Region—but, unknown to us till informed and initiated, reverberates in us all, whether good or bad. The greater the withdrawal the more intimate the touch with the divine Sound Current and the greater the uplift. This is to be practiced regularly every day for about three hours. The test of the extent of the withdrawal is the numbness or apparent lifelessness, first of the lower limbs and then of the entire body. Of course, this is not accomplished in a day. It is a lifelong process.

The numbness of the body is a temporary phase, lasting only during the meditation period and does not involve any harm to, or mitigation or abrogation of the functions of, the body or the mind. On the other hand, the mental powers are strengthened with this practice, because we acquire the habit of concentrating our thoughts and attention at one point.

In the human body the spirit has its seat or headquarters in the center which is above and behind the eyes. Here it is coupled with the mind and irradiates the whole body. Our first and immediate problem is to withdraw (for the time being) the spirit and hold it there as long as possible by means of dhyan, that is, contemplation, pref-

erably of Master's form. It is a slow and even tiresome
process and requires patience and perseverance. Once
this hurdle is crossed, the rest is comparatively easy.
Then it should be possible to withdraw the spirit to its
center or bring it back into the body as easily as the sword
can be taken out of the scabbard and then put back into
it. Only Adepts or Gurmukhs can do this perfectly.

At the time of initiation, the Master joins the pupil to
the Shabd or the Sound within, and when the pupil withdraws his spirit to this center, the Sound begins to draw
him up. He may hear the Sound before too, but the
Sound, though pleasing and exhilarating, will not be able
to pull him up. There are five stages, and every stage has
a sound of its own. The Sound which we catch will gradually lead us from one sound to another—depending on
our past karmas, our earnestness and zeal, the time and
effort we are able to put in and not the least, the grace of
the Guru—till we reach the stage whence there is no coming back, that is, no rebirth.

This is, in brief, a resume of our faith and practice.
"Radha Soami" is the name of God as revealed by Swami
Ji. He has also called Him "Anami," that is, without any
name, or Nameless.

Now as to your questions:

(1) The initiation is given by a Satguru or Master
who, besides instructing you on all points, joins you to
the Sound within. He may also authorize somebody to do
so on his behalf in the case of deserving pupils at a distance, but he himself supervises spiritually. You can receive initiation in this manner after you have been on the
diet for six months.

(2) The full and correct technique, as well as the description of the internal sounds or Shabds and the stages,

are revealed to the disciple at the time of initiation and not before.

(3) You concentrate your thoughts and attention, with eyes closed, between the two eyebrows. You can imagine a point there if you find it helpful, and also mentally repeat "Radha Soami." In due course you may see points or flashes of light too.

You may start practicing along these lines and see if you can keep to a strict vegetarian diet. Then after six months you may be initiated.

Hatha Yoga, I may point out, is an excellent discipline for the body. Raja Yoga is better but that too does not enable you to control the mind fully nor does it finish your series of births and deaths, for the seeds of karma are not destroyed by that method. Surat Shabd Yoga enables you to 'roast' the seeds of karmas, as it were, so that they cannot sprout again. Mind can only be fully controlled by a Power which has its origin beyond the mind, and that is the Divine Sound.

After attaining the highest stage, one may get absorbed in the Deity and thus share this fuller life, or one may return to this or some other sphere on a mission of mercy, but there is no obligation to come back.

I hope I have made myself clear, but if there is any point on which you require further elucidation, I shall be glad to help you.

* * *

107.   According to Sant Mat we have to turn our attention inside and gradually weaken our love for external things. The course of simran or the repetition of the five Holy Names, with attention at the eye center, is very necessary as it is only with the help of simran that our attention currents are turned inwards.

The mystic vision, the love, the Shabd, are all there inside and have always been there, but we have to go in to contact them. This also evokes His blessings and love. The first part—the simran—which enables us to come to the eye center, has to be done with effort. Then the fountain of love and grace will begin to flow. I am not angry or displeased, but you have to work your way up. Faith is a good thing, but it must be turned into a living faith.

* * *

108. I note your interest in Sant Mat teachings. This is the easiest and surest way to spiritual development and union with the Ultimate Reality. You do not have to give up your normal vocation or change your way of life except that you have to abstain completely from meat, fish, fowl, eggs and alcoholic drinks. There are no dangers. The outer and inner guidance of the Master rules out any such possibility.

I can understand the fears of your husband because he does not know that real spiritual practice is not like the usual occult practices and that no danger is involved. However, you should not offend or annoy him but should do whatever you can in the meanwhile in the way of studying Sant Mat literature and getting accustomed to sit for an hour or more in one posture—any comfortable position—and meditate, that is, concentrate your *attention* between the eyebrows. There should be no strain whatsoever on the physical eyes. They should be closed and remain relaxed. It is the attention which is to be concentrated. This will enable you to get a theoretical mastery of the subject and also start you in an humble way on the path, at the same time preserving peace and harmony in the home.

* * *

109.   The fact that you have been practicing yoga is good, as it is always better to do something rather than nothing. However, without proper guidance, one can so easily be deceived.

Sant Mat is not like yoga in the ordinary sense. It is a real spiritual yoga. In a nutshell, the aim is to realize God within ourselves. He is always within us, but because our minds have become scattered by being dominated by the senses and attachments of the senses to the things of this world, we have forgotten our Source and do not know how to rise above the nine doors of the body so that we may realize God. The way back to our Home—while living and performing our duties in this world—is to concentrate our attention at the eye center by means of repetition of the Holy Names given to us at initiation. Thus we contact the Sound Current, and with the help of the Sound we shall be taken to the place from where it comes, and that is from Sach Khand. There is never to be any strain on the eyes as it is not the physical eyes which see inside. So in a way this is also yoga, but in a practical, spiritual sense.

In order to work on the path and travel in the right direction, diet is very essential, and it is necessary that one completely eliminate all meats, eggs and alcoholic drinks, or anything containing eggs or meat. Cheese and milk may be taken. Therefore you may try to remain on the diet for six or seven months and then write to me. Meanwhile you may study Sant Mat literature.

These teachings never cause a split between husband and wife. It is only when we do not correctly understand the teachings or do not properly follow them that it may cause the partner some concern. I never want these teachings to cause any misunderstanding whatsoever. If Sant Mat is followed with love and devotion, it helps one to become patient, tolerant, kind and in every way improves our nature so that we become better life partners and can render better service. We are taught to do our duty first and always as a loving service, and that also applies to husband and wife.

* * *

110.   Yes, the five Holy Names have to be repeated one after the other, in the order in which they have been given to you; and at the time of repetition, effort should be made to keep the attention at the eye center. In fact, one of the important results of simran, or the repetition of the Names, is to draw up the consciousness from the body and concentrate the attention at the eye center, after which the real spiritual journey begins.

Please do not mind the visions, that is, the colors and lights, or whether they represent any shape or form or not. That is immaterial. The important thing is to concentrate the attention and then to catch the Sound which will lead you up. Meeting the Master inside and talking to him is a question of steady, regular practice. As said before, the consciousness is first to be collected at the eye center, then the Sound Current will take it in and up. It is after crossing the regions of the sun and the moon that you meet the radiant form of the Master.

The best time for meditation is early morning when you wake up fresh and have nothing on your mind, and the surroundings are also quiet. But this is not absolutely obligatory. If you cannot get up early in the morning, choose a time which suits you best and when you will not be interrupted. While doing your simran, it is immaterial whether you face east or west.

As for trying to help others, one should carry out his civic duties but should not get unduly involved in such

matters. There is a time for everything and when your
time came, you came to the path. The important thing is
that you have come. True love springs up when you go in
and contact the Shabd or the Master.

* * *

111.   You are right in saying that your meditation, that
is, simran and bhajan, will determine to a great extent
how soon you go in. The help and grace of the Master
are, of course, always there. A bird flies with the help of
both wings, and in this case the two wings are the Master's grace and the pupil's efforts. But you had a good
start in hearing the bells. Now it is for you to keep it up
and advance further. It was not imagination. For the time
being your attention was inside.

* * *

112.   I compliment you on your realization of the importance and significance of Sant Mat, and it is doubly
fortunate that both husband and wife tread the same
path. There cannot be progress or happiness when the
two pull in opposite directions. Now you should give *regularly* the required time for bhajan and simran, and pay
particular attention to simran or the repetition of the five
Holy Names, which is our technique for withdrawing the
consciousness from the body—gradually—and concentrating it in the eye center. The course of Shabd begins after this. One may hear the Sound Current now and then,
but it does not pull until all the attention has been concentrated at the eye center.

* * *

113.   It is a very encouraging start that you have gotten.
It is the result of your devotion, sincerity and *sanskaras,*

that is, tendencies resulting from past karmas. It is now for you to develop it by regular devotion to bhajan and simran. The experience was correct and no delusion. There are whole worlds inside as a microcosm, and as the disciple goes in, astral sights and sounds are seen and heard, and these create a desire to go further in and make one indifferent to the world. One should not get attached, even to them, but keep his attention in Shabd, which is the royal road to the Supreme Goal.

Please continue with simran and bhajan, and increase the period gradually so that you can keep up without strain. You may write to me whenever you like about your experiences but should not speculate too much about them.

* * *

114. Your effort is laudable, but unconsciousness of the body is not achieved in a day. In some cases it is a life-long work to reach even that stage. We are accustomed to go out and have been doing so for ages; therefore it is very difficult to completely turn the attention in a short time. However, your experiences are quite encouraging. As regards the sounds which you hear, you should just take note of them but should not run after them, so to say, or pursue them. The attention should always be concentrated at the point between the two eyebrows. It is not a process of repetition with the vocal cords nor seeing with the physical eyes nor hearing with the physical ears. It is the *mind* that is to do the meditating and there should be no strain. The *tattwic* phenomena which you saw is an encouragement. But for one who wants to achieve real spiritual progress this should not mean much.

* * *

115.   Please do not mind the ups and downs which are almost unavoidable but carry on with faith and confidence. It is not for us to judge the progress. Ours is to do our duty faithfully and leave the rest to the Master. The soldier's duty is to fight and to obey the commands. It is for the generals to plan the strategy and evaluate results. If we but do our duty faithfully and carry out the instructions we received at the time of initiation, we have nothing to worry about. The Master will do the rest.

Please keep on with your bhajan and simran, and try to be regular. Do some simran before retiring to bed and read Sant Mat books when you get time, but never strain yourself.

* * *

116.   At one time or another in our life we all feel that something is lacking and look out for this or that *ism,* for some escape from the evils and hardships of life, but the real answer for us is to *seek within ourselves.* This is what all great Sages and Masters have taught, and it is what our Great Master, Baba Sawan Singh Maharaj Ji, taught and insisted upon. "Go within," he used to say. But we must know how to enter within ourselves. This is the technique which the Saints teach their disciples. Once the disciple does it, there will be no more trouble and no "conference" would be needed.

* * *

117.   We should try to make as thorough a search as possible to find the path to God-realization. The time spent in sincere search for Truth is never lost. But when one is satisfied that the path he has selected is the correct one from every point of view, then he should put everything into practice. We are not to change our religion as

Sant Mat has a much higher aim and in no way interferes with existing orthodox religions. One is free to practice whatever he chooses, so long as he adheres to Sant Mat principles. Of course it is necessary to abstain from meat, fish, poultry, eggs or anything containing them, and alcoholic drinks. If you wish to follow this path, please try to put this into practice for six months and see how it suits you.

* * *

118. I appreciate your resolve to do your best; and if you do your best, the Power which is within you will not fail to reward you. If you find difficulty in getting up early, you may shift the hours to suit your convenience. Early morning time is calm and quiet but it is not absolutely necessary. If one has had rest before sitting in bhajan, it is helpful.

Please ignore the breathing and all sensations like the one you mentioned, and keep your attention in the center between the two eyebrows, and repeat the Names mentally and rhythmically. You may write when you have time and there is something to write. It is not very necessary.

* * *

119. As for the lights and the colors which you see occasionally, it is right and encouraging; but you should see them disinterestedly. That is, if things do not happen before you, you should not miss them, and when they do come, you should not become overjoyed and get interested in them. For all these are phenomena on the way. As you see these things you should not try to follow them but keep your thought centered at the eye focus, just as one looks at the cinema screen while keeping to one's chair.

* * *

120.   You will see Jesus when you reach his region, but you can feel his influence and contact him in his Shabd form even lower. In fact, Saints and great Teachers assume the physical form only for the purpose of guiding and teaching, but their real spiritual form is the Shabd, called also the Sound Current or the Word. If one wishes to contact Christ or realize the truth of his teachings, he can succeed in his object by following the path of the Saints under the guidance of a living Master. But if you do not mind, how will it profit you to know the truth of his birth and teachings? Your first and foremost aim should be to go in. That is, by means of intensive repetition of the five Holy Names you should try to vacate the body and draw up your consciousness to the eye center so that you might be able to start on the spiritual journey with the help of Shabd, and the rest will follow in due course.

To speed up your progress, you may try repeating the five Names mentally at any and all times when you are free and are not mentally occupied with your work, such as when you are waiting for an appointment, traveling in any conveyance, doing some routine work that does not require the full attention of the mind, or even for a few moments in between appointments, etc. This will help you to concentrate your attention more easily when you sit for meditation.

* * *

121.   As regards smoking, in the interest of health and the nervous system it is best eschewed, but there is no absolute ban. However, it may be given up gradually.

* * *

122.   The company of satsangis, if the topic of conversation is spiritual and relates to bhajan and simran or the Master and Sant Mat principles, is good and helpful. Satsang topics canalize the attention inside, more or less.

* * *

123.   You should go on working steadily, giving as much time as you can to simran—repetition of the five Holy Names—with the attention fixed at the eye center, and at least one-half hour every day to listening to the Sound. This will clear up several things and help your spiritual advancement. There should be no hurry. The attempt should be to consolidate what you have already got. The experiences which you get are encouraging but that is not the goal. The aim is to get into intimate touch with the Sound Current, which will ultimately pull you up. The feeling of having spiders about the face or the body sometimes comes to satsangis or even to other practitioners when the concentration begins in right earnest. It is nothing to worry about. Just pay no attention to it.

* * *

124.   As for the problem of useless bulls on the farm, since you cannot make use of them nor can you afford to feed them on your farm, the only thing to do is to dispose of them. But you do not do so with the object of slaughter. That is, you sell them to some buyer and not direct to a slaughterhouse. You do not ask the buyer what he is going to do with them; and once you have sold them to him, the disposition of the animals is his concern and not

yours. However, under no circumstances is a satsangi
permitted to raise any animals or poultry for slaughter.
That automatically takes care of the question of what to
do with pigs and poultry. They do not even enter into the
picture for a satsangi, as that would be deliberately accumulating bad karma. Many farms, not only in India but
also in America and other countries, are profitably run
without resorting to raising pigs, poultry or any animals
for slaughter.

If you work diligently and manage the farm well, it
can bring in good returns materially without putting you
in great debt spiritually; in fact, it would help you to work
off karma instead of accumulating mountains of it as you
would be doing if you undertook to raising pigs and
poultry.

* * *

125.   It is good that you have adopted other and better ways of supplementing your income. If you will carry on with your meditation *regularly and faithfully,* with
love and devotion every day, most of your difficulties
will be solved automatically and you will develop such
courage and strength that the rest will all be easy.

* * *

126.   Your writing direct to me in view of your eagerness and search after the Truth is quite correct, and
please do not worry on that account. The Truth, however, is to be found within you and it is there that it
should be sought.

What are known as psychic powers and occult or su-
pernatural powers, however attractive they may seem,
are not to be confounded with Truth or Reality. They are

only an evidence of the superiority of the mind over matter and a proof that the mind, if properly disciplined and
trained, can exercise almost complete mastery over matter. The real problem, however, is to free the soul from
the dragging influence of matter and take it back to its
Source, the Supreme Father. Whatever we behold is phenomenal, transient, illusory, and cannot make us really
happy. We should seek what is True and abiding. This
cannot be achieved in a day, but to work under a Spiritual
Adept or a Master is itself a privilege; and as one walks
the road he realizes the Truth and feels the uplift till he is
able to ride his mind and let the soul feel the spiritual love
of the Supreme Father. Mind is the great obstacle—the
veil between ourselves and the Deity.

The Deity as well as the mind, say the Saints, are both
within us. By proper spiritual discipline we have to control and nullify the mind. We have to go in and accomplish this great design within us. Thinking of outward
things brings the attention out and creates attachment.
By concentrating attention on an inner center we take
our attention inside and develop control over the mind.
When the concentration is complete all the consciousness
will be drawn up to the eye center and, for the time being, the body below the eyes will be like a dead body—
but only temporarily. Then will the Word Divine, which
we call Shabd, be contacted and draw up the disciple, and
bring about the glorious union in course of time.

Desire and attachment are the cause of sorrow and
pain. These spring from the result of our own actions in
this life and in previous lives, which we inherit in the form
of tendencies and inclinations. We can overcome these
tendencies by attaching ourselves to the Divine Shabd
and thus work out our karmas under the guidance of a
Master.

127.   It is the Divine plan to send Saints and Masters from time to time so that they may be able to connect devoted and deserving people to this spiritual link. So it behooves us, when once connected, to persevere on the path without caring for difficulties or obstacles and thus reach our Home. Yes, it is true that slow and steady wins the race. How many times do we stumble and fall when we learn to walk. But as we grow older we forget the struggles and enjoy the performance. So it is with spiritual work.

* * *

128.   Your deep desire to pierce the veil and contact the Reality is appreciated. Saints and prophets are the Divinity clothed in flesh, to facilitate the task of seekers and travelers on the path and offer them help and guidance; but all the same, Reality is within you. The misguiding factors are also within you and sometimes they disguise themselves cleverly and lead the aspirant astray. Hence the Saints have prescribed the acid test—the repetition of the five Names, against which no power that is not in harmony with the Master can stand. Please, therefore, do not forget to apply this test when necessary. Try to catch the Divine Melody and plunge into it, as it were, so that you may *see* things for yourself instead of receiving messages.

* * *

129.   Not only is it best that seekers are supplied with all available information, but the Masters have always enjoined satsangis to spend some time daily in reading Radha Soami books or anything pertaining to Sant Mat teachings. This advice was particularly given to those who could not attend the Master's daily satsangs.

The reason for the necessity of keeping the mind occupied as much as possible with the teachings of the Saints is quite evident. It is the *mind* which is to be subdued. Therefore, when it is not possible to meditate properly or to attend the Master's satsangs, it is best to engage the mind in dwelling on his teachings. Otherwise, the mind creates notions of its own and these are very misleading. Until the mind has been conquered, it is our own worst enemy.

You might also impress on others that we cannot read these truths too often. Each time they are read, they seem to contain a new and more meaningful message, especially to the sincere and devout souls.

* * *

130. Please allow me to emphasize that under no circumstances should a photo be used for the purpose of contemplating on the Master's form, whether he be a living Master or a Saint who lived in the immediate or distant past. The late Masters have often cautioned us not to try to visualize the Master's form from the photo, for even if we do see the Master inside as a result of this type of contemplation, it will simply be a mental image of the photo and cannot communicate with us. The photo is only to remind us of him and for the purpose of identification for those who have not seen him in person. But the best and only foolproof test when we see anything inside—whether it be the Master or some other person, place or thing—is to *repeat the five Names*. That which remains is True, and all things false will immediately vanish. Of course this test can be used only by disciples who have been given the five Holy Names at initiation, and it indicates how necessary it is for all of us to do simran to such a great extent that it practically becomes a habit.

131. I am glad you have read *Sar Bachan* and read it still. It contains the basic teachings of Radha Soami faith and will bear several readings. No wonder you find something new every time you read it. The essence of the system is to withdraw your consciousness gradually from the body by means of repetition of the Holy Names. That is also living what you learn. This is the way of living a really detached life in the world—being in the world but not of it.

* * *

132. You are really beginning to awaken out of this dream which we call 'life' and qualifying yourself for the real eternal life. Simran and bhajan constitute the passport to this new land.

Your experience was quite correct and reflects your ardent love and progress in bhajan. Your mind and you —the soul—are two separate entities. It is by means of spiritual and meditative exercises that we free the soul from the clutches of the mind. This is done gradually and automatically, and involves no risk or danger. It is perfectly correct and natural to find yourself quite normal in the morning (after your experiences). Let it not disturb you. It should rather spur you on to more simran and devotion to Shabd.

We repeat these five Names because they represent the lords or rulers of these spiritual regions through which we have to pass on our way up. By repetition and meditation we cultivate their acquaintance, as it were, and facilitate our spiritual journey.

True humility comes with bhajan, as our attention is fixed more and more in Shabd. However, our dealings in life also should be marked with humility and modesty, that is, negation or abrogation of egoism and pride.

Do not mind your inability to visit this country. Satguru is within you.

* * *

133. The eye center is the window opening into the astral world and may present wonderful panoramas. But the disciple should not get interested in these sights, for this also gives an opportunity to the mind to play tricks. Just watch as a spectator. There are angels, but we are to keep our attention on the goal.

* * *

134. I am pleased to learn that you are devoting so much time to bhajan and simran, but the main object should be to draw the attention currents up to the center behind the eyes. (We merely concentrate the attention between the eyebrows by means of simran, and the Sound Current will take it in and up.)

(a) Numbness of the lower limbs and the extremities follows successful concentration of the attention between the eyebrows. But this is only temporary, resulting from the withdrawal of the spirit current. When the attention of the mind comes down again, the numbness disappears and a person can go on with his work in the normal fashion; in fact, more successfully.

The creeping feeling or the feeling of pins pricking is also experienced in some cases. All these things are correct but they should not worry the disciple. However, the generation of gas is more the result of the food that one takes and also incomplete digestion. The meditative exercises have nothing to do with the generation of gas. For relief from this, one should look for a suitable change in the items of food, namely, take the right kind and the proper combination suitable to the individual.

(b) In simran, the five Holy Names should be repeated only mentally. All the attention should be kept at the center between the eyebrows, without putting any strain whatsoever on the eyes. It is the mind which is to do the repeating at this center, and that is what will draw the attention currents up to this point. When all the attention is concentrated there, the Shabd will automatically pull it to the center behind the eyes and up to the higher centers.

When the spirit current is properly focused at the eye center, you will see some light—perhaps points, flashes or some other sort of light—and as you go on, withdrawal will be quick and the pain in the lower limbs will disappear. The numbness of the legs, far from disappearing, will be achieved more quickly; and the return of the current, after the meditation period is completed, would also be comparatively quicker.

(c) You may arrange the number of hours for meditation according to your convenience, but should not tire yourself to the extent of getting negative results. At that stage it would be better to stop and begin another sitting. It is your better mind which goads you onward and you should not worry about it, but also perform your worldly duties and obligations.

* * *

135.   God showers his gifts unasked and does not expect anything in return. Nevertheless the recipient should appreciate the gift and make full use of it.

The foundation is simran. Therefore, if you have been doing good simran, you will find it easy to contact the Shabd and to develop it within yourself. It is hard work in the beginning, but by practice everything comes easily. When you are able to withdraw your attention and to keep all your thoughts at the eye center, the body will automatically obey. The body is a willing instrument and always obeys the mind. It will also give you a greater sense of peace and strength and poise. All you have to do is to go on with your meditation with devotion and faith.

* * *

136. I would advise you to read the Sant Mat literature carefully and thoroughly before seeking initiation. You will find that in carefully studying this literature, many of your questions will be answered therein. If you have any doubts or further questions, you may unhesitatingly refer them here for clarification.

* * *

137. You must have been told at the time of initiation that we seek Nam *not* for any personal gain or worldly advantage, but for spiritual uplift and to secure liberation. This means that the dragging forces of the karmas have to be eliminated. This can be done by paying the karmas off actually and by spiritual meditation. In Sant Mat it is done in both ways. The more one carries on the meditation practice, the lighter the karmic debt becomes.

Another effect of meditation and the loving repetition of the five Holy Names whenever and wherever possible is that it makes the will strong and strengthens the faith of the disciple. One should make the effort to the best of his or her ability, not only in meditation but also in carrying out one's daily duties; *then* leave the results to the Master. It is good that you are undergoing all this willingly and turning to the Satguru inside. That is the best method of paying off karma.

Please do not feel worried or helpless, but go on lovingly with the repetition of the five Holy Names and as much of the Sound practice as you can conveniently do. More stress is to be laid on repetition of the five Holy Names, which should be done not only at the regular time of sitting, but can also be carried on at almost any time when you are free and have nothing to do. This will facilitate inner contact.

The posture given to the disciples at the time of initiation is the standard, normal posture, but it does not always suit Western people. The idea of posture is to keep steadily in one position long enough to continue the simran practice, and then to hear the Sound Current. If you are unable to keep in this position or to sit for long conveniently in this position, you may sit in a chair or adopt any other position which you find convenient and helpful.

* * *

138.   It is our consciousness which has the experience, and that consciousness now pervades the entire body. Unless it is drawn up more or less to the eye center, it cannot have inner experiences or see the Master within. The Master is always there. All we need to do is to go up and meet him. This is accomplished by engaging the attention in simran or repetition of the five Holy Names at the center between the eyebrows. In addition to the simran at the time of meditation, one might engage in a sort of subconscious repetition of the Names at any time during the day. This will not interfere with the normal routine. For instance, we may thus utilize the time while waiting for an appointment or waiting at any station or office, or while riding or driving, or when we are more or less at leisure and not doing anything in particular.

As to the Sound, if the simran or the repetition is strong, the Sound also will become strong and clear and attractive; but it should always be heard from the right side and later from the center, but *never from the left.* If the sound from the left persists, you should remove the thumb from the left ear; and if it still persists, you may revert to simran or even end that particular period of meditation for the time being and devote the remainder of that period to reading some Sant Mat literature, preferably *Sar Bachan* or *Spiritual Path,* Vol. II. But most probably the sound from the left will cease if you just ignore it and keep the attention fixed at the center between the eyebrows.

* * *

139.   As you know, our spiritual journey starts from the toes and ends at the top of the head. The most important portion of it is concentrating our attention at the tisra til or third eye, and going up. Then it is that our past karmas, past achievements, past affiliations, etc., begin to show themselves more than ever. By and by, with patience and courage, the disciple makes headway with the overall protection and guidance of the Master.

In the beginning it is not always easy to stand the force of the Shabd or Sound, which is not always gentle or soothing but may also be terrific in its strength. It is then that the difficulty comes. The physical frame is attuned only by and by to enable it to stand that Divine Energy. In the course of time the Sound or Shabd itself brings about a quiet but useful change in the physical body and makes it more fit and adaptable to receive the Divine Message.

There is no reason for being dismayed or discouraged. You are doing quite nicely and adapting yourself to that great blessing. Yes, it is right that you turn to the Shabd in a spirit of loving submission. It will permeate your body and also take you up. But there should be no attempt at analysis. That defeats its own purpose, for the mind then does not go up with *all* its energy because part of it remains to analyze and explain. As the mind submits to the Shabd, it will acquire new strength and new power of penetration, and many things which had seemed inexplicable would of themselves become clear. The feeling of confidence would also grow.

It is good to hear the Shabd in the center or top of the head. That is the place to which it belongs. Yes, you may hear it also with the eyes wide open or shut, or even when listening or talking to others. It is a question of attention. It is kept in the background only in order that one may go on with the ordinary duties. Otherwise, if all the attention is absorbed in the Shabd, it is impossible to do anything else.

The gradual numbness of the body during bhajan and simran is an indication or a proof that the attention is being directed elsewhere, and you should not be startled at this nor at. . . . Remember the Guru and the simran, and nothing can harm you.

* * *

140. It is certainly a hard life, but you will realize that most of our troubles are of our own making. It is our own past karmas reacting on us and taking one shape or another.

For your physical condition I would suggest that you resort to some natural remedies and try to contact a good doctor who can give you advice along this line. Diet also plays an important part; and even on a vegetarian diet, each one has to observe what particular foods and combinations of them are the most easily digestible and then adhere to them for the sake of health. One should not pamper or give too much thought to the body, yet we should do whatever we can to maintain good health.

I quite understand how physical disappointments and ailments stand in the way of meditation, but that is a karmic debt which has to be paid off sooner or later. The best thing is to mitigate the ill effects of these pralabdh karmas by doing as much simran as possible. As you cannot go to work in your present state of health and probably cannot sit for a long time, then do the simran or repetition of the five Holy Names at all times and under all circumstances, even while lying in bed. When devoting your regular time you have only to see that you do not fall asleep while repeating the Names; and with that caution in mind, you may remain in bed and go on slowly repeating the five Holy Names *with the attention of the mind,* focusing same at the center between the eyebrows. The eyes, of course, are to be gently closed and there should be no movement of the muscles of the throat, for it is the attention of the mind that is to do the seeing and repeating. That will take your attention upward.

As you have a lot of time at your disposal, you ought to make the best use of it by repeating the Names almost at all times, not only in the morning and evening; and pray to the Master inside who is with you always.

* * *

141. It is on account of our divorce from Shabd and our affiliation with the mind that we have been born over and over again into this world.

The sound you have described is correct. The object of repetition is to enable us to withdraw our attention completely and to be in contact with the Sound. If the Sound is almost compelling at the time of repetition, it is perfectly permissible to turn your attention to it—but the center should not be lost; that is, you should not try to run after the Sound, so to say, but listen to it with love and devotion while keeping your attention at the eye center.

Yes, the withdrawal is quicker if one is listening to the Sound with all his attention. The body-jerking which you experience is a physical sensation purely due to physical causes. It can and should be overcome by diet regulation or other methods. It is unfortunate that the connection with the Sound should be interrupted by these physical disturbances. The darshan will come when you are uninterruptedly joined to the Sound for some time. Keep the yearning in your mind and this will help you a lot.

Your attitude towards simran during the rest of the day and the working hours is quite all right. Having simran in the subconscious is very important and helpful. The Master is always within and ready to help; in fact, he waits every moment for his disciples to turn to him. The more you develop this attitude and at the same time do your worldly duties to the best of your ability, the more will the help be forthcoming.

Yes, absolute faith is a wonderful thing but it is not easy to attain. Even when we feel we have attained that state it is usually an illusion of the mind. It is only when the real test comes in life that we can find out whether we have absolute faith or just how much faith we have.

It is perfectly all right to switch on to listening to the Sound before going to sleep. Simran is the base and Sound is the effect.

* * *

142. Satguru is within you and it is he who will answer all your questions and problems if by concentration and simran you withdraw your consciousness and reach the center behind the eyes. Till this is achieved, your procedure is correct, namely, meditate on him and then do according to the best of your light or ability. You have, in this way, the blessings of Satguru. I realize your difficulties which spring chiefly from lack of personal touch, but the *daya*, 'mercy', also is in proportion to your difficulties.

The object of satsang is twofold: To non-satsangis it provides an opportunity of seeking the Truth, removing their doubts, and arriving at a correct understanding, thus realizing the importance and significance of Sant Mat principles. For satsangis it creates or strengthens the yearning for going in and helps to concentrate the mind. The real satsang is the hearing of the Shabd within. We should find as much time as possible to devote to simran and to bhajan. This is the secret of progress.

* * *

143.   As to my coming to America, it is not for us to wish one way or the other but to leave it entirely in the hands of the Master in whose care we are and in whose name and under whose orders we are working. If he wishes that I should go to America, it will come to pass and the plans will be made known sufficiently in advance. In the meantime, the best way to cooperate with the Master is to devote as much time as possible to bhajan and simran.

I am glad you have had a nice holiday. That will enable you to attend to your work of the world and your bhajan with greater vigor. We have to take care of both. Progress is rather slow, but that should not worry us. If you go on boring steadily, no matter how thick the wall, one day you will be able to bore through, even though you cannot see the light on the other side till you break through. Effort is never wasted.

* * *

144. Regarding the center itself, please do not strain yourself in order to find any particular point but keep your attention fixed at the spot between the two eyebrows, and in course of time it will be automatically guided to the right center.

* * *

145. I am pleased to learn that you keep your attention in Shabd and simran and do not worry about the trouble. That is the right attitude and it is not difficult to adopt this attitude when one has perfect faith. The Master knows what is for our ultimate good and how best to make us work out our karmas. We do not feel the pain too, or feel it very little, when we put our attention in Shabd. We should start with simran and then pass on into Shabd. If it is painful to sit, you can do your simran while lying in bed or in any other position that you find comfortable. This applies also to Shabd. Plenty of rest is desirable, and when you are in Shabd and listening to the Sound you are having very good rest.

* * *

146. As regards your illness, take all the precautions you can and follow the doctor's advice. Then with faith and love, leave it to the Master to deal with it as he thinks fit, and that would be in your best interests. Above all, devote all the time you can spare to bhajan and simran. Do as much repetition as you can—this can be done at any time—so that you may easily catch the Sound Current. Pain and worry also would decrease as you keep your attention in the Shabd Dhun.

* * *

147. Please continue in your efforts on your own behalf and do not waste time in bemoaning the plight or fate of others. It is only after we have extricated ourselves from the wheel of reincarnation that we are able to help others. When their time comes, they will also be called and will have the opportunity to extricate themselves with the help of a Master. There is no need to be discouraged or disappointed, as there is a time for everyone. In the meantime, we should continue in our own efforts. There is no better way in which we can help than by first reaching the goal from which we are able to render effective help.

* * *

148. I note your difficulties and your distress over having had to take liver injections on medical advice. Do not take it so much to heart. The effect will pass off—that is to say, spiritually—within a few months. However, *under no circumstances* should we ever knowingly and willingly partake of meat, eggs or alcoholic drinks. It is never permissible to take any of these things by mouth. Please regulate your diet, keeping in view the energy requirements of the body.

If blood transfusions are necessary, there is no objection and you need not worry as to who the donor is as long as the blood is your type and is medically suitable.

* * *

149. If you wish, you may fast once a week, but it has no spiritual significance other than if it aids your health, which ultimately helps you in carrying on your spiritual duties. Regularity in diet is best; that is, one should partake of the properly selected diet but never eat too much. Some bodies require more food than others. The thing to do is to find out what agrees with you and then eat a sufficient quantity of the properly selected foods, but do not overeat. You may fast for a day whenever you feel the need of it, but do not make it a habit. Regular light meals are much better and more healthful than periods of overeating followed by fasting.

* * *

150. I can understand your distressed feelings at the events narrated in your letter. It is unfortunate, but let me make plain to you that Sant Mat does not countenance or encourage such things. The alleged justification for such behavior is even worse. Sant Mat insists upon the discharge of our obligations as a matter of duty, and this should make us better citizens, and better husbands and wives. Happy homes—all working towards the same goal and walking the same path—and *not* broken or ruined homes, are the rule in Sant Mat. But, and this is important, a true and earnest disciple seeking to go in and reach the goal should not bother himself or herself with what others do. We should not look upon any disciple as the ideal or model of Sant Mat and judge Sant Mat thereby. We should follow the path with a clear grasp of the principles that have been pointed out to us by the Master. We should give ourselves up to Shabd and not be worried about any individual.

A seeker should make all the inquiries he likes and thoroughly acquaint himself with the teachings, thrashing out anything which he does not understand; but once he understands and accepts the teachings and is on the path, he should bend all his energies on going in.

* * *

151. Why should you feel lonely and forsaken when the Master and Shabd are always with you and within you, and waiting for you to come up? You respond when people want you, but it is time now that you respond to the call of the Master, which will end forever your feeling of loneliness. The indifference of the people and their intolerance, as you have rightly remarked, are blessings in disguise and should help you to turn away gradually from the world. Those who do not fit in anywhere in the world, if given an opportunity, fit inside very well.

Simran—the repetition of the five Names—is the key. By simran draw up your consciousness or try to keep your attention fixed at the center behind the eyes and you will find it easy to contact the Shabd. Simran may be done not only at the regular hours but at any time of the day and especially when you feel lonely. Try at that time to reach the unfailing Friend within.

Your ambition should be to cross the portals of death during life, that is, while living in this world. Then there is no fear nor uncertainty.

"Faith in the feet of the Master" is an oriental devotional expression and means the same thing as faith in the Master.

* * *

152.   I appreciate your sentiments and am very pleased to learn of the peace and contentment that you have begun to feel. Real peace, bliss and understanding come when we are able to go in and be one with Shabd. But even clearer understanding of the law of karma and the value of suffering, if properly taken, goes a long way in satisfying our conceptions of justice and mercy. The Supreme Father *is* merciful.

Paradoxical as it may seem, even suffering can be a source of power, and it has a chastening and cleansing effect if gone through with understanding. It is enough if the disciple follows the directions of the Master with love and faith. Please be *regular* in your bhajan and simran.

It is good to keep the books in circulation. Thus you bring the teaching of the Saints to the notice of the aspirants. It is not in a spirit of propaganda, but for information. Only those who are marked will heed.

As regards marriage with Negroes, we have no objection. Saints do not recognize such barriers. The *spirit* is the same. The rest is a question of social and individual convenience.

* * *

153. Coming to India is not necessary. The thing is to go 'in' and contact the astral form, for which distance is no bar. One should be interested neither in remaining in the world nor in leaving it but in devoting oneself to Shabd, and leave this problem to the Master, who knows best. By devotion to Shabd, our karmas, which keep us tied down to the earth plane, are gradually worked out, the spirit becomes lighter and lighter, and tends to rise up towards its Source.

The words *spirit* and *soul* are used by us synonymously. We mean the imperishable part of us which has come from God, the Source.

Those who are tied down to the earth plane by desires and cravings want to stay here longer. It is the experience of the Saints that those who follow the path of Shabd gradually begin to see through the hollowness of this phenomenal world and, in the course of four lives at the most, they finish with this world and go to the spiritual region—the Everlasting Abode—whence we originally descended. This is made possible by the vigilant help and guidance of the perfect Master. People do not realize the importance and need of a living Master and hence lapse into all sorts of practices. It should not bother you, however. You have got the path and are treading it.

* * *

154. Affording a chance to read about the path and get acquainted with the principles of Sant Mat is good *seva*, 'service', but the result is not in our hands. Only those who are ordained to tread the path in this life will do so. Others who merely read books, make inquiries, etc., create good karmas which will help them in the next life. Do not feel so sorry for your friends.

If one is able to concentrate all his attention at the eye center by means of simran and is able to go in, distance becomes immaterial. That should be your aim. If circumstances are favorable and you are able to take the trip, you are welcome; but why not try to contact the astral form within? Labor is never lost.

* * *

155. I am pleased to have such an honest and accurate analysis of the simran as you have given in your letter. In the beginning it is like that. As you persevere, by and by the success would increase, and you should not think it unsatisfactory. If it is 60 percent successful and 40 percent struggle, then that would mean that the tables have been definitely turned and you have gained the upper hand.

Mind has been accustomed to roam about for many ages and it is only slowly and gradually that it can be properly subdued. Constant—subconscious—repetition of the five Holy Names, in addition to the simran at the appointed time, is the secret, and I hope you will succeed.

* * *

156.   We all judge things from our past experience and in the light of inherited tendencies. That is what makes so much difference between man and man, that is, in the attitude towards life and its problems. Some people have a definite goal and a definite urge, and work towards it. Others are striving to find what they should work and live for.

Mind is a very important factor and a very powerful force too. Uncontrolled and undisciplined, it might lead us into trouble and spoil our prospects of a successful worldly or spiritual life. Controlled and disciplined, it leads us on to success and prosperity—worldly and spiritual. In this respect it is like fire: a good servant but a terrible master.

Life has a meaning and a purpose. The grand aim of human life is to foster, develop and guide those spiritual homing instincts and try to return to the spiritual Home whence we came. It is only in human life that this is possible. This is the aim of evolving and perfecting that wonderful instrument, the brain, which has spiritual centers. These centers can be developed by proper means. All realizations come from *within*. The kingdom of God also is *within*. We must therefore go *in*, that is, turn all our attention and thoughts to the proper inner center so that we might realize ourselves and then realize God.

Mind is a great obstacle and, as you have already said, fools us into believing that we are acting according to the Supreme Father's Will, while all the time it is carrying on with its own egotistical desires and wishes. It is here that the Saints and Masters come in. They warn you of this danger and help you to make the mind a friend and co-operate with you in your best interest. The vision of the Saints is boundless. The supreme cosmic purpose is revealed to them. They can thus put us on the right road and lead us back to our Supreme Father. The greater the faith and confidence of the disciple, the easier it is for him to overcome the obstacle and traverse the path. But it is he himself who must work his way up. Saints only guide and help.

This is to give you a brief, general idea of Sant Mat, but you are always welcome to ask any question which you want to have clarified, and write to me here unhesitatingly.

* * *

157.   I am pleased to read your letter and appreciate your devotion and the idea of dedication to Sant Mat. But you know that we can give away only those things that belong to us, and here is the rub. We constantly think and talk of our mind as if it belonged to us, but the truth of the matter is that in 99.9 percent of the cases we are under the grip of the mind. We discover this painful fact when we are advised to do something which the mind does not accept. Then the struggle begins. The supreme mystery lies within us, but the mind rebels and refuses to go in or does so only for a short while because it is accustomed to enjoy the phenomenal sensual world.

The first step, therefore, is to go in by simran or constant repetition of the Holy Names, which are given at the time of initiation, and to withdraw—if not all the body consciousness, then as much of it as possible—to the center between the two eyebrows and then catch the Divine Melody, the Shabd or the Word, which is ringing in all of us.

You can serve me best by serving yourself, that is, by cultivating a detached outlook and attending to the spiritual practices known as bhajan and simran, which will be explained to you at the time of initiation.

Your devotion and your determination are praise-
worthy. Please remember that the Satguru himself steps
forward to help such people when difficulties arise, if
they keep up their struggle with faith.

* * *

158.   The feeling of never belonging anywhere is conducive to spiritual progress, for then we are not apt to cling
to things of this world and can perform our duties to the
best of our ability, but with complete detachment.

I note your experience and will say that sometimes
one sees many odd faces, and even distorted and horrible
things. They are all due to sanskaras of past lives or some
suppressed thoughts. The main thing is to give your *full
attention* to simran, that is, repeating the five Holy
Names, and by and by all this will vanish. There is
nothing to fear, howsoever horrible anything may seem.
Nobody can do you any harm or come near you as long as
you go on repeating the five Holy Names. That is why it is
good practice to repeat the five Holy Names at every
opportunity possible throughout the day, even when not
sitting in meditation and whenever the mind is not occupied with duties which require attention, for then we
form the habit and are more likely to be on guard even in
our dreams.

* * *

159.   As for meditation, everyone, at some time or
other—some more and some less—meditates, but without conscious effort. They think (meditate) on their troubles, on the unknown, on what is to come or what is to
happen, etc. But a satsangi cheerfully meditates for the
development of the mind and spirit. Meditation of the
right kind makes one a better person, for—as even the

most worldly person would concede—one should think before one acts.

* * *

160. What you have written about your bhajan is all right except that you are not to pay attention to anything on the left, whether it be the bell sound or any other sound. You will see many things and scenes, and hear different kinds of sounds as you proceed. The best thing is to watch rather indifferently all that you see and hear, and not let your mind run after them at any time. Of all these, the bell sound is a substantial step forward. The other sounds which you have mentioned are sometimes heard in the beginning, but by and by you will come up and stick to the bell sound.

I am glad you are accustoming yourself to the posture, but do it only gradually and do not feel panicky about anything that may happen. There is no danger. The Guru is always with you and you have nothing to fear. He watches every move, but the disciple is not conscious of this until he goes within. It is very difficult to take the consciousness completely away from the body, or even half of it. When the attention is being kept upward, only automatic actions, which are cared for by the *pranas*, go on in the body. When you have vacated the body or even part of it, you will see more things inside, and the light too.

If you apply yourself earnestly and regularly to bhajan and simran, and carry on your worldly duties to the best of your ability, your worldly life too will be regulated properly. Love is the one thing essential on the path. The more you can give, the quicker and easier will you achieve results. This would also be reflected in your daily conduct and dealings with fellow men.

161. There is no harm in dividing the period of meditation in two shifts, that is, morning and evening, instead of sitting for two and a half hours uninterruptedly. It is also good to establish a regular schedule and stick to it. In fact, in the beginning it is more or less necessary. (But one should gradually and eventually try to meditate for at least two and a half hours in one sitting). It would not, however, do to follow the practice of Indian yogis and others by keeping yourself confined in the room all day long. I would advise you to concentrate all the attention on yourself and your own meditation, and not mix much with others, especially the members of the opposite sex.

As regards the experience you have had and what followed, that was to a great extent a reflection of your thoughts and feelings and past impressions. On all such occasions you should try to take your thoughts to the eye center and start repetition, even audibly or semi-audibly if necessary. The sex energy is very useful if it is transmuted, that is, turned inwards and utilized for bhajan and simran. This is the real transmutation, that is, of the lower self into the higher self. Seeking relief in any other manner would establish wrong tendencies and deprive you of the advantages of that energy.

Yes, a diet of fruits and vegetables, judiciously selected, is helpful, and in winter if necessary it might be supplemented by nuts. But above all, repetition at the eye center is the remedy for all such things.

* * *

162. Please do not feel sad or worried, but use all your eagerness and love for going in. Distances exist only as long as we are in the outward, phenomenal world; but when we go in and up, there is no distance. And how much more valuable is that meeting!

163.   Your dream, although I would ask you not to
dwell too much on dreams, is symbolic and tells you how
the Master brings out what is latent within the disciple
and tries to cure it. In this way the disciple knows his own
weaknesses, knows that they should be gotten rid of and
also feels and enjoys the protection of the Satguru.

You should, however, place confidence only in the
Master, and whenever you are in any difficulty or have a
sense of fear you should repeat the five Holy Names and
leave the rest to the Master. Anything which should not
be there will have to leave the scene if you repeat the five
Holy Names with love and faith, and all the more so if
you carry on regularly and faithfully with your daily
meditation.

I would also advise you not to think too much of the
world and worldly things, but do your duty, earn your
living and keep as much of your attention as possible in
bhajan and simran and in the Master. Idleness and bad
companions are not conducive to spiritual progress.

As for the repetition of the Names, you should repeat
only the five Names which were given to you at the time
of initiation. When the disciple has qualified himself and
reaches the fifth stage, it is then that the Sat Purush
speeds him on. The correct thing now is to repeat only
the *five* Names.

* * *

164.   It is true that our relationships in this world are
based upon our past karmas and associations, and cannot
be considered absolute because they are changing in
every life; but in this life we must carry on the duties that
devolve upon us according to our present conditions. The
True Father is in Sach Khand.

As for your dream experiences, you had better not

dwell upon them. Sometimes the Master makes one undergo certain karmas in this state, but more often it is either a more or less spontaneous coming up of old associations or a psychic pull of karmas and associations under certain conditions. Anyway, one should not take too much interest in these things, and whenever one finds himself in a dangerous or risky position, he should think of the Master and repeat the five Names.

* * *

165.   I appreciate your studies and aims of higher life. All that one can do in this world is to try, but very few have been able to accomplish all that they desired. When one thing is achieved, other desires and ambitions and aims show up. We should try to do what we can, always keeping in mind first our own devotion to duty, by which I mean the prime duty of meditation, and then do whatever good we can. The guidance of the Satguru is always there.

There is no objection to your carrying on your business or profession for the sake of livelihood, but you should not put your heart into it to a great extent. Carry it out only as a matter of routine or to make a living, and keep all your mind and attention in bhajan and simran. "Laying on of hands," however, is not advisable.

Sant Mat does not favor asceticism but advocates the carrying on of one's duties in the world; then, as the taste develops and the mind longs for it, increase the time for bhajan and simran. The basic period of two and one-half hours each day must, however, be devoted to it in every case.

* * *

166.   The basic philosophy of the economics of life is to stand on one's own legs, earn one's own living according to one's capacity and not be a burden on anybody else. If one is not able to earn as much as he would like, he should decrease his needs. The Sant Mat way of life helps this attitude.

* * *

167.   Truth is one and is present everywhere in varying degrees. In fact, Truth and mystic doctrines are at the bottom of all religions but have been overlaid with a thick crust of ritualism. In the Radha Soami system you attempt to pierce this crust and contact the Truth—the Shabd.

* * *

168.   Faith and courage solve many problems. Do whatever you like, whatever suits you, but let bhajan and simran be your main work. We seek a job because we have to earn an honest living, without which spiritual progress is difficult.

* * *

169.   Regarding the repetition of the five Holy Names, it is not just repetition for the sake of breaking the habit of the mind and inculcating obedience. These Names, if properly repeated with devotion, stir up spiritual vibrations and bring you in contact with those inner regions through which the soul has to pass on its way up to Sat Lok.

* * *

170.   The best and most satisfactory explanation of the experiences and also other questions that crop up from

time to time come really from within, after one has gone
in at the eye center. The more you devote your time to
listening to the Sound, the clearer your spiritual understanding will become. This is the most important part,
although simran or the repetition of the five Holy Names
is the foundation.

Now to answer your questions: Since you are accustomed to praying, you may continue to do so. However,
when treating your patients or invoking the blessings of
the Master on them, you should do it in an impersonal
manner. Do it for the good of the patient as one of the
particles of humanity, and do not stress the idea of his
being your patient or that he should be cured. Naturally,
everybody cannot be cured. They have all to expiate their
karma. But a general desire to be good and helpful and
render service to humanity is laudable.

Yawning has no spiritual significance. It has a physical
and, to some extent, mental basis and is connected with
the flow of pranas. But that does not concern us.

As you proceed in your bhajan and develop the habit
of one-pointedness, you will see many such things; but
these should not arrest nor divert your attention. The aim
of a true satsangi is to take his mind away from other
things and to merge into the Sound or Shabd, so that
after being rendered pure by contact with the Sound,
he might be taken up along with it to purer and higher
regions.

Regarding the quotations from "Light on the Anand
Yog," the idea seems to be that the life on this earth, if
properly lived under the direction of a competent Master,
is a very enviable life and certainly preferable to life in
paradise, because in paradise, when the merits of one's
karmas are exhausted, he is again thrown down on this
earth by being reborn according to his residual karmas.

But a life well lived on earth not only makes you happy here but entitles you even during your lifetime to high spiritual spheres from whence there is no coming back to this earth.

By "translating spirituality into physicality" is meant the incorporation of the spiritual principles in your physical body to such an extent that you are a source of light and help and comfort to those around you. This has been the case with all great spiritual men and Masters. But this happens only when first we have risen above the earthly conditions and attachments, have gone in at the eye center and been in free association with the spiritual Source.

Yes, going in at the eye center is certainly a hard task because for centuries and centuries we have been accustomed to going out. But once one is convinced and sees the necessity of such a course, it should not be so difficult. Patience and perseverance win in the end. The mind, however, likes more to be persuaded and coaxed than to be goaded and driven at the point of a bayonet. If thoughts go out too much or seem to rush in from all sides at the time of bhajan and simran, gently push them aside, reason and say firmly, "We'll discuss these things after meditation." Then by and by you will be able to follow a healthy means of going in at the time of bhajan, and attending to the worldly duties at other times. This is an ideal worth striving for.

Of course it is necessary for parents to be firm and properly discipline their children through love and understanding, but one should never be carried away by anger. The most important thing is that nothing should be forced, but opportunities should be offered and suitable literature should be available. Last, but not the least, your own life should be a shining example to the rest of the family. Children are quick to imitate their elders.

171. It is true that everything is predestined; but this is a general statement and it can have a number of exceptions, the exceptions themselves being a part of the rule of predestination. For instance, when a perfect Saint initiates a person and takes him into his fold, the course of destiny is appreciably changed. This statement also needs a lot of clarification. It is highly involved and difficult for the mind to comprehend. Suffice it to say that the Master helps not only the satsangis themselves but all those whom they love and serve and those who love and serve the satsangis. A satsangi should work earnestly with faith and devotion, which will develop in him an intense love for the Master. True love does not mean possessiveness, but complete and unconditional surrender to His Will. He alone knows what is best for us. If, however, one goes on doing his duty and following the instructions which have been given him by the Master, he need not worry nor be concerned about anything.

It is true that real love for the Master wonderfully disinfects the mind and washes off a good deal of the accumulated filth. But when this is not possible or it is difficult, then one ought to work towards it by concentration at the eye center by means of simran, that is, repetition of the five Holy Names, and thus gradually vacate the body.

Yes, conditioned reflexes which have been grooved in the brain for years are difficult to overcome. But I think you know the other side of the picture too, namely, they can be modified and have been modified. Those who are fortunate enough to attend the satsang of Saints or Sadhus or Adepts find it easier. Even without such exalted company, the study of Sant Mat literature, thinking of the Master and visualizing his form, and then the repetition of the five Holy Names with the attention of the mind, cumulatively have the same effect. We should not forget that it took some time for these grooves to be formed in the brain and it will naturally take time to obliterate them and make new ones.

Yes, the Sound Current does cleanse and purify, but ordinarily it is not easily caught by the impure and distracted mind—except in the presence of a Master.

The sounds which you hear are undoubtedly very elementary and cannot be classed in the category of Shabd. These sounds are only the beginning, the lower end of the rope. If you persist in paying attention to these sounds (seemingly from the right ear or the center only and *not* from the left side), they will ultimately develop into something finer. Then by and by, in the course of time, you will reach the bell sound. In the meantime, take hold of what is available, work upon it and make yourself deserving of higher things. This is my advice.

In order to feel the love and friendship of the higher regions, one must try to reach those places, unless one is satisfied with speculation on and contemplation of what happens there. The way to reach those places has already been given to you by your Master. You could certainly see Master Jagat Singh and talk with him if you had intense love or if you could raise your consciousness to the center between the eyebrows, from where it would be taken above and behind the eyes.

* * *

172. Drowsiness is really something to guard against. If you feel drowsy at the beginning, you might wash your face and then start the practice. If you feel drowsy during the exercise, give yourself a shake and look up; then start again. If drowsiness persists too much, get up, walk a few steps and then sit down again for the meditation practice. Drowsiness comes when the attention has slipped downward from the eye center. If you keep your attention up at the eye center and repeat the five Holy Names with the *attention* of-the mind, the problem of drowsiness will be solved. Yes, the problem of drowsiness and falling asleep during meditation will surely be solved after a little persistence.

* * *

173.   Once a Master has accepted a disciple, he never leaves him but is ever ready to guide him on the path. He does much more for us than the human mind can comprehend. All that is asked of us is to follow his instructions with faith and devotion, and he will do the rest.

* * *

174.   You may certainly have novocaine injected, in order to have painless extraction. There is absolutely no objection whatever to it.

Regarding your progress, the rate varies with each individual and depends upon one's previous background, the present effort, the time devoted to meditation, the attitude of mind, etc. There is definitely no reason for being dejected or discouraged. Everything in good time.

You find only darkness within because the conscious currents have not yet been concentrated inside. As you vacate the body by withdrawing the consciousness to the eye center by means of simran (repetition of the five Holy Names), flashes of light will be visible.

One way of speeding up the progress is to keep on repeating the five Holy Names mentally any time—whenever you are not particularly busy or are engaged in work which does not require presence of mind, such as when traveling in any conveyance, waiting at a station or in an office, or anywhere for that matter. You may do this without attracting attention or inviting comment, but the moment something has to be attended to which requires your attention, you may stop your mental repetition and attend to the work at hand. This will enable you to concentrate more easily when you sit for meditation at the appointed time.

* * *

175.   As regards smoking, it is not a good habit though it is very much prevalent in social circles. While it is not taboo altogether, it is desirable that you try to give it up gradually. Anything which weakens our will or makes us depend too much even on apparently innocent stimulants is a disadvantage. The more you are able to concentrate your attention and go *in*, the more you will be inclined to give up all such things and be independent in the true sense.

* * *

176.   Sant Mat, especially if one tries to live up to the teachings, should and does improve the home life and the relationship between husband and wife because now they can look on all such relationships more objectively than before, the mind being really set upon the spiritual goal. Husband and wife should follow the path together, for they can be extremely helpful to each other.

It is a rare privilege that both husband and wife can be initiated, for many there are whose husbands or wives are not interested or designated to take Nam in this lifetime. Even then, that is no excuse for shirking one's duty as a householder. When both are initiated, they know well how to live in the world and perform their duties, and there should be no difficulty whatsoever in continuing marital life.

It is true that differences sometimes do arise in married life, but if we take a rational and normal view and remember that we have to pull through life together, the differences are soon made up and understanding develops. On the other hand, separation or divorce really sets a bad example and hinders rather than helps the Master's work. I would advise both of you to smoothen any differences that you may have and start life anew, doing your meditations *regularly* as well as your worldly duties. This is what the Master wants of us and this is the most acceptable *seva,* 'service'. It may not be possible to forget, but it should certainly be possible to forgive and start life anew.

* * *

177. I appreciate your desire to serve the Master and the Master's cause, but before doing so one should be master of one's self. Unless we are masters of ourselves, how can we offer what is not really ours? Charity should begin at home and one should serve himself first before serving others. That service is to free the soul from the clutches of the mind, and that is possible only when we devote ourselves *regularly* to Shabd practice, without neglecting our worldly duties. I would therefore advise you, in order to achieve your object of serving the Master and serving others, to start by serving yourself, that is, by devoting the maximum time to bhajan and simran, living your life accordingly, and thus developing Shabd consciousness.

Satsangis should love each other and be tolerant and sympathetic, being followers of the same path.

* * *

178. Please do not take these things to heart. Maybe they exist only to impress upon you the proper value—or rather the nothingness—of things of this world. Man is really always alone but he thinks—and wrongly so—that he has a host of friends, possessions and attachments. At last a time comes when he is disillusioned, and if he happens to be a satsangi he realizes that the only real and true friend is the Master.

If we are not attached and have no expectations or unfulfilled desires, the behavior of other people does not affect us much. After all, it is not the things themselves but the reaction which they produce upon us which really matters. People of the world also ultimately come to this conclusion after receiving hard knocks and crushing disappointments. But a satsangi gradually and almost imperceptibly loosens the bonds of attachment in this world by devotion to Shabd.

Please have courage and faith in the Master. Now that you have learned the hollowness of the world and its possessions and attachments, you will be able to devote all your attention assiduously to simran and listening to the Sound whenever possible. As you very well know, simran or the repetition of the five Holy Names is the foundation of this spiritual practice. It is by means of worldly simran, thinking of the things of this world, that we have become denizens of this plane and strangers to our own home. Therefore, we should gradually, by means of spiritual simran, draw up our consciousness to the center above the eyes, and then the Sound will automatically take care of us. We only have to do our duty and may thoroughly rest assured that the Master will do his duty; that is, he will take us at the proper time. All that is necessary is that we turn our back to the world and face the Master. He is always there to receive and welcome us with open arms.

I think there is some confusion in the minds of many people as to what is a normal instinct. Scientifically, instinct is based upon what the race or the individual has experienced in the past, and aims at survival. As man progresses, instincts change. But deep down in everybody, even in those whom we do not value as very high in society, is an instinct for peace and for union with a higher or superior Power. If nature were left to take its course undisturbed, perhaps this instinct would come to fruition in many centuries or even eons.

Our Great Master used to say that all these so-called normal instincts are common in animals as well as in man. What distinguishes man from animal is his ability to rise above the instincts and go back to his Creator. He would also say that even as animals we had parents, mates, progeny, and experienced all those sensations. Now that we have a human body, we should do something better and use it for the purpose for which it was created, and that is to realize God.

Saints come into this world to help develop this higher instinct. By their personal touch and by other means—inner, spiritual—they put us on the road so that even the worst among us should not have to sojourn in this valley of tears for more than four human lives. The return to this world is only for such as, in spite of all the teachings, have not been able to sublimate the cravings of the mind and senses. Even for such, these cravings would become weaker and weaker in the subsequent births, and the opportunities for spiritual uplift would become greater and greater, thus enabling a 'doubting Thomas' to become a devoted pupil. He ultimately acquires a very holy status and becomes a Gurmukh (highly advanced soul).

To be able to rise above the world and above the mind and senses is no easy job. First of all, the mind has

to be convinced, so that instead of open or silent oppo-
sition, it offers assistance. This also makes the task of
the Satguru easy. Then the contact with the Shabd pulls
us up and completely washes off the dirt of the karmas.
When thus purified, we become consciously united with
the Satguru.

* * *

179.   The world is very unhappy today and the ills of the
mind far exceed the ills of the body, for which there is but
one and only one remedy—Nam.

* * *

180.   But as they do their bhajan and go up, they will
soon realize that the best things which this world has to
offer are as nothing in comparison with the joy and the
bliss of going in and contacting the Divine Sound. Even
when our concentration is not yet complete, but fairly
complete, we begin to receive the thrills of joy, and those
who want to work on scientific or philosophic lines may
automatically receive new and fresh ideas and suggestions. However, these are only mental satisfactions. The
real ideal is to rise above the mind and get merged in the
Ocean of Love. I wish that there be perfect amity and
understanding among all satsangis; and they should all
work together for their own good and for the benefit of
the newcomers.

* * *

181.   I requested better understanding only in view of
the Master's cause and I am glad that it was taken in the
right spirit. Mysticism and symbolism are as much facts of
nature as its other grand phenomena and stand on their
own merit and utility. Neither proving nor disproving will

make any substantial change in the position. Life is so
short and there is so much to accomplish in the way of
breaking through the barriers erected for us by the negative power when we are heading for our real Home, that I
wonder how people can waste time in wrangling. The
path for satsangis is clear, namely, to do what they conveniently can for others in a spirit of service and do *as much
as possible* for their own spiritual uplift. Let us offer ourselves as instruments in His hands and let Him use us as
He wills.

Your lecture work has been responsible for introduc-
ing so many new persons to Radha Soami literature, and
as such it has a double value. Such are the ways of the
Master. You have already taken several rapid strides on
the path of surrender—apparently the most difficult and
yet the easiest way to purify the mind. Liquidating it
altogether will not do, as it also has its function to perform. I wish you godspeed in your interesting and useful
work which has so many useful lines. It should not make
you feel weary, but fill you with satisfaction to see your
efforts being crowned with success.

* * *

182.   The essence of the thing is that one should follow
a career or profession to make one's living but should not
become engrossed in it to the detriment of one's spiritual
attainment. "Hand to work but mind in Satguru," is a
saying here. Besides, one has to balance the karmic account
too. Destiny cannot be evaded, but if gone through
with full understanding and under the guiding and protecting hand of Satguru, it can be made to subserve the
great end.

* * *

183.   You are right in thinking that if we go on lovingly and faithfully with our bhajan and simran many things get cleared up automatically. Yet that need not make you hesitate to write to me whenever you feel like doing so. Satguru is within you and is always ready to help you. Nothing gives the Master more pleasure than a disciple coming up to him and contacting him within. Within us are light, radiance, joy and bliss, and as we go in we feel the peace and blessing.

Your experience is correct and is the result of your previous sanskaras, that is, impressions and tendencies of good deeds in previous lives. You should, however, listen to the sound from the *right* ear only and not from the left. The attention should be kept at the eye center. The Sound, which is Shabd, really comes from the center, but as we are accustomed to listen through the ear we think it is coming from the ears. By keeping the attention at the eye center, the Sound will gradually concentrate in the center and lead straight up. The left side is dominated or governed by the negative power and, though sometimes it may seem more attractive, it should be avoided. Satguru's path is on the right.

* * *

184.   It is a pleasure to read your appreciation of the path. This is only the beginning. As you persevere on the path and give the required time with love and devotion you will realize the glories of the spirit and feel the guidance and protection of the Master.

Your experiences are correct. The normal course is to do your simran or repetition of the five Names given you at the time of initiation for about two hours, or so long as you can, and then devote about an hour or so to hearing the Sound. During repetition you have to keep the

attention fixed at the eye center without caring for the
Sound unless it becomes persistent and compelling. When
the Sound draws you up, yield to it. You repeat the
Names only if at any time during this Sound experience
you feel any doubt, hesitation, difficulty or fear, and not
otherwise during the time you are listening to the Sound.
On account of earnestness and good concentration, the
Sound can be heard at any time when one is a little relaxed, but at such times its pull is usually not effective.
If you find the Sound very strong you can give yourself
up to it, but *never* to any sound coming from the left. This
Sound experience is chiefly due to your past karmas. You
will see the radiant form too, by and by. Love, faith and
perseverance constitute the keynote.

Asanas, 'yogic postures', are good for health and
physical fitness, and so is deep breathing. If you have recourse to them only for health purposes and for keeping
fit, without any spiritual significance, there is no harm;
but it is not to be used as a spiritual discipline.

* * *

185. I am glad you realize the importance and significance of the spiritual path. Peace and happiness lie in
going in and contacting the Shabd. A good moral life and
regularity in bhajan and simran make for progress.

If one is unable to overcome the five enemies at once,
he should make an earnest attempt and pray to the Master to give him strength, and be earnest and faithful in his
devotions. When the disciple makes a sincere effort, help
is vouchsafed.

The cooking and purchasing of meat, fish, fowl, etc.,
even for guests, is improper and should be avoided. You
can offer fruits or other gifts.

Be regular in your meditations and lay stress on

simran, that is, repetition of the Names. You can do this at odd hours too and in bed, in addition to the prescribed hours.

* * *

186. Your experience is correct and as you persevere in the repetition of the Names, keeping the attention at the eye center, the sound of the bell which is now feeble will become strong and clear, and in due course will lead to other experiences. The more the mind is concentrated and unattached, the stronger and clearer will be the Sound. Perseverance and diligence with love and faith count a good deal.

As to the second problem, I would remind you of the instructions and directions at the time of initiation. For progress on the path a good, pure, moral life is very necessary. Although continued meditation even in existing circumstances will not be without some effect, it will not be much. By meditation we try to take the mind and soul up, but attachments—and especially sinful attachments—bring them down. We are thus practically nullifying the results of meditation.

I appreciate your desire to be a good satsangi. Take courage in both hands and get out of this ugly mess. Satguru helps those who wish to tread the moral and spiritual path and lead a true satsangi's life. Never mind the past and do not dwell on it or even think of it. Let it be a closed chapter and start life afresh, as it were. The Satguru will forgive the past if you stick to your resolve. This will improve your bhajan and simran also.

* * *

187. Your letter was duly received and I have thoroughly noted its contents. I am indeed sorry to be so late in replying, but this was unavoidable owing to so many things which required my personal attention here. Every year on 29th December we celebrate the *bhandara,* that is, the death anniversary of the founder of this institution. The bhandara is attended by thirty to forty thousand devoted satsangis from all over the country, and means two very busy weeks.

The problem which you have is a very personal one and yours should be the last word in the matter. I am writing to you only in an advisory capacity and in response to your detailed letter which analyzes and partly sums up the situation very nicely.

Marriage, as it seems to me, means complete understanding and cooperation. Without understanding, it is very hard to pull through; but if impelled by love, one decides to cooperate and pull through, understanding follows. To find a *perfect* partner, according to one's ideal, is almost impossible because there are several factors which bring people together. Love, however, smoothens and adjusts, and one finds happiness in making the other person happy. Our lives and relationships are based to a very great extent upon karmic adjustments and factors beyond our control. We come close to each other because of this background and sometimes have to go through situations and experiences for the sake of karmic adjustments, whether we like it or not. In fact, life in this world is like acting a part, and if we do not forget this and play our part well, we should be happy. Marriage is no exception to this rule.

Besides, we should not be too analytical. It leads us nowhere eventually. The more we analyze, the more we will see the hollowness of it and court disappointment. If we go on subjecting people to tests all our life, we will have no friend to lean on. Let the mind be made up and then stick to it, stressing and dwelling upon the points of agreement, and belittling and ignoring the points of difference and disagreement.

So far as diet is concerned, the idea of marriage is perfectly satisfactory, providing you help him in his vegetarian diet. There is no compulsion or obligation in the matter of bringing up the children. It is left completely to the parents. In fact, Sant Mat does not advocate force or pressure of any sort in any matter. It offers its protection and solutions of the problems of life and death to those who ask for it and are ready for it. Sant Mat does not thrust its teachings upon persons unwilling to accept them, even though it stresses the importance of the human life and the opportunity for keeping the Truth open to us as human beings. Only in human life is it possible to seek the Truth, and to find abiding peace and happiness by seeking God-realization or Truth. But there is almost the whole of life before you.

Actually, one is always lonely in life and hence tries to make someone his or her own. But again the time comes when one realizes that nothing is his or hers in life. Personally, I welcome that feeling and even think that the sooner it comes the better. It is only then that we begin to search for some One who is really our own and is going to be ours forever. This search is the main object of our life on this earth.

* * *

188.   I am glad to know that you enjoy your meditation, even though the joy of it is sometimes interrupted by worldly anxieties and thoughts. As you no doubt know, the meditation according to the teaching of the Saints is simply to disconnect the soul from the world and to connect it with the Supreme Being. This is done only

gradually and takes almost a lifetime. But as you persevere regularly in the meditation, you get ample joy and
peace, which compensates for your labors and makes you
cheerfully and patiently look forward to ultimate victory.

I would ask that before you sit in meditation, you
make up your mind not to worry about these things
nor give thought to anything else until you have finished
your period of meditation. You know that when these
thoughts invade your mind during your period of bhajan
and simran, it helps neither the worldly problem nor the
abhyas, the spiritual practice. But if you devote yourself
sincerely and with all your heart and attention at the time
of meditation, and do so regularly every day, you will receive help in solving your worldly problems too.

The Guru is always helpful, but the disciple can see
the help only when he goes in. You may rest assured that
whatever happens is for the disciple's own spiritual benefit, even though the disciple may not be able to understand it at the time. Hence the need for implicit faith and
love, which are engendered and strengthened by means
of bhajan and simran.

* * *

189. You are right in thinking that we should put forth
whatever efforts we can, and leave the results to the Master. The more time one gives to the repetition of the Holy
Names and listening to the Sound—with love and devotion—the nearer he comes to his goal. The spiritual
journey is traversed, not with physical limbs but with
attention. And when we repeat the Names, our attention
is turned inwards to the spiritual regions. Idle conversation and gossip, however, tend to keep the attention
outwards.

* * *

190.   You are welcome to this place but I should tell you that distance is no bar to bhajan and simran. You have to develop the proper attitude of mind wherever you are.

* * *

191.   Glad to know that you are realizing the significance of initiation and feeling the all-pervading Power which calls the marked people from the multitude. It is now for you to respond to the call and cooperate with all your zeal.

There should be no strain at the time of simran. Just keep your attention in darkness in your forehead with eyes closed, of course, and try to prevent the attention from sliding down or going out. If it does, bring it back. When you find yourself calm, one-pointed and introspective, utilize the time for listening to the Sound.

Sound or Shabd is the Power that will in due course pull you up, but the ground must be prepared by simran, or the repetition of the Names, now that you have received the initiation.

At the time of a special experience like the one described, reverently repeat the five Names for a few minutes. Then if it remains, submit to the Power or Presence and receive its influence.

* * *

192.   You seem to have been rather upset. Things do sometimes take a strange turn, but as you know, it is all what we have sown at one time or another. A satsangi should face all situations with faith and courage and never lose heart, and above all never be lax in bhajan and simran. If there has been any laxity, the sooner it is made up the better. Regularity in meditation gives confidence and strength that are difficult to acquire in any other way. Then you would also realize how the Master is helping you and, in fact, molding you.

* * *

193. Truly, Nam is the greatest gift of all, and one can only begin to have some idea of the magnitude of this wonderful blessing after going in.

Yes, to control the mind *is* the real problem. It is not an easy job to still and control the mind. One may do so to an extent, more or less, by study, contemplation and other means; but the mind is really controlled and becomes a friend only when it comes into contact with Shabd and begins to enjoy its bliss.

Controlling the mind by other means is like putting a poisonous snake in a basket (as snake charmers do here in India). It may seem harmless as long as it is in the basket, but as soon as it gets an opportunity it will surely bite. However, if the poison sac is taken out of the snake, there is no need of even putting it in a basket and one may handle it freely, as he likes.

One may approach the Shabd through intensive simran, that is the repetition of the five Holy Names. One may hear various sounds, as you are hearing—and this is good too—but one will be *joined* to Shabd only when *all* the attention is concentrated above the eyes. (You are not to strain nor try to put your attention there, but simply keep it at the center between the two eyebrows; it will go in and up of itself.)

The bliss or the enjoyment of Shabd is superior to any other pleasure which one can enjoy in this world. Once the mind begins to enjoy this bliss, it will be harnessed to it and will not turn back to worldly pleasures. It will then be like the snake whose poison sac has been removed.

Please go on working, and with faith and devotion attend to the spiritual practice regularly. By and by everything will be all right.

* * *

194. You are free to ask a million, million questions if you like. Why wait for your coming here or my visit there? Start right now, study the books thoroughly, attend the satsang, begin your meditations; and whatever is not clear to you, write to me by all means. Most of the questions are automatically answered when one begins meditation and study earnestly.

The light is within you and when you concentrate your attention at the eye center and go in, you will be able to see the light. Simran is the key to the whole practice and the foundation of the system, as it were.

* * *

195. Your candid admission of your slackness in performing your duty and acting up to your promise stands to your credit, but this is an omission which has to be made up. The time lost can never be regained but we can sincerely aim to do better.

Initiation into Sant Mat is a privilege, and this privilege should be fully utilized. Diet also is an important factor, but meditation is the chief thing. Of course, unless one abstains from meat, eggs, alcohol, etc., it is impossible to concentrate properly.

The object of meditation is to transfer the center of attention to inner and more real things, compared to which the outward shows are like shadows. The door to those inner realms is above and behind the two eyes, and it is by persistently knocking at those gates (concentrating *the attention* between the two eyebrows) in the manner taught to you at the time of initiation, that admittance is gained.

The easiest way to achieve this, without disturbing normal existence and upsetting existing relations, is to practice meditation for *at least* two and one-half hours *every day* so that one learns to withdraw the attention gradually and voluntarily and also to *hold* it there. This preliminary work is hard, and in the beginning it is tiring and boring also, for the tendency of the human mind is to go out, and not in. It is only by going in that we can reach the kingdom of God. Once concentration has been achieved, the rest becomes comparatively easy, for then bhajan is delightful. However, for the average individual, this is almost the work of a lifetime. But when this has been accomplished, one literally rises above the world.

The eye center is the door that leads up into higher regions, and down into this body or the world as well. The world exists for us and influences us only when we play through the nine doors, but when we make for the tenth door we rise above the world. It is then that we acquire strong faith in the Master and realize that in whatever we have to face, to go through, the Master is always with us and guides and protects us. The Master always guides and protects—though he seldom interferes in pralabdh—but at this stage we see and know what he is doing, and that inspires faith, love and courage in us. It is then only that knowable contact with the Master is made at will (whenever we wish).

I have written to you at some length because these small doubts and stirrings are the signs of dissatisfaction and longing for something better than the world affords. Most of your problems will be solved automatically if you apply yourself to the practice with *diligence* and *faith*.

I do not wonder if the idea of future prospects sometimes fills you with anxiety. It is but natural as long as we
depend entirely on our own resources. But in this matter
too, while following the path which prudence and experience dictates, you should depend upon the Master and
not neglect any inner promptings that come to you *un-
sought and without any effort.*

As regards the course of psychoanalysis, we have no
prejudices, but the same result can be achieved, as you
rightly guess, by a *continued* and *faithful* course of proper
meditation. Hundreds of people seek interviews with the
Master for their internal problems and this, combined
with the exposition during the satsang, solves their difficulties and secures for them even greater results than psychoanalysis. You may continue this course (of psychoanalysis) as long as you find it helpful, but do not depend too
much on it.

* * *

196. Saints and Masters are the "Word made flesh."
The Word or Divine Sound pervades everywhere, but it
is up to you to make effective use of this initiation, and
that is by withdrawing your attention and your consciousness from the body up to the eye center.

The more you are able to detach yourself, the better
you will be able to hear the Sound. Sometimes you may
hear several sounds. Choose the finer one and hold onto
it till you get the bell or the gong sound, but never go after the sound and always keep the attention in the center
between the eyebrows. The Sound will itself pull you in
and up. You may have to work for it for some time but do
not despair. Continue to go about your meditation with
calmness and devotion. Please also remember that no

sound, however sweet, is to be heard from the *left* side. If
it persists, it ought to be ignored.

Yes, you may use a stool and make yourself comfortable. The point is that the *attention* should be concentrated and fixed at the center between the eyebrows, but
if the body is in an uncomfortable position it will constantly draw the attention down. But by and by you
should try to accustom yourself to the posture, as it would
be helpful.

* * *

197.   Sometimes frail health does affect the meditation
practice but if you are able to contact the Sound and gently submit to it, it has an invigorating effect. For the present you may divide your meditation period into suitable
intervals and keep the idea of the Master and Nam in
your mind throughout the day.

It is true that the Shabd or the Sound initiation is really earned only when a person has been able to vacate the
body at least up to the navel, but in view of the short span
of life and other dangers and difficulties, the Great Master, Huzur Sawan Singh Ji Maharaj, made very lenient
conditions. You should not omit the Sound or Shabd
program from your daily meditations and should make it
a point to devote at least half an hour to it daily, whenever and wherever you conveniently can. You may practice this even while sitting in a chair when you are alone,
simply closing the eyes and lightly putting the hand up to
the face and covering the right ear. Listening to the
Sound also helps withdrawal in due course. When sitting
for Sound, please keep your attention *not* in the right ear,
but between the two eyebrows, the same as for simran.

As for karma, it is best not to bother about it but just
do your duty and then leave everything to the Master. No

use blaming yourself or anything else. Ours should be a positive approach, and that is covered by the Master's instructions.

As for social activities, there is no ban upon them and you may certainly meet your friends. But all the while you should not forget that you are a satsangi, and avoid partaking of or doing the things which a satsangi should not do. If you remain firm and true to your principles and still meet your friends politely and cheerfully, it will be helpful to them as well as to yourself.

* * *

198. Your Master is even now within you, and by intensive simran and bhajan you may go up and have a glimpse of your dear Master. Satguru never dies, and is only waiting for the disciple to turn to him. This, I hope, will be a consolation to you.

* * *

199. Do not feel disheartened, please. The progress is slow but it is there even though we may not realize it at the moment. The music at the right ear is one such manifestation. By and by you will have closer and more intimate contact with the Sound Current. The practice of dhyan, i.e., contemplation of your Satguru at the eye center, will help you a good deal. You should contemplate on the form of your Satguru, Maharaj Jagat Singh Ji. For you he is not dead, and you have only to reach the eye center to contact him. There should be no feeling of frustration.

* * *

200. It is evident that you *are* making progress although you seem to be doubtful or modest about it. A definite lift inside is not a mere fancy, nor is the feeling of great joy inside throughout the day whilst at your work imaginary. It comes when the chief attention is inside. You do very well in repeating the Names on such occasions, even when the feeling or emotion is that of joy. This again gives you a lift and enables you by constant practice to rise above joy and sorrow.

The experience of being flooded with bright sunlight at the eye focus is quite correct, and the progress of numbness higher up in the limbs leaves no doubt whatsoever about the progress in withdrawing. Yes, the feeling of having the Master about you is genuine. As you make more progress, you will be able to see the Master directly before you and, in course of time, may even be able to talk to him. All that is really worthwhile in this life is realization of the Master's form within and perfect contact with the Sound Current, which will ultimately lead you to your goal.

I am very glad you have learned the method of using the Names at all times during the day, even while attending to the other work. This is, in fact, the key to the solutions of most problems.

Crowds, scenes or other substances do sometimes pass before our vision at the time of simran or meditation. To these and to all other such things you should be an indifferent and not an interested spectator. Then your progress will be more rapid.

* * *

201. As to bhajan and simran—the most important work—that, of course, can be carried on anywhere. It does not depend on geographical conditions but is chiefly a discipline of the mind. The Shabd is within you and so is the Master, and it is you who have to contact them—

space making no difference—whether in America or in India.

* * *

202. It is the duty of the husband to support his wife and children quite as much as it is the duty of the wife to minister to the needs and comfort of the husband, and work for peace and domestic happiness. Husband and wife are like two wheels of a chariot. Smooth running of the domestic chariot depends on *both* the wheels, and the two should cooperate together. Sant Mat strongly advocates domestic peace and harmony, as it makes for spiritual progress, among other things. Where there is discord, much time is wasted.

* * *

203. All our improper urges, desires and attractions can be overcome or controlled by *regularly* giving time to simran and bhajan, particularly to simran. If you carry on the simran (repetition of the five Holy Names) regularly, for a minimum of two hours every day, by and by you will feel a sense of detachment. Simran helps in drawing the attention up and therefore loosens the ties consequent upon living in this world.

* * *

204. Shabd and Nam are the only real, everlasting and unfailing friends, and these we should try to cultivate. Shabd never deserts, nor does the Master. It is we who become indifferent. Worldly affections and other entanglements claim too much of our attention, and we lose touch with Shabd. It is always there in spite of all this and can be contacted any moment by simran. We have to turn our face that way, and help is forthcoming.

This world is the field of karmas, and we should discharge our duties and obligations but we should not, at the same time, forget the Eternal Reality. We meet and part according to our karmic background and should not break our hearts over these lapses, but turn to Nam and Shabd instead.

Please begin your meditations as faithfully and regularly as before and turn to Shabd as the only real friend, and you will be happy. It is good to be forgiving.

* * *

205.   I am glad that you are devoting yourself to meditation more regularly. We feel the ills of the body and the shocks of the world in proportion to our attachment. By meditation, that is, by repetition of the names and devotion to Shabd practice, we increase our love for the real and the permanent, and loosen our attachment for the impermanent.

Individuals are brought together or separated according to their past karmas, just as pieces of timber floating on a river are brought together by one current and separated again by another. In the behavior of your . . . and your . . . and the consequent pain and suffering, behold the play of the karmas. Behind this fleeting show of karmas is the permanent Reality—Shabd—and your own consciousness. Both are of the same essence and differ radically from the entity we call mind, which finds outer expression in our loves and hates, attachment and indifferences, etc., all of which makes us miserable here. Shabd alone has the power to detach us from these. When we are joined to the divine current of Shabd we rise above phenomena and, knowing the Reality, cease to be unhappy and miserable. Hence, the insistence of the

Saints upon devotion to Shabd and to repetition of the Holy Names.

The repetition of the Names has an uplifting effect, counteracts the downward drag of the karmas and, by enabling us to concentrate our attention and consciousness at the eye focus, helps us in contacting the Shabd. By devoting yourself to meditation more regularly and assiduously, you would be able to see the how and why, and the sting will be taken out. Then, if it is so ordained, things may improve. But whatever happens, you should transfer your devotion and affection to the inner reality, the Shabd Dhun within you. That is the road to peace and happiness. It does not imply any sudden break. One may go on doing his or her duty to everyone and by everyone, but the heart should be elsewhere.

By ill will, we only complicate matters and forge new bonds of karmas. Do your duty, act rightly and truthfully, but without any malice or ill will; and conquer by love.

* * *

206.   Age does not matter so much if the mind is willing and the application is steady. You will also feel that if you keep yourself in the Shabd, most of your problems will automatically be attended to.

The object of human life is to be able to attain salvation and return Home, and for that it is necessary that we give as much time as possible—as we can, consistently, with our duties in the world—to learn to withdraw our attention from the phenomenal world and to raise it to the spirit center. Of course it requires time and effort. Hence the need is steady application.

* * *

207.   Sorry to hear about your illness. Have recourse to
whatever treatment suits you and appeals to you. Our
diseases and illnesses are the result of our own actions,
and much may be done by changing the course of our
mental currents. Some of it may have to be worked out.
The proper attitude is to put all your heart and attention
in devotion and meditation, and love even your enemies
and detractors. That may be too much, but you can at
least ignore them and seek consolation in the goodness of
the spirit and the mercy of the Lord. Think how good and
merciful God is, when you are inclined to be disgusted
with the treatment meted out to you. That is the best
healing ointment.

What we are paying for or working out in this life are
not the karmas of one life, but several lives. We should
not try to analyze these things but should think instead
how to pay them off and be free.

You may pray as you like but the best prayer is to ask
the Lord to give us strength and courage to face gracefully whatever He wants us to face, and submit to His divine
Will.

Attachment is the root of all trouble. One can help
without being attached.

* * *

208.   I understand your difficulty but am glad you realize that the remedy for all these ills lies in self-control and
in devotion to bhajan and simran. Sant Mat does not encourage ostracism, but at the same time it does not want
us to strengthen our ties, which subsequently we may
have to loosen.

As for the Radha Soami science, you may certainly
tell people, but generally a few broad hints are enough
for those who are really interested. They are sure to ask

for more. As for those who do not feel any interest, no amount of haranguing would be useful.

Regarding the wandering mind, it has been out for thousands of lives and it has become its nature to flit from one subject to another. Simran and Shabd are the only remedies. One should not despair, but apply these remedies steadily and it will yield in due course. You are not alone in this respect. Most beginners complain of the mind wandering.

You should not meditate upon the photo but try to visualize the form mentally, with your eyes closed. That will partly solve your difficulty. The photograph can remain in the room and you get the impression in your mind, but do not look at it at the time of meditation. The Sound Current is always there, but for lack of attention (mind wandering) we cannot catch it.

As for you, you are on the path and the more progress you make the more you will impress your friends and relatives. Sant Mat believes only in gentle, loving persuasion rather than any severe criticism. And this too will carry conviction only when the time is ripe.

* * *

209. It is good that you are now on the path and have been initiated into the way of working in Shabd, which is the royal road to our True Home. The more you pay attention to bhajan and simran, and especially to the simran which is the repetition of the five Holy Names—with *attention* at the eye center—the more will the feeling of love and confidence spring in your heart; and you will feel that you are not alone.

The Master is always with you. His real form is the Shabd, and that is within you, and it is for you to work your way up and contact the radiant form.

When you are away from satsang, read Sant Mat literature, which will also help you in meditation.

* * *

210.   I am glad that you are firm in your principles and
do not yield to temptation regarding drinks and the like.
But it is much better that these things which are prohibited to us be not served to our friends also. I understand
your position and your problems, but once your friends
come to know of your principles, they will understand
your position and even appreciate it. It is possible to render service to our friends in other ways than this. This was
also the advice given by Huzur Maharaj Ji [Baba Sawan
Singh Ji].

* * *

211.   The Master is always with his satsangis and protects them. You just attend to your bhajan and simran
daily, as you have been told at the time of initiation. You
put forth your best efforts *regularly*, then leave the rest to
him and he will take care of everything.

In your associations, always try to keep good company and do not do anything that you would not do in the
physical presence of your Master. He is always watching
over you, though you may not always be conscious of his
presence. Since you are a satsangi, you should not do
anything which would give a bad impression about the
sangat in general. The best way to impress others is to
actually *live* the life yourself. That counts far more than
all the preaching. It is much better to keep silent and
personally live up to the teachings of Sant Mat in all our
actions.

* * *

212.   I note that you were initiated by Huzur Maharaj Baba Sawan Singh Ji at a very young age. This is your great good fortune, for initiation from such a Master is bound to bear fruit when the time is ripe. It does not matter now if you did not utilize the opportunity in the past, but it will not justify your continuing to neglect the present opportunity. The best way to make amends is to properly utilize the time from now on.

After initiation, the Master is always present within the disciple. All that the disciple has to do after that is to take his attention from the outward things as much as possible and turn it in.

It is very good to have love and regard for your brother satsangis; but this is one thing, and trying to teach them is quite different. Before trying to explain and teach things, one ought to know them himself. An imperfect teacher would turn out only imperfect students. When the Saints appoint someone to carry on their work, it is their (the Saints') force behind him which works, and that is wanting in the case of any other person trying to take up that work.

The advice that was given to you was for your own ultimate benefit, and you will realize this in the course of time. By your behavior, conduct and loving treatment, you can be helpful to satsangis and inspire in them a spirit of love and devotion; but the first and the most important thing is that you should do your own bhajan and simran, which means that you should devote at least two and one-half hours every day—two hours to simran, and one-half hour every day to bhajan, or listening to the inner Sound.

I shall always be glad to hear of your efforts in this direction and to give whatever help is possible. Please also do not neglect your studies. The two things go together. Duty first. One who does not attend to the worldly duty, very often does not care for the spiritual duty either.

* * *

213. You asked advice and blessing in the first letter. I advised you to carry on your business and earn your living wherever it suited you but always to keep the principles of Sant Mat in view and to do your bhajan and simran *regularly*. It seems that you have not acted upon the advice and have even broken your vows by taking meat, etc.

It is true that Satguru is always with his disciples; however, if a disciple were never to glance inward and try to contact him, and violates the very principle of Sant Mat, what can be done? If you cannot do your bhajan and simran, at least you should refrain from further adding to your karmas by violating the vows of taking meat, etc. Sit in meditation and pray to the Satguru within.

* * *

214. I am glad that you have been able to stick to the diet without any difficulty. This, incidentally, gives you an opportunity to explain to inquirers—curious or otherwise—about Sant Mat. Read those spiritual books yourself also when you get time; and before going to bed, sit in bhajan. Simran can also be done while in bed. The more you keep your mind and attention in the Satguru, the more help will you receive. This, however, does not mean that you should neglect the work for which you have been sent there.

As for talking to other people and explaining your point of view, be as gentle, as courteous and as accomodating as possible. This is the way to win the hearts of the

people and secure respect for your views. Besides, your
own behavior speaks louder than words.

* * *

215.   I am in receipt of your letter about the passing
away of ———— . This is the way of all flesh; however,
satsangis have no fear of death because they rest in the
Satguru.

Good people are released early from this prison because the karmic debt which they have to settle is light. It
is a natural desire to be near those whom we love when
their time of departure comes, but such was the *Mauj*,
'Will', of Him who knows best. Please accept my condo-
lence and assuage your grief with the idea that such was
His Mauj, and also that for him at least all the troubles
are over.

* * *

216.   I am in receipt of your letter so full of devotion
and affection, and am happy that you feel so strongly
attracted towards Sant Mat. This is really the object of
life. Your past sanskaras incline you so strongly towards
it, but all the same you should study it thoroughly; and if
any clarification is needed, please do not hesitate to refer
the matter to me.

* * *

217.   I well realize that you have great longing for initiation. This was, however, withheld by me intentionally
with a view to enable you to complete your research
about Sant Mat. Even if one has to spend his whole life
on research alone, it is not time lost but gained—because
the stronger foundation will bring a sound structure. It
is therefore essential that before accepting Sant Mat

principles, the inquiry and investigation should be complete and thorough.

After you have made up your mind, the inquiry should be abandoned and the knowledge applied to practical experiences. This physical body is a rare privilege and opportunity because the main object of life, which is self-realization, can be attained in this human body. We have to carry out the duties of the worldly life and live as normal human beings, but the goal and destination must not be overlooked.

* * *

218. I am glad that you have both come to the path of Nam. That makes life easy and facilitates meditation, as both pull in the same direction.

Yes, God does work in His own mysterious ways, and it is not for us to question how and why. It is His grace alone that really opens our eyes and stirs our hearts, for He is within all of us. It is within, and not in the outside world, that we must try to realize Him with the aid of Master and Shabd—the Divine Harmony that created and sustains us.

What Dr. Johnson means is that if we start our meditation in a spirit of love, faith and reverence, which may also take the form of a short mental prayer, we put or tend to put ourselves *en rapport* with the Master.

3:00 A.M. meditation, if one can practice without difficulty, is definitely better than 6:00 A.M. meditation, because not only is it quiet all round and is the mind free from distracting thoughts of the day, but the atmosphere is also full of divine currents. It depends upon the individual temperaments and circumstances, however, to a great extent. It suits some, while others may find it difficult.

It is good to increase the meditation period gradually,

till the maximum period is reached, consolidating your gains. There should be no sliding back. Slow and steady wins the race.

The mind is like a monkey and does not wish to be confined and be still. It is its nature to be flitting from place to place and thought to thought, seeking—as it were—the bliss which it once enjoyed in the region of Trikuti. When it is able to catch the Shabd, the Divine Word, it will be still. It has been going out for ages and naturally finds it difficult to go in. Simran is an invocation, an appeal and a gradual turning inside. Persevere on, then the periods when you, the real you, are in control will increase.

You may meditate in the same room, but it would not be advisable for you to exchange experiences, not for the present at least.

* * *

219. Your search for Reality is really the aim and object of existence, and as this search can be made successfully in human life only, we should spare no trouble in seeking the Truth. It should be sought within ourselves. It has been well said that the kingdom of heaven lies within us. Without the help and assistance of a guide we cannot sail these uncharted seas.

* * *

220. Nam is, indeed, the *summum bonum* of our life, and blessed are those who have been shown the path and are treading it. Nam, Logos, Word, Shabd, all mean practically the same thing. It is by means of Shabd that we can gradually withdraw ourselves from the phenomenal and contact the Real. The path of the Saints enables you to do so without disturbing your normal course of life.

Whatever and wherever you may be, you can spare some time for your devotions and meditations; then in the course of time the entire life is reorientated.

Simran, or repetition of the Holy Names given to you, does the trick. In fact, too much emphasis cannot be laid upon simran, which should be done faithfully, regularly and with attention between the two eyebrows. By simran we concentrate our attention at the eye center and then contact the Divine Word which leads us on.

The physical form of the Master is also an embodiment of Shabd. He teaches and instructs in the physical form outside, and helps and guides in Shabd form inside. Love and devotion to the physical form and faithful repetition of the Holy Names lead to contact with the Shabd form inside. Satguru watches the progress of the disciple, but the disciple can realize this—as well as the help and protection received—only when he goes inside.

Bhajan and simran also constitute Master's seva, and that is the best and most acceptable service.

* * *

221. Abstinence is of course the best solution, but *only* if it is practiced by mutual consent and without any pressure. The course recommended by ——— , that is, safe phases, is next best. Domestic peace and harmony should not be affected.

I am glad that you are keen on following the path. You will find in your meditation a true guide and friend.

* * *

222. Unsatisfactory meditation may be due to faulty methods, too much worldly interest or too many worldly attractions which make it difficult to concentrate the attention at the time of meditation, or to strong karmic disturbances. All these can be overcome in the course of time. Simran, that is, repetition of the Holy Names, if carried on long enough and with persistence, would take care of all these difficulties and also develop love for inner life. Simran is, in fact, the foundation of the whole system. The essence of simran is to withdraw all thoughts from outer things and hold the *attention* at the eye center—without any strain.

Marriage is no bar, but excessive indulgence is to be avoided. The best way of working off karma and, at the same time, of avoiding the accumulation of further karmas is by doing things in a spirit of duty. This attitude in life, along with regular meditation, that is, bhajan and simran, is the best way of overcoming the drag of karma and getting spiritual uplift.

* * *

223.   The mind is scattered not only throughout the body but in so many things in the world, because we have been accustomed for ages to look outwards and not inwards. The entire problem is to draw our *attention* from the outside things, and from the body as well, and fix it at a point between the two eyebrows. The eyes should be closed, for it is not the physical eyes which are to look at this point but it is the attention which is to be concentrated there. Talking of the Master and his work, and attending satsang, also help in concentration.

* * *

224.   You have referred to "unconditional surrender." This is certainly the foundation of spiritual progress in Sant Mat, but it is a hard thing to attain. Until we have vacated the body and met the Satguru inside, unconditional surrender is not really possible, although the outward surrender also is very desirable. Strive for that inner darshan. Then "unconditional surrender" shall once and for all time solve all problems. Please devote *all* your available time to bhajan and simran in order to achieve this desirable end, and do not worry about other people. Incidentally, the best way to help other people is to first help yourself and thus be a model to others.

The best and most acceptable service you can render is to do your bhajan and simran regularly and at every available moment.

* * *

225.   The most important thing is to go in and get first-hand spiritual contact. Not only will this solve all your problems automatically but it will also speed you forward on the road to Realization. After all, it is individual practice, or effort, and Realization that really matter. In my opinion you will thus help yourself and at the same time carry out the instructions of the late Master by keeping aloof from all these things, and that is what he meant when he said, "But nothing should stand in the way of your meditation." I can well imagine what you are feeling. That is due to weakness of the mind, and it is this very weakness which you have to overcome by devotion and practice of simran and bhajan. It is only those who have satisfactorily solved their own problems who are really in a position to help others.

Nothing in this world can help at the time of death or in the period after death except devotion to Shabd, and this is the only thing that really matters. You have had enough of clairvoyance and experience of other attachments. It is now time that you devote all your attention and available time entirely to meditation and to Shabd, which alone will stand by you.

Please remember that your own inner experiences are entirely your own private property and are not to be divulged to or shared with anybody else. Every individual should keep the inner experiences to himself or herself and should discuss them with no one nor write about them to anyone except the Master. This advice is for the disciple's own good.

* * *

226.   I am very glad to know that you are at peace and busy with your own work, which is bhajan and simran. This is the only thing that is important and will be of any use to you. Worldly approval has hardly any value. Our main business is to break the shackles that tie us fast to this world and prevent us from escaping from the dominion of Kal. This can be done only by keeping all our attention in the simran and Shabd—the Shabd alone being able to take us beyond the dominion of Kal, to Sach Khand. But as long as we have any grievances, unfulfilled desires and wishes, we are pulled down at the most inconvenient time.

Whatever experiences you have, you keep to yourself. What you have described is only the beginning. The important thing is to get into intimate touch with Shabd and almost lose yourself in it, so that it may take you to higher regions. One's devotion and practice of simran and bhajan is reflected in outside conditions and behavior in everyday life. We have light and colors and sounds at so many places. It is best not to dwell much on them, for they are not our aim and goal. Our aim is to be one with Shabd and to reach the place from which it comes through the intermediate centers of Shabd. Please devote your attention to the bell sound for long hours.

When one leaves the body, even for short periods,

one does become indifferent to the world and to the previous attachments. But this attitude of indifference is maintained only if one *continues* working regularly and for long periods, for a long time.

* * *

227. I am glad to know that your outlook on life has changed and that you now realize that the only true friend is Shabd. In fact, you had a practical experience during your recent journey, as you have described it.

Worldly attachments and worldly connections are not only temporary but are the cause of pain and loneliness. We are all lonely in this world but do not realize it. The sooner we realize it the better, for only then can we attach ourselves to something which is *really* ours. That, of course, is Shabd.

* * *

228. I am glad to learn of the improved conditions in bhajan and simran as well as in your health. Peace comes from within and not from the outward satisfaction of desires or cravings. There is no peace like that which flows from Shabd. The foundation of the system is withdrawal of consciousness by simran. Students sometimes neglect simran—the repetition of the Holy Names—and do not pay requisite time and attention to this important aspect, with the result that withdrawal is incomplete. There is no peace, no joy, no bliss, greater than that which comes from the consciousness of being joined to and merged in Shabd. All those who have been initiated will one day reach Sach Khand by means of devotion to Shabd and to Satguru. The real form of Satguru is also Shabd, and the faithful carrying out of his instructions is Satguru bhakti, which leads to Shabd bhakti.

229. As to "sounds," I would ask you not to bank too much on sounds unless the consciousness has been withdrawn and there are other confirming signs. Quite often one may hear sounds—apparently of higher regions—which are really only imitation sounds sent by the negative power to deceive the applicant or the new disciple. (Hence, the warning to listen only to the Sound that comes from the right or the center.)

* * *

230. I would like to call your attention to that particular translation sent to you on the subject of each one looking to his own Master for dhyan. That is, those who have been initiated by Huzur Maharaj Ji should yearn for his dhyan only, and those who have been initiated by Sardar Bahadur Maharaj Ji should long to see only him. No doubt you are also aware of the fact that neither of the late Masters permitted photos of themselves to be sent to satsangis until the last years of their lives, and even then they cautioned over and over again that the photo was not to be used for the purpose of 'visualizing' the Master within but simply for the purpose of identification.

* * *

231. People judge a philosophy not by its exposition so much as by its effects upon those who profess it, by the changes it has brought in the lives of its followers. The leaders of all movements—social, religious and philosophical—are constantly in the eyes of the public and open to public criticism. What is more, their actions and motives are not always interpreted charitably. The more one can stand this public gaze, the better he can serve the cause. And nothing makes a person so detached, so noble and so high as a life of continued and uninterrupted

devotion to bhajan and simran, especially bhajan, that is,
listening to the Sound. We can never have too much of it.
(But of course, simran comes first.)

* * *

232.   Old relations do come in our present lives, but it is
wrong to revive old relationships (from past lives) as that
would involve us in the meshes of Kal and karmas. Mind
is quick to recognize such relationships, but it is risky and
may lead to our downfall. Our attachments and affections
have brought us into this world and have given us birth
into this vale of sorrow from which we are trying to escape. Saints teach us to finish and destroy the karmas
and, thus freed from their dragging and restraining influence, rise to our Lord and Master.

* * *

233.   You know that all of us have to work out our pralabdh karmas. The law is inexorable, but by the practice
of Nam and Shabd we are enabled to rise above the sufferings and to face the situation with confidence and ease.
The more we practice simran and Shabd, the more we rise
above the body and therefore are indifferent to any sufferings to which the body may be subject. The account,
however, must be settled by everybody.

* * *

234.   Regarding surplus bulls on the farm, it is a very
difficult and ticklish question and was also discussed with
———— . If the bulls are of no use on the farm, they have
to be disposed of. Just sell them to a buyer, but without
the idea in your mind of selling them for slaughter. Whatever the buyer does with them is then his concern and not
yours. In other words, one should not sell them for the

purpose of slaughter but need not be concerned what the purchaser does with them. Under no circumstances are animals to be raised for slaughter, nor should a satsangi go in for raising pigs and poultry.

* * *

235.   Sant Mat meditation does not send the mind away from the body but takes it up to higher centers *within* the body and, in due course, gives the practitioner complete control to go up or to come down. However, in order to reach the stage where one can go up *at will* to higher centers requires a lot of time because the mind has been accustomed to go out for eons and eons.

The body is the microcosm and hence it has all the features of the macrocosm. Taking the mind and attention up to the higher brain centers is done under the overall supervision and protection of the Master. This is accomplished gradually and without giving up the normal vocation. There is therefore no sudden break or change, which sometimes constitutes danger.

The first stage in this practice consists of focusing the attention at the center between the two eyebrows and *keeping* it there—if not wholly, at least to a great extent—during the rest of the day. This requires a lot of time and practice, as one has to accustom himself to this condition. The Persian saying goes, *"Dil ba yar, dast ba kar"*; that is, "Apply your hands to your work but let your mind be with your Friend."

When the attention has been sufficiently concentrated at the center, the upward journey is undertaken by the help of Shabd. The Satguru, who is really Shabd, helps and guides.

* * *

236. Regarding Scientology and all its claims for improvement in the outlook and conduct of people, it does not take you beyond the reach of the mind. Rather, it makes you more and more dependent on the mind, though in the higher form; nevertheless, it falls far short of the ideals of Sant Mat.

* * *

237. What you have asked about the *sunnas* is more of an academic than practical nature. The word *sunn* is a Prakrit formation of the Sanskrit word *shunya*, which means a void or emptiness. They are, however, far from being mere voids, and to one who has not completed his spiritual journey, it is not only of no use but may even be of some risk to dabble in the lower sunnas. The Master gives us knowledge and information only about those sunnas which are helpful in our journey upward. It is only after having reached Sach Khand that the abhyasi may be allowed to see and go about anywhere, for then there is no chance of his being misled.

* * *

238. The *Mystic Bible* seems to have been well received. The author thoroughly understands Sant Mat and explains it from the Christian point of view; that is, from the Holy Bible—the Old Testament and the New—in the same way as it is explained here in India from the Granth Sahib, the Ramayana and other sacred writings. Yes, it carries suggestions and inspirations especially for the Jews and the Christians, and will help them to understand Sant Mat.

As for your remarks about the reach of these saints,

Om is the beginning of creation of mind and matter. Saints—that is, Saints of Sant Mat—take us higher. We appreciate their greatness and glory only by comparison.

* * *

239. This is indeed a great opportunity and everyone who is so fortunate as to receive initiation ought to devote his best time and attention to making progress on the path. The Master supervises the efforts of the disciple, but the effort has to be made by the disciple himself.

In the beginning you should start with love and faith, and keep the mind away from worldly things so that you might be able to draw your attention inside and concentrate at the eye center. It is by means of our thoughts that we have become attached to the outside world, and it is by the same means that we ought to withdraw ourselves and concentrate our thoughts at the eye center. The Master is never happier than when he sees the disciple working honestly and faithfully, trying to reach his goal. And of course, his blessings always go out to such a disciple.

* * *

240. I was very glad to read what you wrote about your experience at the time of initiation. Though it is the preliminary stage, it will convince you that you are on the right path. By devoting the full time to simran, this will become permanent; and after going beyond the stars, the sun and the moon, you will see the Master within. But of course it takes time. It is a good beginning but you should persevere.

It is good that you are both satsangis and are trying to follow the path. It is comparatively easy when both husband and wife pull in the same direction. Difficulties do come in and sometimes obstructions crop up when we start on the path of goodness and righteousness; but if we are firm and have faith and confidence, everything is right. Resort to simran and pray to the Master in case of difficulties, and persevere on steadily with your meditations.

* * *

241. It is our own karmas that are worked out on our bodies in the form of ill health or disease, and it would not be in our better and ultimate interest to adopt wrong methods and wrong foods. I appreciate your sincerity and your devotion in seeking advice, and your anxiety to do the right thing; but I regret that it is not possible for me to make a compromise upon this point and advise you contrary to the principles of Sant Mat. Love and devotion can do much more than people sometimes think. Regularity in bhajan and simran will help you in paying off your karmic debt.

When your sleep is disturbed, please try repeating the Holy Names while in bed. This brings rest and sleep.

* * *

242. The best way to appreciate the gift of Nam is to utilize all available time for working on the path. It is only the early stage that is difficult to negotiate because we have to withdraw the consciousness, now scattered throughout the body, and collect it at the eye center. That is why you feel pain in the legs after an hour or so, but generally you will get used to it and there will be no more difficulty. It is a good plan to increase the time gradually so that you are able to consolidate the gains. While repeating the Names, try to keep your attention between the two eyebrows.

What you have read in *Sar Bachan,* about having one meal a day only, does not apply to you—not even to all the satsangis here. It is meant for very eager and enthusiastic disciples who are fed up with this world, have practically no responsibilities and are anxious to reach Home in the shortest possible time. But of course, eating too much, that is, more than necessary for health, makes us slothful and stands in the way of mental concentration.

As regards children, parents have a responsibility. Animal products such as eggs, codliver oil, etc., are not necessary and are best avoided as far as possible. Good natural food, including vegetables and dairy products, helps nature in building up young bodies. Their highest good and yours are not different.

* * *

243. Alone one can only roam about but cannot escape the wheel. Shabd is the silken thread which can lead you Home if you continue to stick to it. The first thing is to vacate the body by simran, that is, regular and persistent repetition of the Holy Names, and concentrate your consciousness at the eye center. Here you will contact the Shabd and also meet the astral radiant form of the Master. The knotted mind will be straightened by Shabd practice only.

* * *

244. We have to carry on as the Great Master wishes, and our happiness lies in submitting to his all-knowing will. Radha Soami faith indeed gives you the best means of reaching Home—Sat Lok—and nothing gives more pleasure or happiness to a Master than to guide willing souls to their goal.

As for the position, the squatting posture with thumbs in ears and fingers over the eyes is useful, but you should continue to meditate in the position which suits you best.

The main idea is to concentrate all the mental currents at the eye center.

When you are sitting at the eye focus, as we say, the conscious 'you' will have left the lower part, and therefore the body below the eyes—or a given part of it—will temporarily become numb or without any feeling.

I would suggest that you continue to sit in a chair as you do now, but at the same time try to accustom yourself to the squatting position for five or ten minutes every day.

* * *

245. I appreciate your keen desire to progress on the path and the fact that you enjoy your meditation. Nothing in this world can give so much happiness as following this path. The more you are able to withdraw your attention to the eye center, the happier you will feel, and it will also be easier to catch the Sound Current. Please persevere on the path with love and devotion. Do not try to force the pace but be regular and consolidate your results.

* * *

246. Regarding your studies in astrology in order to be able to help others, I would say that the best way to help others is to first help yourself. How to do that? By devoting your time to the spiritual practice and continuing to do so with love and faith. We cannot help others to understand themselves until we have first understood our own self. And self-realization leads to God-realization.

It is also a good practice to devote some time every day to reading some Radha Soami book, particularly the chapters that inspire the feeling of love and devotion. It helps to put you in the proper mood for meditation.

Yes, as we look back we can see that it is usually the difficulties in life which help to strengthen our desire for liberation and enlightenment, because they enable us to realize more and more the transitory nature of this world and its contents.

* * *

247.   The trouble you mention is all due to past karma and will disappear after sufficient time has been spent in bhajan and simran with faith and devotion, *regularly*, every day. There is nothing to fear. The posture itself would never throw your back out of line; if anything, it would put it back in line.

When sitting in meditation, be perfectly relaxed in any comfortable position and do not strain any part of the body nor the physical eyes. They should be gently closed and relaxed. It is the *attention* of the mind that is to do the repeating of the five Holy Names. This is an individual proposition and you should not depend on the company of others. It is you who have to attain self-realization of your own self before you can attain God-realization. To be able to sit calmly and concentrate the mind at the center between the eyebrows is the first step.

As you have been told at initiation, listen only to the sound that seemingly comes from the right ear or from the center and pay no attention whatsoever to any sound from the left ear, even if it is the bell sound. In the beginning, various sounds may be heard before one hears the bell sound.

* * *

248.   Sorry to learn of your illness. There is no reason why you should not try to get well and get yourself treated properly. Karma should be fought by taking your mind away from the body and putting it in simran on the one hand, and by getting yourself treated on the other. The more the attention is fixed in simran, that is, the repetition of the five Holy Names, the less will you suffer, and the karma will be paid off gradually. You should think of simran and not of karma. Help is always available but it comes from within. So once again, the more you do your simran, the lighter will you feel.

You can prove the Radha Soami truths by going in and not by reasoning. Follow the instructions *faithfully*, then knowledge will come too. Faith and deed both are necessary. You can do your simran while lying on your back and trying to fix your attention between the eyebrows with your eyes closed.

* * *

249. I am sorry to find you downhearted and despondent. Help is always there but you have to look up and see it. It is just the load of karmas which you have referred to in your letter that makes things look so bleak. The thicker the wall, the longer it takes to bore through; yet everything will be paid off. The light will shine through. One should not give up hope and courage. As you increase your repetition period, the Sound will come of itself in due course.

The proper thing for you now is to do as much simran as possible. Devote half an hour or so to Shabd and the rest to repetition of the Holy Names. At other times also, when you feel confused or despondent, begin repeating the Names mentally—without taking up the usual posture.

Why should you think of madness? Think of the Master instead, and repeat the Names, read some Sant Mat books or seek the company of some good satsangis.

250.   A person who devotes himself to the repetition of the five Holy Names and contacts the Sound has absolutely nothing to fear. What are you afraid of? Whenever any feeling of fear or uncertainty crosses your mind, think of the Master and repeat the Names, keeping in mind that you have his help and protection at all times.

What you are experiencing is probably the result of past associations and other karmas which are coming up to take their toll. With faith and courage, dismiss all such feelings boldly and say that you have nothing to do with them. You are now with the Master. Please do not think and argue as to what is happening or what will happen, but feel secure in the protection of the Satguru and Nam. There is no peace except in Nam.

Your experience of seeing a large bright star and merging into it is very encouraging. Yes, it has a significance and a very happy one. You should have a feeling of peace after this experience.

* * *

251.   The rule in Sant Mat is for a disciple to get all the help and advice from the living Satguru and also to render him service, but the Master who initiated the disciple continues to be the Master for that disciple and will guide the soul on the inner planes even though he may have left the physical body. Yes, Master Jagat Singh, who initiated you, is still your Master.

Radha Soami is the highest goal. Living up to the Radha Soami standard and devoting all the time possible to simran and bhajan is more than enough for a lifetime's work. Our first aim should be to perfect ourselves or at least to achieve some substantial progress in our spiritual efforts before we try to interest other people. The Radha Soami practice is not like other philosophies, and one need not try to go out of his way in order to interest other people unless asked to do so by the Master. Those who are destined to tread the path will be attracted sooner or later. There need not be and there should not be any spirit of aloofness or superiority—not even a suggestion of it—in your contact with your friends and other people, except that *your* conduct and *your* dealings should now be of a very high order, based upon Sant Mat principles.

You may meet with satsang groups and satsangi friends whenever you find it convenient to do so, but do not worry about it when you cannot conveniently do so. Please read the Radha Soami books and other such literature, in addition to devoting as much time as possible to simran and bhajan.

* * *

252.   Anything that reminds us of Him is a blessing indeed, and helps to engender an intense longing to be at His holy feet within. That in turn spurs us on to greater effort in bhajan and simran, of which we cannot do too much.

* * *

253.   For us, Maharaj Ji [Maharaj Sawan Singh Ji] is still living, though we undoubtedly miss his physical presence. You do well to reflect on what he said—all solid, unchallengeable truths. It brings comfort and solace to sufferers when they think of him and dwell on his words. Our human relationship, even at its best, is short-lived, but the bond between disciple and Satguru is indissoluble. He will not rest till he has taken the disciple to his final resting place. This should clear the clouds away and cheer you up.

I can understand your loneliness and sympathize with

you. Even this sense of loneliness can be turned to good account, for in such circumstances one looks for a true helper who would befriend him or her. And in this respect you are lucky that you have such an unfailing friend and companion. And what is more, he is not far. You have only to turn in and realize what he is doing for you and how he is washing and cleansing your soul.

Please devote as much time as possible to simran, not only at the regular hours but also at any time of the day when you are free, when you are feeling unhappy or when unhappy memories crowd upon you. But while doing this, the attention should be centered as much as possible between the two eyebrows. This practice helps you to go in and forget the earthly woes. Do not strain, however. Adopt an easy, relaxing attitude.

Maharaj Ji used to advise reading satsangs and Sant Mat books when one is physically far from the Satguru and satsang. Reading such literature tends to bring the mind in tune with the Satguru and the Shabd.

* * *

254. It gives me great pleasure to learn that you are now feeling more at peace inside. In fact, our Great Master used to say that peace can be found only inside, and the more we go in and stay there, the more at peace and happy we will be. The karma, of course, has to be wiped out—both by going through it and by means of meditation. That is, intensive and constant simran mitigates some of it, and then one goes through whatever is unavoidable. This should be done with perfect faith and confidence in the will of the Satguru. Then no bitterness is left behind.

* * *

255. I am glad you enjoyed the New Year message. It contains the essence of Sant Mat and should be studied and acted upon. Satguru is within us, and if we follow the instructions and do our bhajan and simran faithfully, we can meet him. Peace and happiness are to be found within.

* * *

256. Dreams, as you well know, do not always come true. They are both good and bad, and those who carry on their bhajan and simran usually get good dreams. If more people come to Sant Mat and follow it, it is all very good, but the important thing for us is to make sure that we ourselves are following the path.

Regarding your visions, you should not pay much attention to them. The main thing is to carry on with the simran intensively and then to switch over to the Sound. Scenes and visions of past relatives do come sometimes, but the proper thing at that time is to think of the Satguru and repeat the five Holy Names. Simran is the remedy for all these things.

* * *

257. I note your difficulties in your search for Truth. The search is beset with difficulties, even dangerous ones, and sometimes—as you say—black despair does stare us in the face. But the brave man should not give up this struggle. If one but perseveres, he will reach the goal. There is a time for everything.

We are too much engrossed with our little struggles, desires and disappointments, to think of the grand purpose of our coming here. To be born as a human being is a great privilege because it is only as a human being that you can strive to work for your emancipation and thus get out of this endless chain of birth and death.

The mystery of creation and other spiritual mysteries cannot, however, be grasped only by discussion and reading books. It is only by actual practice and by traveling on the path that man understands the core of things and grasps the Reality. Yet, some sort of mental attitude is necessary. Above all, one must have faith in and be devoted to the path which he wishes to follow. This should not be a blind, unreasonable faith, but one should study, discuss and then try to follow a particular path. Having once chosen the path, he should work on it earnestly and with faith.

Hence, I would suggest that you study the principles of Sant Mat from the books and other available literature as well as by contact with satsangis; also, continue on the diet, eliminating meat, fish, fowl, eggs, and anything containing them, as well as alcoholic drinks. When you are convinced that you wish to travel this path, you may apply for initiation through the representative. By first making certain that what you really want is God-realization and that you are willing to make the necessary effort, it will enable you to travel the path without any doubt or hesitation after receiving initiation.

This world is founded upon karmas, which is a very comprehensive term for 'cause and effect'. Having come into this world in the form of a human being, gifted with brain and thinking or reasoning power, we ought to try to scan this mystery as far as we can and then endeavor to rise above this earthly existence so that we may finally rest in our eternal home in Sach Khand. We can go back almost by the same way that we came. Our desires and our ambitions—fulfilled and unfulfilled—brought us into this world, and when we have been convinced of their hollowness, we are ready to turn our back upon them and begin the homeward journey.

This return journey is entirely inward, for man is a sort of microcosm; that is, whatever exists without, exists within himself. The first step is to withdraw the thinking and feeling power, or consciousness, which now pervades the entire body, up to the center above and behind the eyes and then begin the inward journey. The method of reaching the center is explained at the time of initiation, but I might add that this center is reached only after concentration of the attention at the center between the two eyebrows, when it will automatically be taken in and up.

The first part of the journey is the most difficult and takes a comparatively long time. When the consciousness has been completely withdrawn from the body, the limbs and the entire body below the eyes will be the same as dead. It is actually a process of dying while living. One is unconscious only without but completely conscious within, whereas before this one is conscious without and unconscious within. This condition of the body is only temporary, and when the consciousness returns at the close of the meditation period, you will again be as living and as active as before—even stronger.

The idea is that we should be able to withdraw ourselves *consciously* from the body. Then we would be able to live in the world and perform our duties without being affected, just as a duck lives in the water without getting its feathers wet. That, in a nutshell, is the philosophy of Sant Mat, to be in the world but be not of it, and to go on working and rising above the world while living in it. This is done, of course, with the help of the Master and your own persistent efforts. As previously mentioned, the technique is given at the time of initiation.

If there are any further questions, you may feel free to write to me and I shall be glad to help you.

258. The source of peace is really in you yourself, but there must be someone to guide you to it, and for that a living Master is needed. The treasure is buried within you and you must have a chart and a guide in order to dig it out and utilize it for yourself. It is kept for you and is always there, but that unerring Power sees to it that you get it only when you can properly utilize it.

The peace and the bliss in the Supreme Power's house is unending and unabated. We too are of the same essence as our Supreme Father, but the light of the soul has been clouded by mental aberrations and desires. These are the only things which keep us back. Our object is to withdraw our attention from the outside, concentrate it at the eye center and then bring it into touch with Shabd. This Divine Sound is of the essence of God, and we are to travel along with it through all the intervening spiritual regions up to the Divine Source itself.

Insistence on a strict vegetarian diet and on non-killing, etc., is to prevent us from accruing more harmful karmas, which would greatly impede our progress. This is only the first or the introductory part. When you get Nam, you will receive the instructions and will be given the proper technique. Then progress will depend on your efforts, devotion, faith and confidence in the Master.

* * *

259. Yours is an interesting letter, too, in that it portrays graphically the condition of the mind, swaying now to one side and now to the other. Your own mind, that is, the higher mind, in moments of calm reflection, should tell you which is the better side. Cast your vote on that side and make it decisive. Realize your strength, seek good company, read good literature—that which helps you to realize yourself and makes you go in—and it will no longer be fifty-fifty.

Sant Mat does not enforce or even recommend asceticism but asks you to learn the true value of everything and then hold on to that which is of lasting value. When you read Sant Mat literature, frequent the company of satsangis and practice meditation, you will be able to see through this game we call the world and its pleasures. You will then *realize* the truth of the saying, "All that glitters is not gold."

Sant Mat welcomes earnest and sincere seekers with open arms. Above all, pray in the quietness of solitude and meditation, and the Inner Power will hear.

* * *

260. Yes, it is not easy, but the Master is always there to guide us and help us if we but turn to him. The Master never leaves his disciple and is ever bestowing his grace and mercy, even though the disciple may not be aware of it.

To wish to be worthy is a lofty ideal, and the way to do so is to put as much time as possible in bhajan and simran, but not less than two and one-half hours daily. Slow and steady wins the race.

Even in the face of seeming failure, one should continue the practice with faith and devotion. The mind has been going out for countless ages, and each time it has become more scattered. The object is to collect the mind at the point of concentration, contact Shabd and begin our homeward journey. The first step is the most difficult of all and takes a long time, the length of time depending on the results of our own previous actions plus the sincerity and amount of steady effort we put forth in following his instructions. Effort and grace go hand in hand. The more effort we make, the more grace we receive to make more effort until the goal is reached.

* * *

261.   I would suggest that you depend not upon such external aids for your spiritual progress, but upon the method of meditation and concentration which was given to you at the time of initiation.

The fact that you find some days better than others depends mostly on your own mental attitude. Simran or repetition of the five Holy Names is the foundation of bhajan because it is only by means of simran, performed with faith and devotion, that we can draw up our consciousness to the eye center. You should therefore devote two hours—or about that—to simran, and a half-hour to bhajan (listening to the Sound) every day, without worrying yourself whether or not on a particular day your practice was good, very good or indifferent.

* * *

262.   Surroundings, especially in the beginning, do have some effect on meditation, but as you lay more and more stress upon simran and give more time to the repetition of the Holy Names, you will not be disturbed so much by outside circumstances. However, if you can move to a better environment without much difficulty, you surely may do so.

Simran is really the foundation. It is by simran that the consciousness and the attention currents are concentrated at the eye center, whence the real spiritual journey upwards begins. One should take reasonable care of one's health, as bhajan and simran become easy when the health is good.

If breathing exercises are very necessary, they may be

performed, but only for the sake of health. Breathing exercises should not be linked with bhajan and simran. Do as much simran as you can and keep the attention at the center between the two eyebrows while repeating the Holy Names.

* * *

263. Kal's activities are also with the consent of God or Sat Purush and depend upon our karmas. If we devote ourselves to Shabd practice and keep in touch with the divine Sound Current, we need not fear Kal. We then place ourselves outside the jurisdiction of Kal. By our karmas and desires only do we put ourselves in the grip of Kal.

Please do not send any money. We have enough to keep things going by the grace of Maharaj Ji [Baba Sawan Singh Ji]. We want only your time and devotion to bhajan and simran. By devotion to Shabd, try to meet the Master inside.

* * *

264. I am indeed sorry to learn that you took the matter so much to heart and felt so disconsolate over it. I did not mean to cause you sorrow or pain in any way but simply wished to tell you that this was quite unnecessary as we have sufficient funds for the postage account—nothing more than this. Please do not feel unhappy over it but turn with love and faith to the Satguru within, wherein is all life and love and happiness.

* * *

265. The main object of our coming into this life and receiving Nam is to relieve ourselves from all past bondages and karmas and thus be liberated from the cycle of birth and death. This can be done only in the human form, so we should take full advantage of the opportunity. It is indeed a rare privilege to receive Nam, and the way to make the best use of it is to devote as much time as possible to bhajan and simran in addition to carrying on your duties in this world.

There is no objection whatsoever to your keeping the dog and the cat. We are to continue the use of the proper means of protection and hygiene in matters pertaining to this world. It is the soul which the Master takes under his protection and guidance. While he greatly reduces our karma, there is some which we must undergo, and the more we devote ourselves to the spiritual practice with devotion and faith, the less do we feel the effect of karmas. The real form of the Master is Shabd, and that is always with you. So you should try to be in touch with Shabd as that will always protect you—everywhere.

* * *

266.   I appreciate your kind thoughts and note your apprehension about karma. Please do not worry. As long as one regularly devotes the required time to the spiritual practice and otherwise carries out all other duties cheerfully and to the best of one's ability, there is no room for concern nor should one feel the least bit perplexed. All such thoughts scatter the mind, whereas that energy should be used for concentrating it.

I have carefully read what you have said about your feelings and sensations during the course of bhajan. I think it would not be very useful to tell you what it is due to, unless at a later stage, but it shows the attempt of the spirit to rise. These chilly feelings, or sometimes feelings of pain, are experienced by some disciples but not by everyone. It is not wrong.

I would advise you to be careful about your diet and

avoid straining your eyes. The diet should be light, easily digestible and nourishing. There should be absolutely no strain at the time of meditation, but just gazing (with the attention) at the eye center with the eyes gently closed and without any expectation or speculation. Watch whatever happens. During simran or repetition of the Holy Names, repeat the Names mentally, slowly and rhythmically, with a feeling of love and devotion, and *discard* all other thoughts or concern about anything or anyone during the period set aside for meditation. Slow and easy is all right, but one should try to do one's bit without thinking and worrying about what comes.

* * *

267.   As a citizen you have to perform jury duty, and you may do so. Try to be perfectly impartial. Before starting deliberations and giving the verdict, you may quietly, that is, inwardly, repeat the Holy Names and think of the Satguru for a minute or so.

We neither use nor recommend non-vegetarian food for babies. They get their nourishment from the mother who should be well fed, and her diet should not lack in calcium, the chief need of the growing baby. Doctors here sometimes advise a spoonful or two of orange juice or some preparation of lime water for the baby, and the doctors there can be consulted about it. Milk is a perfect food and the juice supplies vitamin C.

The best way to help the child is to repeat the Holy Names as often as possible and sit in bhajan. The mother, in particular, may repeat the Names mentally while suckling the baby.

* * *

268. I too am pleased to find satsangis happy, contented and devoted to spiritual meditations. Yes, it is a trust, and by loving submission to the Great Master and by regular and loyal devotion to bhajan and simran you can best discharge your responsibilities. In worldly matters one should act according to the best of one's light, but always depend on the Satguru within. In course of time one begins to receive light and guidance consciously. Regularity in spiritual exercises with faith and love is the keynote.

* * *

269. I note your difficulty regarding the wandering of the mind at the time of repetition. It does happen with people who are very conscious of their activities and their daily duties, that thoughts of them invade their meditation period. Another reason is that we are accustomed to think outwardly, and very rarely go in.

However, this should not discourage you. In course of time you will succeed in controlling the outgoing or wandering tendencies of the mind; in fact, you have already made a start in being conscious of the fact that your mind was not in the repetition. You should call it back the moment you discover that it has gone out.

Before sitting for meditation, pray to the Master for a few minutes and firmly tell your mind not to bring in any extraneous ideas during the time you expect to devote to bhajan and simran. If you feel too disturbed during the meditation period, you might open the eyes for a while and repeat the Names semi-audibly, say for ten or fifteen minutes, and then again continue with the quiet, mental repetition with eyes closed.

* * *

270.   It appears that you are really confused. Meditation and mental illness are two quite different things.

We are all either making karmas or paying off karmas. Satsangis, by virtue of meditation and concentration at the eye center and contacting the Sound Current, develop a detached attitude and are also able to pay off their past karmas more easily. Their minds and brains, far from being deranged, are sharper, more acute and under control. You will appreciate this if you give the full time to simran and bhajan, that is, the repetition of the five Holy Names and listening to the Divine Sound within. Psychiatrists deal with consciousness at a comparatively lower level and are not able to evaluate and understand the Sant Mat technique.

Please do not feel startled, worried or frightened if occasionally you have a feeling that the mind—or rather the spirit—is floating into space. At that time, instead of feeling frightened, you should do your simran and *relax*. There should be no tension, please.

The headache may be due to physical causes, that is, constipation, indigestion, etc., or wrong meditation also. In the former case, a change in diet, etc., will improve the condition. In the latter case, avoid straining at the time of meditation. Look easily and naturally in front of you— with eyes closed, of course—without putting any strain on your eyes or the facial nerves.

Yes, milk, cheese and vegetable proteins, with fresh fruit, constitute an adequate diet.

Please go on with your bhajan and simran and do not have any fears or doubts. Loving faith and trust are a great help, but if you have any difficulty or experience which you cannot understand and which disturbs you, do not hesitate to refer it to me.

* * *

271. I note that you are hearing a steady humming sound in the right ear during bhajan and even otherwise occasionally. This is correct and you should continue to hear it. In due course and with constant practice, the sound will become more refined and distinct.

The experiences gained by you during simran—while in a state of drowsiness—would appear to be actual phenomena and you need not be perturbed about them. The unclean thoughts are destroyed mostly by simran.

As you are aware, we have strict injunctions against the use of forbidden food and drink, like meat, liquor, etc. We have to observe these principles in our daily life, scrupulously and with care. If you are sure of your ground and you are able to withstand the temptation offered in the society in which you have to move, there should be no harm in attending such social functions as mentioned by you. Otherwise, it will be desirable to avoid them.

* * *

272. After all, it is the practice which matters. The inner journey must be traveled by you yourself. Now that you have received the instructions and were given the technique, you should utilize all your leisure time—that is, whatever time you can conveniently spare in addition to the regular time—in accomplishing this task.

Before starting on any journey, one packs up his belongings, and all his thoughts are turned towards his goal. It is this part of the process (simran) which is rather difficult and takes a long time unless one is extremely eager and zealous. Hence, love for the Master and love for the goal play a very important part in facilitating our progress. The Master is always ready to help. It is the disciple who must be ready to receive.

* * *

273. I am glad to learn that you are practicing your meditation regularly and have even cut down your engagements to find time for bhajan and simran. It may seem a sacrifice, but if you persist, it will bring enough reward. Sleep should not be sacrificed, for it gives rest and recuperation. Later on, when you are firmly established in the Shabd Dhun, you may require less sleep. It will be adjusted automatically.

Progress in the beginning is generally slow, but there is no universal rule. It is individual and depends upon so many factors. Practice and perseverance never fail to bring their reward; and by our standard, two and one-half to three hours is the minimum.

Satguru cleanses the mind in a variety of ways, and molds and fashions it so that it becomes a fit companion and useful friend.

You have already begun well, and by and by as you lay stress on simran and try to draw your attention up to the eye center, you will have more experiences. Light will become steady and the Sound more distinct, and the Sound will exercise a pulling effect too. You should not be too anxious or try to hurry the pace.

* * *

274. I am glad to know that you are now finding concentration easier. As you go on, it will become more easy still. The secret is persistence and regularity with a devotional attitude of mind.

We sleep when the attention slips down from the eye center. When we go on repeating the Words consciously —with the attention of the mind—and keep the attention at the eye center, we will not sleep while so engaged.

Here in India we prefer the morning hours for meditation because the mind is then fresh and undisturbed, and the body has had the needed rest during the night. However, the early morning hours do not suit some Occidental people. If you find the morning time is not convenient, you may do it at any other time when you find it easy and convenient to do so.

* * *

275. I am glad that you value the teachings so much. In fact, Nam is such a blessing that there is nothing in this world that can be compared to it, but one can realize that only by going within. As one practices regularly and conscientiously, and the attention goes more and more inward, many things for which we felt a longing and which we were eager to do before, automatically lose their charm.

You need not discontinue being an actress. There is nothing wrong with the profession itself, but one should not succumb to the temptations incidental to it. I might add that all of us are actors on this stage of the world. So in life too, they do best who look upon themselves only as actors and do not get involved in worldly entanglements. Similarly should you also follow acting as a profession. The most important point is detachment. If one can do things in a detached and cheerful manner, and does not feel or miss them afterwards, it is all right. You may carry on with your duties, but always, as you have said in your letter, in a detached manner, thinking that this is only a phase of life in order to provide you with the necessities.

I am sorry to learn of your illness and operation, and the fact that you were obliged to take animal food about a month before initiation. But I am very pleased to note that you stuck to your principles and brought the doctor around to your point of view in your case, thus permitting you to adhere to the vegetarian diet. No blame is attached to you in this connection. Please go on with your bhajan and simran lovingly and regularly, and everything will be all right. Incidentally, if properly selected, the vegetarian diet can be very satisfying and nourishing.

As for the time, 3:00 A.M. does not suit most of the Western people, and you may certainly change the timing to suit your convenience. If it is not inconvenient, you may start your meditations at 5:00 or 6:00 A.M. If, however, you find that midnight suits you best, you may practice even at midnight; but the regular period of meditation should always be at the same time. This creates a sort of mental preparedness and is helpful.

As to whether or not you were initiated in a previous incarnation, it may have been so, but there is no use speculating upon these things because then one question leads to another, and one loses so much time and energy. However, when one goes in, one sees and knows many things firsthand, and that should be our aim.

* * *

276.   I appreciate your difficulties as well as the fine stand you have taken, and am glad that you stick to your principles and have not only perseverance but faith and understanding also. Self help, coupled with faith, invokes help from higher quarters too. As you travel on the path, knowledge will come—knowledge born of bhakti and devotion to Nam or Shabd. The path may be narrow, but love and faith are great assets.

Yes, you may help and explain things to persons in need, who require consolation and seek the Light, but in a detached and impersonal manner.

Regarding your personal problem, I note that you tried to change over to business but found the business world far worse, and feel that on the whole, your own profession, which you had followed so far, is better. I agree with you. So long as you stick to Sant Mat principles and steer clear of the dangers and temptations incidental to the profession, you may continue to follow your old profession. With your objective view and your firmness in dealing with such situations, it should not be difficult for you to earn an honorable living.

> *Honor and shame from no condition rise.*
> *Act well your part—there all the honor lies.*

Then does it matter what role you play? When you are off the stage you are no longer the part you played but are yourself again. Acting is acting after all, whether one acts the part of a good character or a bad character. It is not *you,* and that is enough; but while acting, you should not lose yourself. Your agents should help in contacting the right type of men and get work for you; and more than anything else, you have the power of simran with you, particularly when there is "no opposite desire," as you have very well put it.

Do the work for which you are best fitted, with faith and courage and simran in your heart, and without compromising Sant Mat principles even in such an atmosphere. That is how a satsangi should work in life. This wide world is a stage and we are all actors, playing the parts allotted to us according to our karmas. Just as logs of wood floating in a river are brought together by currents and then parted by other currents, so do we meet and part. That is all there is to our relationship in this life.

* * *

277.   Yes, you may continue your vocation as an artist and vary your themes to suit your social and political conditions and the market. There is no harm in pursuing your career, but always remember that this is only a career and occupation, and never be slack in your bhajan and simran, which means you should try to give the promised time regularly. The Master is within you and showers his grace on earnest and struggling disciples.

* * *

278.   I am glad that you have received the Sound initiation and now you will undoubtedly find that you will be making better progress. There is a time for everything, and our own karmas stand in the way. As you felt that the wall had crumbled and the path was cleared, now when you devote yourself to the hearing of the Sound, you will find your experience even more wonderful and elevating.

I am glad you feel that you benefited by having had your initiation in two parts and appreciate your suggestion that future applicants would likewise benefit by having a two-part initiation. In fact, this was the practice adopted by the late Master; but as against this, we have to consider the risk of human beings in this world. Death may overtake a person before he has reached the eye center, or other karmic difficulties and circumstances may make it impossible for him to get the Sound initiation for a long time. A disciple gets full protection and the Master accepts full responsibility only when the Sound initiation has been given, for the all-pervading Shabd is the link between the Master and the disciple. Anyway, it cannot do one harm but may do immense good to receive full initiation. Hence, it has been decided to revert to the former practice of giving the complete initiation.

* * *

279. The Sound initiation is a wonderful thing and is the very soul and essence of the Radha Soami faith, the Sound being the *real* form of the Master. It is in the Shabd form that the Master exists everywhere and offers help and protection and guidance to his disciples.

You should try to forget your mental obsession through devotion to Shabd. If you cannot get the Shabd at all times, then at the time when these mental currents bother you, repeat the five Holy Names—even semi-audibly, in private. Quick and constant repetition of these Names will pin the mind more or less to them and prevent undesirable ideas or emotions.

The Master is always willing and glad to help, if only the disciple will turn to him. Hence, it is very necessary to work intensively on the path and contact the Master inside. I hope you will take full advantage of this Sound initiation and devote all available time to bhajan and simran.

* * *

280. Yes, it is a long path, and they do best who go on with their meditation slowly and steadily and do not want to hurry things. Putting the attention between the two eyebrows helps concentration, but even this should be increased only gradually so that you may be able to hold onto what you have achieved.

The pain in the legs is partly due to the position to which Westerners are not accustomed. After some time the body will get used to it and the physical cause of the pain will disappear. But there is another reason also, and that is the beginning of the struggle, so to say, between the spirit and the flesh. As one begins to move up towards the eye center, no matter how slowly, this pain is felt like cramps or creeping sensations, first in the legs, and then creeps up a little higher. But this should not worry anybody, as it is automatically conquered. And when you see the light within, the joy of it will make you completely unmindful of any pain or inconvenience.

It is too early yet for you to guess where you are. You are still in the body but you have begun to move, and that is quite satisfactory. It is always useful to take whatever one experiences as natural and not to speculate upon it, for that scatters the mind energy.

Regarding marriage, it is not prohibited by the Saints. It is a question of one's personal needs and temperament, etc. If one feels like getting married and can do so, one should. But all the same, one should continue with the diet and the spiritual practices. When one lives up to the principles and teachings of Sant Mat, one is automatically a better citizen, wife, husband, etc. Only one thing need be stressed in considering marriage, and that is to find a life partner who would be a help and not a hindrance.

* * *

281. After all, this is the most important work in the world. As this can be carried on only in the human life, we should give it top priority so that we may not have to wander again in this ocean of existence but go back to our Father and rest in peace and bliss.

I am sorry about your husband's passing away but assure you that your faith, love and devotion in bhajan and simran will help him also.

* * *

282. Thank you for your letter—stating that you are on a strict diet and asking permission to meditate while waiting for initiation.

Yes, you may sit quietly in any comfortable position

and try to concentrate your attention at the center between the eyebrows, with the eyes gently closed. In order
to achieve concentration, you may *mentally* repeat any
name that is sacred to you, during this period. Please be
sure there is no strain on the eyes, as it is the attention of
the *mind* and not the physical eyes which are to concentrate at this point. You may practice this for fifteen minutes or half an hour at a time, then gradually work up to
one hour daily. Any time of the day or night is all right,
but the early morning hours are best if that time can be
conveniently utilized.

When you feel that you can conveniently remain on
this diet and have resolved to do so for the remainder of
your life, you may kindly send your application through
the representative.

* * *

283.   Yes, sometimes our latent karmas do turn up and
disturb or frighten us in the form of unpleasant dreams,
but there is nothing in the least to be frightened or worried about. When you have strongly developed the habit
of simran or the repetition of the Holy Names, the simran
would come up at that time too and scare away anything
evil or frightening.

* * *

284.   Karma is really the problem, for the entire existence depends on karma. We are kept chained to the
world and its relationship by karmas—past and present.
It is for this reason that we are enjoined not to interest
ourselves too much—not more than is necessary—in people and things. Of course, we must do our duty in every
sphere of life but in a spirit of duty, without being unduly
attached. One may pray for the good of all humanity.

That is elevating. By praying for specific persons, some amount of karma is shared. One may pray to Satguru about such persons, to help them, if it be his will. Dr. Johnson's book sheds much light on these problems, and after initiation you will understand them more thoroughly.

Your experiences are correct and betoken an aptitude for spiritual life, based upon previous karmas. Their full significance will be realized and appreciated after initiation. Continue on the diet and then apply. In the meantime you may write and ask anything if necessary; and keep your experiences, whatever they be, to yourself.

* * *

285. Yes, you have the privilege of asking for help and having your questions and problems attended to.

Our life is based upon karma but we have also the right and the power to meet the karmas in various ways. You may continue to pray as before, when in trouble, and *at that moment* surrender yourself to the Master and pray to him for strength to endure cheerfully and gracefully. You may, however, consult other doctors and it may be possible to obtain relief. Silent prayer in bed, to Satguru, is quite good.

A person on the diet and with an earnest and sincere longing for initiation is also under the care and protection of the Master to a great extent.

* * *

286. Sant Mat is extremely simple, and the emphasis is on meditation and living the life, which does not require any organization or ritual. A living example is no doubt the best incentive, but we attach great importance to satsang also. Real satsang leads to bhajan and promotes that attitude of mind which makes meditation, that is, bhajan and simran, easier. It induces self-introspection, and the exposition of the Sant Mat teachings enables us to judge ourselves, to discover our weaknesses and remove them. We are influenced to a very great extent by the company we keep or the society we move in. Here again, satsang is helpful in molding the mind and providing an atmosphere for bhajan.

But satsang is for all, that is, members as well as non-members, and sometimes people may behave strangely. These things should not be taken too seriously. They should be ignored, but the seekers must be encouraged, as that is one of the objects of satsang. As satsang is open to all sorts of people, we need not be too critical. We should pick up what is good and keep our attention in Shabd.

Master is within all of us and hears our cries and prayers, but we should pray to be granted strength to face calmly what is in store for us, and to enable us to keep our attention in simran and bhajan. You can refer your problems either in meditation or in a letter to me, just as it suits and pleases you.

Probably you are putting too much strain on the eyes in trying to see within. This should not be. You do not see inside with these eyes. Please adopt the posture which is convenient and comfortable, and do not put any strain on your eyes. This is the path of slow and steady progress. *Regularity* is a great thing. Persevere on steadily, without trying to force things or even dwelling upon whether all the karmas can be wiped out in this life. This is the Master's responsibility. He will do what is proper and correct. The disciple should carry on the meditation according to instructions and leave the rest to Him.

* * *

287. Most of your difficulties will disappear if you lay more stress on simran; that is, by intensive repetition of the Holy Names, try to draw the consciousness up to the eye center. It is true that we are very small persons in the midst of a big expanse, and that is why we need concentration on particular sounds all the more. This vast expanse is full of all sorts of sounds, but we have to attend only to those particular sounds which will lead us up. They will become clearer and more definite as, by means of repetition of the five Holy Names, we withdraw ourselves and approach them.

When we hear a concert from a distance, all that we hear is a sort of jumbled echo, but as we draw nearer we are able to identify the notes of the particular instruments. It is almost the same in this case. The object of simran is to withdraw the consciousness from the body and bring it up; and the more we succeed in it, the clearer will be the Sound.

It would be very helpful if you cultivate the habit of repeating the Names mentally at all hours, *in addition* to what you do at the appointed time. That provides work for the mind which in no case remains unoccupied, for it is running after one thing or another. When you acquire proficiency in simran, you will find that even when you are talking to other people, simran goes on automatically in your subconscious mind. That will facilitate concentration and withdrawal when you sit for bhajan.

The throbbing of the blood is physical, while the spiritual sounds are of a higher order. The high-pitched sound or the bell sound are both good. Please be sure that you never pay attention to any sound whatsoever from the left ear. In listening to the sounds, a very important thing is selection of the right sound. You should preferably try to attach your attention to the bell sound. Then the rest will automatically vanish.

You are 'within' when you see the light and have these experiences; but the star, etc., referred to by ——— is higher up. That is when you are nearing the first stage. The bluish light with lighter swirls and other sensations of light are correct. First we go in and then we go up.

As for undesirable sounds which seem to disturb you, all that you have to do is not think of them—withdraw your attention from them. You are doing well and if you persist with love and faith, Maharaj Ji [Maharaj Sawan Singh Ji] will be merciful.

Regarding the sights and sounds, and the dancing of particles which you see now and then with your physical eyes, please do not mind them but think them to be of no particular consequence to you. Keep your attention in Shabd and simran, and go on steadily with your practice.

* * *

288. I am glad to learn from your letter that you have been treading the path since your initiation from our late Master, Sardar Bahadur Jagat Singh Ji. It does not matter much if the progress is slow. Slow and steady wins the race. One should persevere with faith and love, and be regular in the practice.

I expressed in my inaugural address what I felt. I am only a humble follower of the Great Master, Baba Sawan Singh Ji.

* * *

289. Another posture for listening to the Sound is to sit on a cushion on the floor, with legs crossed as in the simran posture; and facing a chair or low bed so that you may place your elbows on the bed or chair seat, place the thumbs in the ears and cover the eyes with the hands. This should not prove very trying.

* * *

290. I note that you are both concerned about the diet of your child. I would not recommend any force or compulsion, even though milk, cheese, vegetables and fresh fruits constitute an adequate diet. He can be persuaded, but he must make his own choice. I am glad to know that you do not serve meat or other forbidden food and drink to guests.

* * *

291. I note that you are anxious to get initiation into the Radha Soami path and, in pursuance of that laudable ambition, have been on a strictly vegetarian diet for nine months. Your application will soon be considered and you will be informed through the representative. In the meantime you should start practicing meditation from one-half to two hours every day, as you find convenient, in the following manner:

Sit in any comfortable posture in which you can stay for some time, that is, without moving or changing position, calm yourself a minute and say to yourself that you are not going to let any thoughts disturb you while you are meditating. Then close your eyes and keep your attention fixed between the eyebrows, but without any strain. If thoughts arise and attention goes out, bring it back again to the same point, all the while repeating "Radha Soami" slowly, mentally.

* * *

292.   What you say about controlling the mind is perfectly correct, yet by practice and perseverance it eventually becomes easy.

The meditation practice suggested to you[1] is only introductory. When you are duly initiated, which will be very soon, it will gradually become easier. In the meantime, this method enables you to practice sitting, in an endeavor to hold the mind to a point and shutting off all irrelevant thoughts. To that extent it will make your bhajan easier.

The course of every applicant runs differently, according to his or her zeal, earnestness and, above all, the past karmas. But *steady* application *always* brings results.

* * *

293.   I am glad that you value and appreciate these teachings, but I should also tell you that these teachings have to be lived and not only professed. The central point in Sant Mat teachings is to live a detached life in this world, that is, to perform all your duties and obligations, whether personal or social, simply as duties, but without being affected or attached. This is, of course, by no means easy, and it is partly for facilitating the cultivation of this attitude in life that regular bhajan and simran are enjoined for at least two and one-half hours every day.

The practice of simran gradually but surely shifts the center of attention from the phenomenal world to the spiritual world, and helps in the withdrawal of the consciousness from the body and its concentration at the eye center, after which only the real bhajan or devotion to

---

1. In Letter 291.

Shabd begins. Success depends upon several factors, including the past sanskaras, your own effort and intense desire, and the grace of the Guru. The word *success* is used in the sense of achieving appreciable results within a reasonable length of time; otherwise, everyone who has been joined to the Shabd eventually reaches the Source from which the Divine Sound proceeds.

Please remember that it is a lifetime's task or even more than a lifetime in some cases. One should not be hasty or get impatient but should go on following the practices perseveringly and remember that the Great Master is watching our efforts. You are enjoined to give at least two and one-half hours every day to the practice. If you find it very difficult to sit for this length of time in the beginning, you may split it up or divide it into two sittings, but always try to prolong the sittings to as much as you can do effectively—so that eventually you will be able to sit at least two and one-half hours at a stretch. If you feel any difficulty or wish to inquire about anything, you can always write to me.

* * *

294. It is never too late to mend. Begin anew and keep to the schedule. Pray to the Master within you to help and guide you, and above all please do not forget that the incidents of life—pleasant and unpleasant—are only a passing phase. The one thing of permanent value which makes you rise above these things is the path of Nam or Shabd. It is our duty to strive on the path.

* * *

295. The mind, of course, has to be reckoned with, but like all problem children, if properly handled it can always be managed. Persuasion is a much better method

than force or suppression. Above all, simran or the repetition of the Holy Names is the most effective way of
bringing it under control. Devote as much time to simran
as you conveniently can, and get into the habit of repeating the Names mentally at all hours of the day too. This
will facilitate concentration and prevent the mind from
wandering about.

As for the Sound, the first rule is that we should *not*
attend to any sound whatsoever from the *left* side. Whatever sound you hear from the right ear should be attended to, and in due course it will connect you to the bell
sound and lead you further on.

The Master in his radiant form is contacted within; in
fact, the Master and the Shabd are *one*.

Please do not worry about the postage, etc., and do
not send anything, as we have funds for that purpose
here.

* * *

296.   I congratulate you on your earnestness and zeal
for spiritual progress. As to what books you should read,
I would say, now that you have all the Radha Soami
books, they bear reading over and over again so that
these teachings may become a part of you. When your
reading time is limited, I would suggest that you pick
up *Sar Bachan* or Puri's *Spiritual Path* Vol. II and read
at least a page or so from either of these books every
day. That also helps to put you in the proper mood for
meditation.

All the necessary instructions were given to you at the
time of initiation; however, I welcome any questions you
may wish to ask and shall always be delighted to hear of
your progress. You are extremely fortunate to be able to
see the form inside so soon after initiation. I would like to

remind you, however, that often Kal appears in the form of the Master, and for your own protection please do not forget to repeat the five Holy Names whenever you see anything inside. Then whatever remains is genuine and can be trusted implicitly.

Such preliminary glimpses of the Master are marks of special grace. When after diligent practice you have contacted the higher Shabd, you will be able to hear him speak to you and you will be able to understand. Until that time comes, the curtain of one's own mind is the real obstacle. That is controlled and purified after *regular* and diligent application to bhajan and simran. It is usually the work of a lifetime, the length of time depending on our past karmas and our sincere efforts, in conjunction with his grace. The more effort we make, the more grace he extends to us to be able to make more effort until we have reached our goal. So with love and faith, continue the practice and he will take care of the results. No amount of effort is ever wasted. He is ever loving and merciful.

I thank you for your kind offer to do some work for me. The best work you can do and that which will be most appreciated is to devote as much time as possible to the spiritual practice.

* * *

297. I am well pleased to have your letter, in which you mention your experiences. Yes, it is wonderful; but as you proceed further and devote more time, you will see and hear still more wonderful things. We have numerous lights of different kinds within us and come across these lights now and then on our own upward journey. Progress would be even better if you could spend not less than two hours, but preferably two and one-half hours, in one sitting, and you may work up to that gradually, devoting two hours to simran and one-half hour to listening to the Sound.

The Sound or Shabd is the most important thing because the Shabd is, as it were, the spiritual extension of Sat Purush Himself. It is the link which connects us to His throne. In order to contact the real Sound and place ourselves within the range of its upward pulling power, it is necessary for us to vacate the nine doors of the body and concentrate all our attention at the eye center, from where the Shabd pulls us in and up. If we devote ourselves lovingly and faithfully to this Shabd and surrender ourselves to it, it will take us Home. But this, as you know, is a question of time. All of us have different backgrounds and different karmas, and that, to a great extent, determines our rate of progress, though of course the Master is always guiding and helping us on the way.

It is good that you can hear the Sound even without sitting in bhajan. This is a very good indication and speaks of your interest and the grace which is being bestowed on you. This is only a preparation and should make you all the more enthusiastic about hearing the Sound when you sit for it properly. The sound that we hear at other times also helps us in concentration of the mind, but it cannot pull us up to higher centers unless all our consciousness has first been concentrated at the eye center by means of simran. Hence the importance of simran.

The Sound pervades everywhere, and in fact everything is supported by Shabd. However, we cannot hear it because our attention is outside. Once you have been placed in touch with it, the moment you are concentrating yourself or are in an introspective mood, you will hear it. Your experiment was perfectly correct. When you turned to spiritual things, the Sound was at hand to help you; and when you were busy with worldly things, it let you work out your own problems.

Your new schedule of timing for devotion is much better. Here in India we start at 3:00 or 4:00 A.M., but this of course does not suit most Western people. The morning hours are quiet, and at that time there are also greater currents of grace and spirituality, which we automatically utilize when we perform our spiritual duties during the early morning hours.

You speak of the sounds being extremely distinct and loud, but you do not mention what are the various distinct sounds; however, when the Sound is so distinct before you sit for simran and bhajan, then you may begin with hearing the Sound. As mentioned at the time of initiation, you are to pay no attention to anything you may seem to hear from the left ear.

As for conversation with the Master from within, that will also come by and by. Everything in good time. Many disciples first see the Master's form, then it may disappear. Later, when it reappears, it becomes steady, and then conversation may take place.

Now that you have the key to the inner Mysteries and have started so hopefully on the inner journey, what matters it to you how feverishly people run about and how they are engaged. They are working out their own destiny. It is all right to sympathize with them, but you cannot interest them in higher things before the time is right. Even if you were to talk to them of the Radha Soami faith and appeal to them from the results of your own experience (which of course is not permitted), they would not believe. You are perfectly right in your aim of conquering the five enemies and scaling the heights yourself first. These enemies are very dangerous and will lay quietly for some time—in ambush, as it were—only to spring upon the disciple at the critical moment. The disciple must therefore fortify himself and gather enough strength to meet them successfully at all times.

Please do not mind about long letters. I am always interested to hear from those who are working faithfully on the path.

* * *

298. What you have said about the Sound is correct. The Sound is really not in the ear, but in the head. We expect to hear it through the ear only because of our habit of getting the external sounds through the ear. But in your case, most of the sounds seem to come from the left side. As you keep your attention at the center or toward the right, the sound from the left will automatically cease and you will eventually hear it either from the right side or from the center.

The bell sound, either from the right ear or from the center, is the proper sound to which we should pay attention. There are numerous sounds inside, and all these little musical sounds are quite interesting, but the sound that will ultimately lead you up is the sound of the big bell, which some hear first as the sound of small tinkling bells. By paying full attention to simran—at the time of doing simran—and to bhajan or listening to whatever bell sound you may hear at the time of bhajan, it will eventually develop into the sound of the big bell or gong. Hence, a disciple may hear and enjoy the various sounds (however, from the right or center only and never from the left—even if you hear the bell sound on the left, disregard it); but ultimately he should take to the bell sound which comes from either the right or the center. In course of time, this will develop into higher sounds. And the effect of the big bell and the higher sounds will be apparent on the mind and the behavior of the person who hears these sounds.

Yes, they can as a rule be heard at all times; for the Sound is always there and a devoted disciple may hear it whenever there is concentration or the mind turns from the outside world and becomes introspective. One thinks that they may be heard by others sitting nearby, but this comes from within, and non-initiates have no access to it. After some practice, one may hear the Sound almost at all times; but when he has to attend to work, he should turn his attention to that, then finish his work, and again be in touch with Shabd when he turns his attention in. This should come automatically, however, and as a result of continued bhajan and simran, and need not be striven for.

As for the lights, you should just note what lights you see and what effects they leave upon your mind and body. Try to avoid being excited or emotionally upset by any of the lights or visions. Our aim is not to see lights or visions but to go in and up with the help of the Shabd, and be united with the Source whence we came. A good many of these lights and visions may be seen within the orbit of the first stage, namely, Sahansdal Kanwal.

I am pleased to learn of your progress and assure you that when you see heavens and stars and the like, you are far from being crazy. In fact, this is exactly what you ought to see. The concentration is good but it does not seem to last or retain its intensity very long. That is why the Master's form seems to come and go. The Satguru (Master) is within us and may always be contacted after crossing the stars, sun and moon—just below the first stage. In the beginning the form seems to come and go or disappear without any talk. As the duration of the practice increases, the duration of concentration increases and the form of the Satguru will stay longer before you inside and will also talk to you and advise you. You are extremely lucky in having gone so far in such a short time; and through perseverance, in course of time you will be able to converse with the Master within.

You should pay no attention to profiles or faces, nor should you attend to any sound which seems to come from behind, for it may be a trick. Whoever has to talk to you should come before you, and if the form remains after the repetition of the five Holy Names, it is genuine. It is therefore very necessary that one should always keep the simran in mind.

It is very good that you have now developed a habit of getting up early and are devoting two and one-half hours or so to simran and bhajan every morning. Please continue and you will have darshan inside as well as conscious guidance and supervision throughout. Once you are in contact with the Master within, you will feel and *know* that you are being guided.

The real Shabd—the one which pulls you in and up— as remarked before, begins from the big bell or gong sound. The other sounds, the minor sounds—from the right or from the center—lead up to that big bell sound, and as such they are also important. But all sounds must be heard from the right side or the center only, and *never* from the left side. They may be there, but one should pay no attention to them except from the right or the center.

You are not imagining things, and in course of time you will yourself feel and know that what you see inside is more real than that which you see outside. Love and devotion constitute the key to success in simran and bhajan.

* * *

299. I am happy to learn of your experience. It is only the beginning. Persevere on with love and faith, and go on working patiently. There is yet much to come, but please remember that we should not anticipate or expect but just take whatever comes, cheerfully.

Emphasis on simran is necessary and everything will be all right, but please do not listen from the left side. The big bell is a sound of the first region and has a magnetic effect, but you should not listen from the left side.

You did well in using your will and determination. When that does not succeed, you may take the thumb from the left ear and concentrate on the sound from the right. If it still persists, switch from sound to simran, and if necessary you may get up for the time being and temporarily terminate the sitting.

Your guess about banning the left side is correct. The left side is the path of the negative power, and things on this route are designed to delude and disturb us. This is correctly understood and appreciated when one reaches Trikuti.

As for the experience about the dark hole trying to engulf you, please do not be afraid but remember that the Satguru is with you always, even though you may not be able to see him. On such occasions you should think of the Satguru and mentally repeat the five Holy Names.

Please do not worry about taking my time. I am always glad to hear from sincere, earnest and loving devotees. In fact, this is my duty.

* * *

300. Simran is the foundation, though it appears dry in the beginning. Dwelling on worldly things and relations is but the simran of the world, which has made us so attached to it. When we change the character of simran, we develop ties and attachment with the spiritual world. Keep on patiently, lovingly and regularly, and Satguru will bless your efforts. Shabd really becomes effective when we have withdrawn ourselves from the body. Before that it sounds pleasing and delightful, but does not pull.

* * *

301. I can understand your eagerness to be here, but you know all other things also have to be taken care of, and you have to attend to your duties there too. Besides, as you have now yourself felt and experienced, the Master is everywhere and his grace is not limited by time or space. I do not mean thereby to prevent you for all time from coming here. The Dera is open to all satsangis and you are most welcome to come when you feel that you can do so without disturbing your routine or causing any inconvenience to yourself. Also, let me know well in advance so that your coming here may coincide with my being at the Dera.

Thank you for the report on your progress. You may always feel free to write to me whenever there is something to say, but do not mind if I am late in replying to your letters as you know of my various activities here. I am glad that you are going on nicely with your bhajan and simran, giving the proper time to it every day. Simran is the foundation of the Shabd practice, and as the concentration becomes greater, you will hear the Shabd or the Sound even while you are carrying on the simran.

I am delighted to read about your experience in ———, which was so gladdening and elevating. It is the grace of Huzur Maharaj Ji which supervises over the destinies of the satsangis, and he came to your help at the right time. Satguru's real form is Shabd, and that is not

limited by distance. He has proved it to you fully by
coming to your help at the right moment, and that is how
he will come to help us at the time of our passing away.
We can express our gratitude to the Satguru in only one
way, and that is by lovingly giving more time and attention to Shabd.

Incidentally, I may add that a lawyer should prepare
his case as a matter of duty and not make it a personal
issue whether he wins or loses. He should do his best and
that is all.

I am pleased with your progress and confirm your experience as genuine. When you talk with the Master inside, you do not speak with the tongue or lips nor hear
with the ears. It was a genuine experience, and as it
should be. It is a sort of understanding (soul to soul)
rather than hearing with the ear, hence the sense of the
words automatically passing from one to the other.

The experience which you have described about seeing red and a golden image within is interesting. If you do
not find this or any reference to such things in the books,
it does not matter. Experience is something higher, and
all the experiences cannot be put into books. I would only
add that you should not wish nor try to be at this or that
stage, nor particularly try to know where you are, but
give yourself up entirely to Shabd. That is the only way to
revere it. One should not stop and revere it, because that
creates duality; but merge yourself into it and feel one
with it, for then it will carry you up to the higher plane,
which you aim to reach.

During the course of simran your attention should be
entirely in the simran, but it may be that the Sound is so
urgent that it takes your attention away for a while. On
the whole, however, you should attend to the Sound *after*
you have finished with the simran, and then you will find

that you can get to the Sound more easily. If the Sound becomes too compelling at the time of simran, then you may switch over to the Sound, but only then.

Yes, it is not good to be either apprehensive or expectant. Just resign yourself to the Shabd.

* * *

302.   I am glad you are devoted to your bhajan and simran, and get encouraging experiences also. Everything will come in due course. It is a long path—a lifetime's task—but with patience and perseverance everything becomes easy. Go on as you are doing, and do not try to become too interested in what you see or hear, that is, do not follow what you see nor miss it when it disappears, but keep your attention in simran. Simran is the foundation, as it were, and the more perfect your simran is, the easier it will be to catch the Shabd, visualize the Master and meditate on his form. By the way, all other visualization, that is, other than that of the Master's form, is discouraged.

Such dreams are generally a little more than dreams, but after all, they are dreams, however satisfying and exhilarating. Anyway, when the attention goes in, it is a distinct advantage. You cannot get everything in books. Some of our experiences are individual, and it is not practical to mention everything in books.

I agree with your opinion, and in fact it has been like this so far, but now things are changing. In view of the increase in property, some regular administration is necessary. I am lucky to have able and retired satsangis (who are honest) as advisers and administrators, and the work is going on smoothly. Legally and virtually I am the owner of all this property, like my predecessors, and it stands

in my name; but you know, according to Sant Mat principles I cannot and do not use a single pie[1] for my personal requirements. I hold it as a trust for the benefit of
satsangis, and live on the agricultural income from my
ancestral lands.

* * *

303.   Whatever you are seeing and experiencing is correct and is the result of your assiduous and diligent application and ardor for spiritual values. You are indeed
fortunate in having this wonderful experience with
Sound. The spirit as well as the Master, both in essence
are Shabd. The ego stands between the two. By simran at
the eye center we gradually make our surrender to the
Master, thus eliminating the ego, and enjoy union in the
Shabd form. Please go on with love and faith, paying
particular emphasis to simran. It is the key and the foundation. Be regular in this supreme duty and do not get
perturbed even if you sometimes miss any of these exhilarating experiences. Simran detaches the mind from the
world and attaches it to Shabd. Though dry in the beginning, it is absolutely necessary. One may hear the Sound,
but unless the course of simran has been completed, the
soul will not be drawn up. We often devote more time
to Shabd and ignore the simran. This is a mistake.

Sant Mat literature and Maharaj Ji's [Maharaj Sawan
Singh Ji's] letters are very helpful and beneficial and supply wholesome enjoyment to the mind. The mind is only
too apt to be influenced by surroundings, therefore remembrance of the Lord and our spiritual goal is very helpful.
Besides, most of our problems and difficulties being

---

1. A former monetary unit of India equal to 1/192 of the rupee.

common, the literature and the letters suggest solutions and show us the way.

Food is an individual problem and has to be regulated according to the individual needs, but there is no doubt that most of us eat more than is necessary. Light and spare meals are very helpful in bhajan and simran, as you have found by personal experience, but no hard and fast rule can be laid down in this respect. Regulation becomes almost automatic.

You are to be complimented on the time you are able to give to simran and bhajan, but right here I may sound a note of warning too. There should be no attempt to force the pace. One should try rather to strengthen and consolidate what has been achieved so that it may be permanent, and not just come and go.

Books describe only the main outline. Details are not given as a rule.

I realize your and other satsangis' great desire to meet me face to face, but those Americans who have been here and have lived in the Dera with me will be able to tell you how difficult it is for me to go out. At present I have no program, but if such be the will of Satguru it would be a pleasure for me to meet all of you.

Religion, alas, especially as it is practiced today, instead of binding us to God, only creates a cleavage between man and man and thus sows the seed of hatred. This should not be. We are all sons of the same Father, who has no religion, caste or creed, nor is He in any one place or limited to any one nation or people. He is in all of us, and if we hate anyone we really hate the Lord. Our religions say so but do not act upon it. If we were to follow this personally there would be no wars and differences, and the kingdom of heaven would really come upon the earth. Maharaj Ji always preached and practiced tolerance and love towards all, even towards those who opposed him.

* * *

304.   As for your experiences, there is an entire world inside, and a much bigger world too. The entire astral plane—with its sub-planes—is populated, and even in Kal's domain there are benevolent souls and radiant forms. A good, safe rule—when meeting attractive forms inside—is to repeat the Names mentally. The same should be done with the Master's radiant form also, to make sure that there is no false impersonation. The Master's form will stay. As you progress, the Master will speak to you also, but everything at the proper time.

It is good that you hear the Sound now from the focus. When you hear the Sound, you should withdraw your attention from everything else, including the simran, and try to absorb yourself in the Sound, which will—by and by—adopt you, so to say, and lead you on. Dhyan should be resorted to at the eye focus, along with simran.

* * *

305.   I am sorry to learn that you are suffering such great pain at the base of your spine when sitting in bhajan. This is, to a great extent, due to the habit of following yogic practices in a past life, some effects of which are still bothering you.

The Radha Soami way of sending the Spirit Current up to higher centers is not the ordinary yogic way that passes through the six chakras. We concentrate *all* our attention at the eye focus. By means of repetition—constant and intensive repetition of the five Holy Names—

we draw the Current up to this point and *then* proceed onwards.

Please try to devote as much time to simran as possible, and also get into the habit of repeating the five Holy Names mentally during the other parts of the day. This will facilitate withdrawal and make the rise of the spirit easy.

Also please adopt a comfortable position, putting a bolster or some cushion behind your back. You may also get some relief by massaging the affected part with some ointment or preparation, like a liniment.

Simran is the means which will enable us to withdraw our attention from outside things, concentrate it at the eye center and then attach it to Shabd. You hear the Sound all right, but cannot make quick progress in the Sound for want of sufficient concentration of consciousness at the eye center.

The scenery, etc., which you see, relate to regions below the first, and are not of much importance. The most important thing is to merge yourself in the Shabd Dhun. The more you merge yourself in Shabd, the more you will feel the presence of the Master and also a feeling of elation and bliss. Your enthusiasm without any impatience is very good and useful, for it is a long and arduous journey.

We get glimpses of past lives when we have reached the first stage. After crossing the second stage, we will know all the lives that we have passed through. But as Huzur Maharaj Ji said, it is not very important. It may sometimes be rather disturbing.

I appreciate your love and devotion, but you should divert it to the Shabd form of the Master, which will increase it all the more and make you happier. The real form of the Master is Shabd, and the more you devote and merge yourself in Shabd, the more you will feel his nearness and realize that God and Satguru are *one*. These are things not to be written or discussed, but to be *realized*.

I am happy to learn that satsang work is going on apace, and that not only the numbers are increasing but that satsangis show genuine interest in spiritual work. We should welcome each other and show *in practice*, by our conduct, that we are sons of the same Father. If there is any doubt or any difference of opinion, it should be lovingly smoothed out. There should be mutual understanding between satsangis, and those with better knowledge and understanding should try to help the other brothers in clearing their doubts and difficulties. New entrants should be helped and encouraged in having their problems or doubts cleared, and the various aspects of Sant Mat should be explained to them. We should behave in such a way that they should not feel that they are strangers in the group.

* * *

306. I compliment you on your search for Truth, but it is not far from us. In fact it is within us, and all we have to do is to turn within and forego those sensual pleasures that give us not only a short-lived pleasure but also involve us in endless misery. Only a calm and settled mind can perceive and reflect the Truth.

You may meditate, say half an hour or more every day. Sit in any comfortable position and, with eyes closed, try to focus your attention between the two eyebrows. While doing so, you may slowly repeat the words *Radha Soami* mentally and drive out all other thoughts.

You should hold strictly to the meatless, fishless, eggless diet and avoid alcoholic drinks. Then apply for initiation when you have finished dieting successfully for six months.

307. Your distressing letter indicates a very scattered and confused mind. I would ask that you again read my letter sent to you and heed the advice given therein. As you yourself admit, these are weaknesses. As you make the effort to overcome them, you will receive the necessary grace from Him to enable you to do so.

There is no need for you to feel confused or frustrated, but rather perform your duties with renewed determination to do everything to the best of your ability. Your first duty is to be a good wife and serve your husband well. That is your vocation in life, so why worry about teaching or what you will do when he has left this world? If your taking up some studies meets with his approval, then well and good; otherwise devote yourself to the job in hand now—hand in hand with your spiritual duties—and leave the rest to Him. "Do your duty. That is best. Leave unto the Lord the rest." If you are thus engaged, how can you fear mental and physical stagnation?

The mention of one meal a day in *Sar Bachan* refers to those who have made sufficient progress to devote most of their time to bhajan, and they therefore do not require nor want more than that. You should eat as much and as often as you require food, the only restrictions being that you do not partake of non-vegetarian food and that you abstain from alcoholic drinks. The selection of the proper combinations of food is very important from the standpoint of health; but by giving this matter some attention, you will soon find out what agrees with you and what does not. Hindus cannot get along with less food and less sleep than Americans. That is entirely an individual matter.

Love is in itself a gift and comes only after long and steady application to the spiritual practice with faith and devotion. In the beginning, sleep does often intervene

when one sits for practice, but that is gradually overcome
by renewed daily practice.

* * *

308.   I appreciate your devotion, and if you will carry
on with your bhajan and simran with this same feeling
of devotion and faith, it will change your whole outlook
on life by driving out all negative and morbid thoughts.
It will also help you to perform your worldly duties
cheerfully.

* * *

309.   It is true that the correct appreciation and significance of initiation comes only by and by. Gradually, as
we make progress, we realize what it means to us in this
life as well as hereafter. It seems, however, that you have
not correctly understood the Radha Soami technique,
which must have been explained to you at the time of initiation. We are to do three things:

(*1*) Dhyan.[1] This means inner contemplation of anything, preferably the form of the Master. It comes
easily with personal contact; but in case of people who
are far away, they may simply think of their Master,
as if they are in his presence at the eye center, always
with a feeling of love and devotion. This is to be done
simultaneously with simran.

(*2*) Simran, as you probably know, is the repetition
of the five Holy Names. This is also to be done with
the *attention* of the mind fixed between the two eyebrows. The tongue is not involved, it is the mind that

---

1. For detailed explanation, see pages 200–202 in *Die to Live.*

is to do the repeating. At the time of repetition, all your attention should be directed to the point of concentration and no thoughts of any kind should be entertained. The mind is to be engaged in repetition and contemplation, simultaneously, and when it is thus engaged there is no room for other thoughts at that time. This is to be done for two hours. But it may not be possible for a beginner to put in the full two hours, so he may start with one hour or even a little less, but should gradually increase the period so that it is done for no less than two hours daily, in one sitting.

(3) After this, one should immediately change the position to that of listening for the Sound from the right ear or from the center, but *never* from the left. If anything is heard from the left, pay no attention to it. The Sound may come at once, or it may take some time before anything is heard. But the practice should be continued every day, irrespective of the result. This should be done for half an hour.

There is to be no visualization of anything traveling up. As a result of repetition, after some time the consciousness tends to gather up at the eye center; but there should be no such thoughts as imagining the currents going up or something coming out from this leg or that leg. Do not let your concentration be thus diverted. It is not the negative force which leaves the body but just the sensory current or consciousness. That happens automatically, after some time, and you should not think of it at all.

As to the number of initiations, you now have all that is needed. The late Master had divided initiation into two parts: first, giving the technique of simran; then, after the disciple had achieved a certain amount of progress, he was told now to listen for the Sound. This latter was called the second initiation. But now we give both the initiations at the same time, as it was done formerly.

* * *

310. I am glad to learn that you have now grasped the full technique given to you at initiation, and do not feel any further difficulty in this respect.

Your keen desire to meet the Master is good because personal contact is the very essence of discipleship; but under the circumstances, it does not seem possible. One also has to fulfill one's worldly and domestic duties from day to day, as well as to devote the required time to bhajan and simran with a feeling of faith and devotion, which ultimately leads to love. Besides, the Master is within you; and by vacating the body and concentrating *all* your consciousness at the eye center during the spiritual exercises and joining the Shabd, you can go up and have a glimpse of the Master inside. Let the energy of your enthusiasm be turned inwards and utilized to take the mind up.

We came into this body on account of certain karmas. One object of being in the body is to be able to work off those karmas by performing our worldly duties in addition to doing the spiritual work. By surrendering to the will of the Master, we work out our pralabdh or destiny karmas, as well as follow a path which will ultimately release us from the tyranny of karmas—the result of our own past deeds and thoughts—and take us back to our Father's Home.

* * *

311. I am very pleased with your eagerness and determination to go in, and to correct all your faults in order that you may achieve success as soon as possible. It is true that slow and easy or steady is the right method, and to hurry is satanic because it involves the mind factor. It is the mind which goads us on, and in so far as we hold to mind—even in good directions—we are losing part of our independence of spirit. A true satsangi should submit himself or herself entirely and unconditionally to the wishes of the Master and leave everything to him. It is for him to set the pace and reward the satsangi for his efforts. But this does not imply that the satsangi should be lazy. Rather, one should strictly, to the best of one's ability, follow the instructions of the Master and *then* leave the result to him.

Your ambition to sit for six hours at a stretch, if you can achieve it without straining yourself too much and without neglecting other duties, is laudable. You can, if you like, divide the period into two installments. Let the anxiety and the gnawing you feel within be controlled and sublimated so that you may find your bhajan more interesting.

As for your husband being initiated, the best way is not to persuade him but bring about such a change for the better in your life, in your devotion to him and your devotion to bhajan and simran, that it will automatically impress him and change his heart.

It is not necessary to become an ascetic and forego everything, although it must be admitted that cinemas and television definitely distract the attention. Milk, milk products, butter, cheese, etc., may be taken and do not hinder one's progress. The most important of all is to *control the gossiping habit*, for nothing scatters the attention so much and brings in so many unnecessary as well as even harmful ideas into the mind as the habit of gossiping. As you start watching your thoughts and actions, you will yourself feel what is necessary and to what extent, and will no doubt act accordingly. When one starts earnestly and honestly, one receives help from all sides.

As for the experiences which you have felt since your initiation, I can say that they are not common to all satsangis. However, the experience of having tiny currents going up is fairly common. Sometimes, though not in many cases, the automatic repetition of the five Holy Names is also heard at the time of meditation. All these experiences imply a partial repetition of a previous experience and previous karmas, called *sanskaras*. They are all good and there is nothing to worry about. However, when the tension becomes terrific, as you say, you might now and then relax a little in a reclining or lying-down position and, after some time, begin again. There is nothing wrong in it.

As to the sounds, the sound of jingling bells is good, though heard from a distance. But *no* sound should ever be listened to from the left. Any sound that is seemingly heard from the right ear or from the center is all right. The gong or big church bell sound is the best, but it does not come so easily. Stick to the bells, and if the gong comes, put your attention into that deep, melodious gong sound.

Let lights—blue or white or whatever color they may be—come before your eyes, but do not pay much attention to them. Be an indifferent spectator. That will be more helpful.

Do not try to locate the center, for that is a waste of energy and time. Just keep the eyes gently closed and do the repetition with the attention of the *mind*, and the center will be found automatically. The attention should be kept in the darkness between the two eyebrows. When concentration is complete, the Shabd will itself pull it in and up.

The feelings of nerve currents, tinglings, stiffness, etc., are all part of the game. Do not let these things worry you. Simply give your body a gentle downward rub before you get up from meditation, and that will be all right.

The heartbeat, breathing and other functions of the body are under the control of the automatic centers and *pranic* energy. We do not interfere with them. Even when the body becomes stiff during this practice, these functions are not harmed. The stiffness may creep up, right up to the shoulders, but not very soon. Even then, no harm would result.

When the spirit is withdrawn from the body you will see a steady light and, of course, hear Sound too. Nothing is to be anticipated. Nothing is to be feared. Whenever you feel any disturbing or frightening effect, turn your thoughts lovingly to the Master and repeat the five Holy Names.

You may have the picture in your room just to look at now and then or as you come and go, but it should *not* be for dhyan or contemplation.

* * *

312. Thank you for your letter informing me of your having received the Sound initiation. It is indeed a great gift and a privilege. But who can say that he is worthy of it? It is a gift from the Great Father, and the Saints are only the dispensers.

Now you should take the fullest advantage of this initiation and devote time to bhajan—to hearing the Sound—regularly every day, after you have finished your simran.

As to the posture for listening to the Sound, it is difficult, no doubt, but it is very helpful too. Until you can
accustom yourself to this posture, which may be done
only gradually, you may either sit in a chair or sit cross-
legged on a cushion on the floor, facing a chair seat or
bed, placing your elbows on the bed or chair seat, and
with the thumbs in the ears and the hands gently placed
over the face—be sure that there is no pressure on the
eyes—listen to the Sound in that posture until you accustom yourself to the prescribed posture. Or in the meantime, you may adopt any other comfortable position in
which you will be able to remain for at least half an hour.

* * *

313.   No doubt you must have considerably felt the loss
of your Master from this physical plane. That has been
almost everybody's experience. Those who have been
able to see him or realize him inside are indeed fortunate
for they *know* he is not far off. You do well in prizing
those letters which you possess. They are very precious,
and to read them over and over again with love and
understanding is also satsang. If I may, I would suggest
that when you read those letters from your Master, you
should sit in meditation immediately afterwards. You will
find this helpful. It is true that it is a matter of living—and
practice too. If only we earnestly follow his advice, we
will have nothing to regret.

You have already the good fortune of catching
glimpses of him and hearing the Sound occasionally. But
if you meditate regularly for the full period, you will soon
do much better. This is the only way in which we can
properly express our gratitude to our Master.

* * *

314.   I appreciate your high qualities and your earnest
desire to work for spiritual uplift according to the Radha
Soami method. The study of those excellent books would
have informed you that God is realized within and not
without. The path as well as the goal lies within us. We
have only to go in and begin the journey, and if we persevere according to instructions there is no reason why we
should not arrive at the goal. The fact that you are a
vegetarian and have a good background makes things
easier. As you have no doubt been informed, in order to
travel on the path it is absolutely necessary to have a firm
determination to remain on a diet free from meat, meat
products, eggs and alcoholic drinks.

I may say, however, that we do not countenance hyp-
notism, hypnotic practice or healing, spiritualism or anything of that sort, because it is not only dangerous but
also scatters the energies. All the energy should be concentrated and applied to traveling on the path.

* * *

315.   I appreciate your question, for it indicates a desire
to be as correct as possible in the matter of diet. Right
living is the foundation of right meditation.

Conditions in your country are different from conditions here, but as far as possible satsangis' children—even
though not yet initiated—should be kept away from a
meat and egg diet. No force should, however, be used;
but it must be impressed upon them gently and per-
suasively that it is not a wholesome diet—for mental and
spiritual well-being, and that the Great Master does not
like us to kill or cause any living being to be killed. Tell
them that is why you, their parents, do not eat fish, eggs
or meat—and, of course, do not take alcoholic drinks. In-
form them that surely you would partake of these things

if you deemed them good and wholesome, but since you realize that they are not, you also do not wish to serve them to your children. In India, satsangis' children are simply forbidden to take these things, and they understand instinctively.

If strict adherence to the diet makes the children appear so different in the eyes of their companions and makes things difficult for them, please ask them to avoid meat and fish at least. It would lighten their burden and make it easier for them to be good satsangis one day. Sometimes a compromise has to be made, but only in the case of children and those who have not been accepted for initiation.

* * *

316.   Love for the Master comes by having darshan inside, that is, by seeing him *inside*. It is only then that the feeling of real love springs up. In the beginning we have to practice it more or less. If we carry out his wishes and commands and follow his instructions faithfully, a feeling of confidence and love springs up; and it also leads to darshan inside, which further promotes and strengthens this love.

* * *

317.   I would say, do whatever you like but do it in a detached spirit and without sacrificing or compromising your principles, that is, the Sant Mat principles. We should take full advantage of human birth and utilize fully our opportunity to devote ourselves to Nam and realize God. Human life is the highest form of existence, and it is only in this form that we can devote ourselves to Guru bhakti and Nam bhakti (devotion to the Guru and devotion to Nam) and thus secure our release from the chain

of births and deaths. Devote as much time as possible to
simran and bhajan—the repetition of the Holy Names
and listening to the Sound Current—and follow your profession disinterestedly, as a means of earning an honest
livelihood.

* * *

318.   I am pleased to learn that you have been following
my directions to the best of your ability and have benefited as a consequence.

You should have no fears at all. Let faith and confidence replace fear, and the best way to achieve this object is to follow the directions completely and manage to
find at least two and a half hours every day (in two installments if need be) for your meditation. Please try to keep
your attention at the eye center, that is, between the two
eyebrows—with eyes closed, of course—at the time of
simran. If thoughts go out, bring them back again and remind yourself that you are not to think of other things
while doing your simran. As you approach the eye center, a sense of strength and confidence will come to you
automatically.

Bad dreams, nightmares and other disturbances will
cease when the pent-up forces have exhausted themselves. The suppressed feelings, emotions and fears are
coming to the surface. The right thing is to face them
boldly, with faith and confidence in the Master, and realize that now your path is quite different. Do your simran
for a short while before going to bed and even while lying
in bed to give a different orientation to your thoughts.
Whenever you feel disturbed at night and have bad
dreams, repeat the Holy Names and think of the Master.

The success or progress of other satsangis should not
disturb you in the least. It is good that it does not. Every

one has to work out his or her karmas, and they get their
deserts at the right moment. Do not feel frightened but
persevere on with love and faith, and do not hesitate to
write whenever you feel the necessity.

* * *

319.　I am very pleased to learn that you are practicing
the directions faithfully and, as a result, experience inner
peace and a sense of freedom. The practice of the Surat
Shabd Yoga—joining your mind and attention to the
Sound Current—turns your attention inward to the Eternal Reality and makes you indifferent to the world and
its babblings. After all, what really matters is the way
that things affect us or what *we* think of them. Sant Mat
enables you to clear all complexes and puts the ego in its
proper place.

　I am happy to learn that the fear of insanity which
haunted you so much has gone and so has the choky feeling round your throat, also that you have faith and confidence that you are not alone. An initiate who has faith
and love is never alone because the Master is with every
disciple, and when the disciple firmly holds the Master's
hand, he or she can look the whole world in the face. If
the disciple is able to withdraw his consciousness to the
eye center by regular meditation, he may also *see* how the
Master is helping.

　Yes, with faith in Nam and Satguru, you have nothing
to fear. Be *regular* in your bhajan and simran; and when
feeling weak or confused in any way, *turn within* to the
Master and Sound Current.

* * *

320.　It is always a pleasure to hear from those who
were initiated by our Great Master, Baba Sawan Singh

Maharaj Ji, and I hope you are making good use of the spiritual gift received from such a great Saint. The path is, after all, the most important thing and the purpose of human life. All else is but subsidiary.

Art, too, uplifts the mind and enlarges the vision, but it should not be an impediment to our higher goal. Artists and geniuses sometimes have visions and see things as they are. The ordinary artist tries to express that idea in language or pictures or stones, but an artist who has been initiated should try to make it a stepping stone to greater and higher spiritual visions till he comes into intimate contact with the ultimate core of all that exists.

* * *

321. I appreciate your desire to follow the spiritual path and live the spiritual life. But it seems to me that there are some difficulties in the way you propose to follow, and that is your intention to come and stay at the Dera for an indefinite period. If convenient to you, you may arrange for a short visit, but a permanent or indefinite stay is quite out of the question under the circumstances. There would probably be difficulties from the government side, too, for a permanent stay.

I would first of all like to know how much progress you have made in the way of withdrawing your consciousness by means of simran—repetition of the five Holy Names—which method was given to you at the time of initiation.

It seems that your love of art, though it inclines you towards the mystical path, brings you out more than it takes you in. Painting and art of any kind are self-expressions to a great extent, and are surely interesting and useful to society, but as you know, our aim is to *go in*. The energy which we spend in expressing ourselves outwardly should be utilized instead in making us go in and reach the inner center where the Shabd or the Divine Melody takes charge of us, and thus we begin our internal spiritual journey. We do not mean to disparage kindly efforts in the worldly sphere, but the inner journey is long and arduous, and you could hardly call it only one lifetime's job. But, of course, when one has taken to the road, that is, when he has actually begun the journey inside, it goes on and on. This being the case, it is our practice to discourage too much outward activity, especially on the part of those who live more or less permanently at the Dera.

You perhaps know that the inhabitants of the Dera get up at 3 o'clock in the morning and meditate until about 6:00 A.M., before starting the day's work. It is therefore not only a strenuous physical life but it is also a strenuous mental and spiritual life as well. May I suggest that you follow the path; that is, strictly adhere to the meditation routine for some time in your own country before trying to come out here, so that you may be able to find out for yourself how such a life would suit you. If the heart is in the spiritual work, it matters little where you are. Distance does not count. In the meantime, you can devote some—but not most—of your time to your profession as an artist, which will be better appreciated in America.

The rule for those staying at the Dera is that everyone should be able to maintain himself. All our workers from the secretary downwards are honorary workers; that is, they work without pay and arrange for their own board and lodging.

* * *

322. I would like to impress one thing upon you, however, that the Guru is not a person but a Power which incarnates for our good. Man can be taught and instructed by man only, hence the necessity of that internal and eternal Power coming into corporeal form. The physical body perishes, but the Guru never dies; and even today, if you vacate the body and reach the astral region, you will meet him there. The Guru is always within —wherever we might be; but as we do not go in, we cannot see and realize this. When we go in and meet him, we shall then realize his greatness and benevolence and all that he does for us.

As far as you are concerned, Sardar Bahadur Jagat Singh Ji, who initiated you, is your Guru, and it is very essential for your spiritual development that with faith and confidence you continue to persevere on the path, as you were directed to do at the time of your initiation. You should try to vacate the body by means of simran, and go up and have his darshan (see him), and he will take you up—stage by stage.

* * *

323. As to infertile eggs, they cannot be classified the same as milk. No matter what you may add to milk, it cannot reproduce the species from which it came; whereas the egg contains the ovum, whether fertile or infertile. Also, whether fertile or infertile, eggs are known to incite animal instincts, which in turn are not conducive to a calm and peaceful mind. Further, even if what you say about eggs were correct, we are strict on the point lest any relaxation may lead to a possible misuse and thus defeat the purpose.

Now, as to your question regarding the individual and his Master: The real form of the Master is Shabd. The

Masters come from Shabd for the purpose of teaching and helping humanity and ultimately go back into Shabd. It is therefore immaterial whether you meet one particular Master after reincarnation, or not. The Saints are an institution, so to say. If the disciple has not been able to accomplish his purpose by the time death cuts off his earthly career, he will again have another incarnation, but into a better life with more opportunities for spiritual progress, and is sure to be drawn to the Saint living at that time. He will then start his spiritual progress from where he left off in his former life. This is guaranteed.

The meeting of a Saint or a Master is destined, but once you are in touch with or have been taken under the protection of a *Sant Satguru,* your progress is determined by the Master's grace and your own effort. So effort does play a part after one has been put on the path by the Master. Grace makes initiation and effort possible, and effort brings on more grace and help in the spiritual progress.

* * *

324.   As to the children, you may occasionally talk to them confidently of the Power within all, let them go to church and Sunday school, tell them that the kingdom of God is within us, and that those who meditate hear the church bells inside themselves, etc. There should be no forcing, however. Your own life is bound to influence them.

* * *

325.   The five passions, as you know, are a great obstacle and become active when one starts on the path. They should be combated by meditation—simran and bhajan—as well as by appeal to one's moral sense, and by satsang.

The Audible Life Stream, except in the case of those with past sanskaras, is generally faint in the beginning but becomes strong as one gives time to the practice. Yes, what you hear is a form of Shabd. As you pay more attention to simran and concentration, it will change into higher notes and begin to draw you up.

Yes, the Master creates an inner astral image of himself (within the disciple) and helps and watches over the disciple. If the disciple *goes in,* he can realize this fact. He can see the Master in the first region and even at the tisra til. Much depends on love and faith.

It is good that you plan your life with an eye on your meditation, but this should not stand in the way of your worldly duties. Sant Mat does not encourage isolation or indifference to duty. The meditation should be done daily, regularly, in addition to the worldly duties.

As regards sharing your inner experiences with your wife, in your mutual interest I think that this should not be done, at least not at present.

* * *

326. I have gone through your letter and wish to assure you that there is nothing to fear and nothing to be disturbed about so long as you do not forget the five Holy Names. You should also try to revive the memory image of the Great Master, who initiated you. These two things afford a wonderful protection, the extent of which is difficult for an ordinary person to realize.

As you have not met with such experiences before, I can quite understand your feelings; but once again I would ask you to prove the efficacy of the simran—repetition of the five Holy Names—whenever you feel frightened or disturbed, and especially on the appearance of such phenomena, which are due to sanskaras.

We have had numerous lives before this, and all those
past associations leave a mark behind. A time comes,
especially for those who tread the spiritual path and particularly the path of Sant Mat, when they (these associ-
ates of the past) try to claim kinship—of course, for *their*
own good. But they cannot force anything nor can they in
any way harm you or drag you down, provided you do
not feel interested in them but remember the Holy Names.
Please do not pay any attention or evince any particular
interest in the forms and faces that appear before you,
but concentrate on the simran, and they will eventually
disappear of themselves. I think this is quite enough to
put your mind at ease.

* * *

327.   We have to get rid of desires. In our everyday life,
while adopting the principles of Sant Mat as our guide,
we should be content to accept whatever comes to us because things are predestined according to our own karmas. This method we call *bhana*, or submission to His
Will. But this does not mean that we should be lazy or in-
active. The idea is that we should do our duty fully and
conscientiously, but leave the result to God; whereas if
we go on praying for the fulfillment of our desires, we are
not only lengthening the chain that binds us to this world
but will have to come back again and again.

We obtained this human body because of a mixture of
good and bad actions. The result is that in the course of
our life we are bound to have both pleasure and pain. If
we were to feel elated at the time of pleasure or happiness and depressed or sad when in pain, we would always
be praying for one thing or another, and would have no
time for bhakti (devotion), without which our coming

and going cannot come to an end. To complete our bhakti
and avoid repeated incarnations, it is necessary that we
submit ourselves to the Will of the Lord.

When one feels very upset or finds oneself on the
horns of a dilemma, one may sit in meditation and seek
guidance within. The best prayer, however, is to ask the
Lord to give us strength to face boldly and gracefully
whatever is our destiny.

I realize your difficulty. One has to do something in
order to keep oneself alive. The struggle for existence is
very keen. I would say whichever of the two possibilities
appeals to you the more favorably, that one might be
taken up. The one thing that you should always keep in
view is that the principles of Sant Mat are always to be
kept in mind, whatever be your career. Whenever you
feel puzzled, sit in bhajan, meditate sincerely and, after
that, make your decision.

* * *

328. The Sound Current is *the* thing. It annihilates the
karma and takes you up. It is the duty of the Satguru to
assist the disciple in paying off the karmic debt in various
ways and partly sharing it. Please do not mind it.

You will be able to see the Master beyond the stars,
sun and moon when you have taken your consciousness
to that point by means of simran.

* * *

329. Worrying never has helped anyone and it never
will. Instead, it weakens our will power and capacity to
face emergencies. In all such situations a disciple should
do all that he or she humanly can and then leave the result to the Master. One should dwell on his kindness and
grace rather than give way to fidgeting and worrying. But

then, your husband is not a satsangi, hence the difference in the outlook.

I would also give you the same advice about your coming to this country as was given to you by the late Sardar Bahadur Jagat Singh Ji, and that is to achieve a fair degree of concentration before coming over to a new place where the physical surroundings may not suit you. And last but not the least, please remember that the Master never dies. He is always with you. The Master is a Power—an eternal Power—Shabd, and not the perishable body.

* * *

330. You will remember that you promised to adhere to the diet when you were initiated. Such lapses delay the spiritual progress by accumulating more undesirable karmas, and as you yourself now feel, it was probably nervous irritation rather than unsuitable diet which caused your trouble. Thousands of Indian people who do hard manual labor as well as those in the army and fighting on the fronts have been able to keep excellent health on a strict vegetarian diet; however, better late than never.

Now that you have realized your mistake and the Master has graciously afforded you a splendid opportunity to revert to the correct diet, please remain on it and make full use of the opportunity that is offered to you. If you use a little will power and resolve firmly to stick to the diet, especially now that your husband is also vegetarian, you will not only progress in your meditations but will also improve physically. If at all any difficulty arises regarding the diet, it is due to improper selection and combination of the foods and does not require shifting from vegetarian to meat diet. There are many good and nourishing strictly vegetarian foods, but what agrees with one does not always agree with everyone. So it is best for you to select that which you can most easily digest. It is very simple and requires only common sense.

* * *

331.   Faith and love is the very foundation of Sant Mat —faith and love in Shabd and Satguru. Then comes surrender to the Will of the Satguru—not a slavish but a loving surrender. The mainspring of action then changes, and the Will of the Lord or the Satguru replaces mind as the motive power. Then the soul is in perfect harmony with the Lord, mind is dethroned, and God is enthroned. It naturally involves a struggle, even a bitter fight to the last; but think of the crowning achievement too.

Persevere on with love and faith. Gradually increase the time allotted to simran and, after the simran period is over, devote yourself to Shabd and try to be one with it. It is Shabd which will ultimately lift you above matter and maya.

* * *

332.   I am very glad to know that you are no longer interested in the sham things of the world and are devoting yourself to bhajan and simran for three hours continuously starting at 3:00 A.M. However, I may say that Sant Mat does not encourage running away from one's duties, but simply taking the mind out of the glamor of the world. By living in the world and performing our duties and obligations, we can still be above these things, and that is the effect of bhajan and simran. When the mind is at peace and you are no longer troubled by attractions and attachments, you are in a place of peace. Peace comes from within.

* * *

333. It is through the avenue of the senses that our attention goes out and we make contact with the outside world. Thus all thoughts, attachments and memories arise and bind us to the phenomenal world. By means of simran we gradually draw ourselves inward, and the more perfectly we do so, the stronger we feel and the more are we able to rise above these thoughts and memories. Practice this assiduously, and if there is any difficulty, please do not hesitate to refer it here.

* * *

334. All of us have our own time, and when the proper time comes we shall certainly go up. It is true that mind and maya block the way, but if we go on lovingly with our bhajan and simran, our task is lightened to a great extent and our difficulties are removed. The Master also finds it easier to help such followers. The important thing is to vacate the body and to withdraw the consciousness to the eye center. Then it will be possible to go up and see the stars, sun, moon, etc.

When we reach the radiant form of the Master, we are not the physical body but the astral body and therefore can stand the conditions prevailing in that atmosphere quite easily. Likewise, in our further ascent when we reach the Causal Plane, the soul has only the causal covering and therefore finds no difficulty. But the most important thing for the disciple is to go on following the practice with love and devotion and contact the Sound. As you *merge* into the Sound, it will take you up and take care of all other things.

It is very encouraging that gradually you have been able to bring your meditation period up to three hours. You should now try to see that the attention is fixed at the eye center as long as possible; then the rest will follow.

Reading *Sar Bachan* and the letters is helpful and facilitates concentration at the time of meditation.

* * *

335. As in the physical world the exercise of a limb makes it strong, so in the spiritual realms the proper exercise and control of the mental faculties will purify and strengthen the mind—provided, of course, this is done with faith and devotion. The Master watches over and is conscious of the efforts of the disciple and helps him whenever necessary, even though the disciple may not be conscious of it on account of his still being in an undeveloped stage.

The advice that I would like to give you is first of all to remember that you are here for only a short while, and that your aim should be to get the maximum benefit out of the body with which you have been endowed, as well as the surroundings in which you have been placed. This can best be done by conscientiously doing your duty to the best of your ability in worldly matters and devoting as much time as possible to simran and bhajan—repetition of the five Holy Names and listening to the Divine Sound. These are the most important things in this world and the greatest benefit that a man can receive here. It depends upon the recipient as to what extent he makes use of this gift.

* * *

336. Self-control is emphasized in all paths, in all spiritual disciplines and in all religions. This should first be practiced by exercising your will and firmness of mind, and realizing the evils and disadvantages of getting angry.

When one is angry, he lets the reins slip out of his hands and thus heads towards disaster. A person in anger cannot think calmly, cannot reason coolly, and apart from the spiritual loss, suffers in a worldly way also.

The best way to overcome such feelings is to apply yourself devotedly to the repetition of the five Holy Names. Not only should the repetition of the Names be done regularly every day at the time of meditation; but especially at the time when anger seems to be creeping into your mind, you should immediately begin repeating the Names with your *attention* for about five minutes. You will then find that the raging fires will subside. The more you practice meditation and turn your attention inwards, the more you will get rid of these things and acquire self-control.

* * *

337. I have before me your touching letter and wish to assure you that your lack of higher education does not matter at all so far as your spiritual progress is concerned. Even an illiterate person, if he follows the instructions with love and faith, may make more progress than an educated person who is lacking in these qualities. Consideration of rank and position (in this world) count only in worldly matters. You should continue to attend the satsang regularly as you do now, without any feeling of inferiority.

Now as to your questions:

(1) The thumb should be put loosely in the left ear but closely in the right ear, so as to exclude all outer sounds, but not so tightly as to cause ache or pain. When sitting for Sound, the attention should be placed in the eye center, and there should be no simran or repetition of the Holy Names at that time.

(2) The practice of praying for strength and help in meditation is all right and quite in order.

(3) You are perfectly right in not asking any help for material things. When a satsangi devotes himself to the practice with faith and love, he gets help automatically, that is, to the extent that is desirable.

* * *

338. As to your bhajan and simran, progress on the path is not at the same pace with everyone; however, progress is always there even though we are not conscious of it. No amount of effort is ever spent in vain. One should continue to persevere, lovingly and regularly, without trying to check every week or every month how much he has progressed. This one comes to know automatically only when the path has been sufficiently cleared and one is nearing the eye center or appreciably improving in concentration.

It is the habit of the mind to refuse to be confined to one place, but it should be disciplined, and so far as possible the attention should be kept at the focus. If it goes out—and it will go out—it should be brought back again and again without any worry, and the process should be continued.

Sometimes one does hear the pulse beat, but please do not worry about it. Only keep your *attention* at the eye center and everything will be all right. Occasionally it may be due to too much pressure being applied by the thumbs in the ears. There should be no pressure of any kind. The entire position is to be a relaxed one.

The Sound that comes from the top of the skull may be attended to, but anything that may seem to come from the direction of the left ear should be ignored. Please do not try to analyze the sounds at the time of hearing, but just listen to it or to the next one that comes out of it. Follow this program for about a month or two and then you may write again if you find it necessary. The main thing in the beginning, however, is simran or the repetition of the five Holy Names, and full time should be devoted to that before listening for or to the Sound.

* * *

339. It is the nature of the mind to wander, but we should bring it back again and again and tell it that all those things which cause the distraction will be attended to after the meditation period is over. When simran—the repetition of the five Holy Names—is done lovingly, then the mind is stilled by and by. Steady practice and perseverance and, above all, regularity in meditation are necessary.

* * *

340. I am happy to know that the whole family has come to Sant Mat, which means harmony not only in worldly affairs but also in spiritual efforts. The *summum bonum* of human life is to seek deliverance from this constant coming and going and from the clutches of Kal. I am glad that you appreciate this point of view.

Now a good deal will depend upon your efforts, your devotion and your regularity in bhajan and simran. The Master always helps those who help themselves, and the best service which a disciple can render him is to contact Shabd and to go in.

* * *

341. Sant Mat is practically a life-long course, and we should not expect spectacular results in a short time, but should go on doing our meditation lovingly and with perseverance. Regularity is a very important factor. Regularity in simran makes the catching of the Shabd easier.

The feeling of fear that you have mentioned is only temporary, and as you are able to keep the attention between the two eyebrows it will gradually disappear. Whenever you have any feeling of fear, remember that you are not alone, but the Master is always with you; and repeat the five Holy Names for some time.

As for your employer, you should try to do your duty by him conscientiously and diligently, keeping always the Sant Mat principles in mind.

Regarding your friend and your mother, if you see that they are interested in the Radha Soami faith, you may talk to them in a general way and introduce them to Sant Mat literature. But the best way of creating an interest in the faith is to mold your own life in such a way that they would appreciate the change and would be attracted to this faith.

* * *

342. It is good practice before sitting in meditation to mentally repeat the words *Radha Soami* a few times and give the mind a good talking-to, saying that it has had sway for twenty-four hours a day for all these years; now in order to go back to its own home, it is necessary for it to accompany the soul. In order to accomplish that, you are not going to pay any attention to it during the time you have set aside for the spiritual practice. And be firm about it, no matter what tricks the mind may try to play while you are sitting. This is no small task.

Regarding satsang talks, *Sar Bachan* is made up of excerpts from Swami Ji's satsangs, and Puri's *Mysticism, The Spiritual Path,* Volume II, contains excerpts from many of Huzur Maharaj Sawan Singh Ji's satsangs. Some translations have also been sent from here, from time to time, to the representatives, who will be glad to let you and other satsangis read them. The highest form of satsang, however, is the individual's internal spiritual practice. The whole secret lies in the part of the body above the eyes, and the search for truth is to be made therein and within. Therefore the mind has to be withdrawn from the world around and also from the body below the eyes, and concentrated in the eye center.

* * *

343.   It is good if people, even for a short while, develop that high consciousness and try to lose the self. We should try to cultivate this way of living, year in and year out, or from day to day. Those who devote themselves to bhajan and simran automatically get this feeling of love and charity and kindliness, and have no difficulty in trying to cultivate this habit.

* * *

344.   Yes, the gift of Nam does give one an entirely new outlook on life; in fact, that is when life really *begins* for us. Before initiation, all our efforts, good and bad, only served to further entangle us. Now you have been shown the way to liberation, and it is for you to put forth your best efforts with faith and devotion. He will do the rest.

* * *

345.   It is good that bad feelings and malice have given place to feelings of love and admiration. Negative feelings and emotions first of all harm those who entertain them. Love, contentment and admiring the good in others are positive and constructive virtues and make us happy.

Thank you for your offer of service. Realization of that Lost Word, the Inner Shabd, is the greatest service

that a person can render, and this is a lifetime's work.
Dr. Johnson refers more than once to the Lost Word of the
Masonic Lodge in his now famous book, *The Path of the
Masters*, and in accordance with the Great Master's ad-
vice, he devoted himself assiduously to the practice of
Shabd during his stay at the Dera. I hope you are devot-
ing time regularly to the practice of contacting this Lost
Word, which is no longer the *Lost* Word for satsangis.

* * *

346. Anything which is honestly done and fills a need
and does not involve any violation of the Sant Mat principles is permissible. Sant Mat does not stand in the way
of your normal business. Rather, it encourages people to
attend to their worldly work and also find time for regular
meditation.

As for your mother, our sufferings are really born of
our own karmas and involve the payment of a karmic
debt; however, you should serve her and try to get her
whatever treatment is possible.

* * *

347. It is good that you do not hear sounds from the
left side, but they manifest themselves from time to time.
However, any sound from the left is always to be ignored
even if it is the bell sound.

The stinging pains in the toes are due to the temporary withdrawal of the consciousness, as the lower extremities become numb. By and by, this painful sensation,
followed by numbness, may extend higher up. This is only
a temporary feeling, however, and upon completion of
the meditation period, consciousness and strength return
again as before. So there is nothing to be frightened
about. Once the pain of withdrawal has been conquered,

each time it becomes less painful until eventually it is not
in the least painful, and one can vacate the whole body—
at will—without pain. That, of course, takes a long time
and depends on the individual's efforts and past karmas.
The sensation of floating is also a good experience.

* * *

348.   I do not wonder at the interest shown by your four-
and-a-half-year-old little son. Children automatically imitate and follow their parents, and in this way you are
perhaps giving him the best education and putting the
best opportunities before him. He will be initiated in due
time. As you know, the understanding and the intellect
have to be developed and matured so that a person is able
to form his own independent judgment and arrive at a
conclusion. But in the meantime, you may lovingly in-
form him about the privileges and the blessings of Sant
Mat and about the Masters, etc., without giving either the
Names or the technique. If he is already assuming the
squatting and the bhajan posture (but without the hands
up to the face) as small children often do in play, that
may be encouraged because it will prove helpful later on.
Postures may be encouraged in the form of exercise for
the sake of health and need not have a spiritual significance. In fact, that is the attitude to be taken toward all
yogic postures and exercises.

* * *

349.   We come into this world with a definite purpose
according to our karma, but we are born as a human
being with a particular aim in addition. That is the privilege of being able to meet a Master, contact Shabd and,
by working in the spiritual Sound or Shabd, go up to our
spiritual home whence we came.

This grand achievement is possible only in a human life. Therefore we should live in this world in such a way as to subordinate everything to this wonderful goal. That is being in the world but not of it. We have to be in the world, discharge our obligations, do our duty, but not be attached to anything or affected by anything. This is the ideal, and the more we do our meditation—simran and bhajan—the nearer will we come to it.

By 'surrendering' we mean that we should do our duty and make efforts according to the best of our ability and in consonance with the principles of Sant Mat. Then leave the result to the Master or Shabd, without worrying how it turns out. Surrender implies surrender to Shabd, which is the real Master or Guru, and not to any physical form. We should by constant practice not only contact the Sound but *merge* ourselves into it so that it will take care of us entirely, in every situation and in every respect.

Your concentration requires improvement. When better concentration is achieved, the conscious current will be withdrawn from the body—at least from the lower part of the body in the beginning—and then the darkness which you now see before you will melt into light. This can be done by intense repetition of the five Holy Names. You should also cultivate the habit of repeating the Names mentally, without closing the eyes, at odd hours of the day when you are mentally free. This will facilitate withdrawal and concentration when you sit at the regular time.

* * *

350. Only until the mind is under control is the path difficult. When once you are in touch with Shabd, or the Inner Music is easily available to you, you will not feel inclined to bring your attention out and listen to any outer music, however beautiful it may be. But this takes time.

* * *

351. You need not worry at all or think you are bothering me. You naturally have to look for clarification and help from here. Karma certainly has quite a lot to do with it, but that should not make anyone despair. Karma in this context means chiefly inherited tendencies; hence, in some cases, a handicap. By regular effort on the part of the disciple and grace from the Master—loving effort evokes grace—the tendencies can be fought and overcome. This is just the principle of education applied in spiritual matters, and is merely by way of explanation. You have not been at it long. The mind is accustomed to have its own way and go about unrestrained. Naturally it resists. With faith, love, and patience in practice you are sure to succeed.

If you cannot sit for two and a half hours at a stretch, do it in installments—say half an hour at the start and then again half an hour in the evening. Go on increasing the period by ten or fifteen minutes so that you have no sense of failure or frustration. Before beginning, pray to the Master and collect your thoughts. Then sit at ease— rather relaxed; and with your eyes closed, repeat mentally the five Holy Names given to you at initiation. Gaze (with the attention but not with the physical eyes) at the space between the two eyebrows, but without any strain or tension.

Light, easily digestible food is helpful and does not make one feel sluggish.

You may also repeat the five Names in bed before going to sleep. You may write to me after two or three weeks.

352.   Please do not worry about the letter. All is well that ends well. Doubts do assail disciples now and then till they have put in some practice and gone in. Hence the necessity of faith and good company in the beginning. The important thing is that cobwebs have been cleared and the meditation has improved. The more you practice repetition of the five Holy Names, the stronger you will feel and the better you will be able to combat any pull of the negative power.

* * *

353.   I did not intend anything specific by asking you to write after two or three weeks but just wished to suggest that you should feel free to write to me when there is something to write about.

Restraining the breath plays no part in this system. We leave the pranas alone and simply concentrate our attention at the eye center, that is, between the two eyebrows. Sometimes when concentration is going on apace, one may feel a little choking sensation but should not worry about it. You should go on normally by holding the attention at the eye center and repeating the five Holy Names, without giving any attention to breathing. The feeling of pressure between the eyebrows is due to the concentration of attention, but there should be absolutely no strain on the eyes.

The sound which you hear is all right. You should go on attending to it till a better sound comes.

* * *

354.   You have abstained from physical relations with your wife in the interest of your spiritual progress, but it must be by mutual consent and should not be a source of conflict or discontent.

As regards your little daughter, what you have done is right, but the best service you can render her is to keep her on the vegetarian diet.

It is not correct that one has to pass through seven lives (after initiation). Four is the maximum number—not the minimum, and though usual, it is not absolutely necessary. This is in accordance with the teachings of Swami Ji, Baba Ji, and Huzur Sawan Singh Maharaj Ji, who quite often told his disciples, "Why wait for four lives? Why not pay off your karmic debt as soon as possible?" Of course, this depends upon the amount to be liquidated and the time given to bhajan and simran.

One half-hour is not enough. If there is any difficulty, the period should be *gradually* increased every week till the normal period of two and a half hours is reached. We cannot expect to go in and stay inside if the attention is outside twenty-three hours, and inside for one hour or less. You should increase the time of simran—repetition of the Holy Names—so that you may contact the Shabd. This is the most important thing for a disciple.

* * *

355.   Harmonious relations in the family help spiritual life considerably, and your effort should be to have a better understanding with your husband—all the more so because he is so loving and tolerant and you love him too. After all, it is our mind which stands between, and it is this which we have to curb and control. You seem to be quite good at analysis. This should help you to analyze your attitude and quietly give up wrong things. Concentration, born of simran, would provide a desirable check to automatic reflexes. Bhajan and simran help us to be sincere and truthful and enable us to make necessary adjustments.

356. *Sar Bachan* contains the essence of Swami Ji's teachings and is solid gold. It should be read and digested carefully.

The real Satguru is Shabd, which is impersonal but assumes personal shape—the Word made flesh—for the sake of teaching people and making wider contacts and appeal. Thus a large number of people are redeemed. The real form of the Satguru is Shabd, as you will find in *Sar Bachan*.

As you sit in meditation regularly every day and give the required time to simran, or the repetition of the Holy Names with attention at the eye center, the feeling of love for the Master will spring in the heart. When you have a feeling of elation and see flashes of light and hear the Sound, this feeling of love will grow and get strengthened.

By "feeling of love" here is meant a pure spiritual yearning for the Lord without the least particle of selfishness. It is a thing to be felt rather than described.

The feeling of joy and admiration automatically springs from the realization of the unity of God and his creation, and an "inner realization," that is, intimate contact with Divine Harmony, which we call Shabd.

When the inner contact is fully established with the Shabd form of the Satguru, the spirit floats in his grace as the fish in water and even momentary interruptions become unbearable. This is a very advanced stage, and represents an ideal for the average satsangi.

Fear means the dread of the wheel, the dread of death, the dread of the 'unknown'. The consciousness that the Master is always with us and will help us, dispels this fear.

Faith is certainly necessary. Nothing can be done without faith. If we are sure that the road we are treading

will lead us to our destination, we walk firmly and unhesitatingly—without stopping or looking back. But faith
is one thing and blind faith quite another thing. In the beginning you have to take certain truths for granted, as in
the propositions of Euclid, only to prove them later on—
Q.E.D.

You require a special position only for listening to
the Sound. For repeating the Names any convenient posture would do, but it should be done at a time when there
is no interruption, and effort should be made to keep
the attention at the eye center. All extraneous thoughts
should be kept out. In addition, you may repeat the
Names quietly at any time of the day when you are not
doing anything in particular. At that time no posture is
necessary. This will facilitate concentration at meditation
time.

Please keep to the diet. It is very essential. Your
choice may not be suitable and you can try other combinations. Simran and diet improve the health also.

* * *

357.   I am sorry to note what you are going through.
You know that the soul is of the essence of God and has a
natural affinity for him, but mind stands in the way. Mind
alone is our enemy whom we have to fight and control or
win over. Is it good strategy to listen to your enemy's
advice?

You promised to give two and a half hours daily to
meditation. The Master is within us and is always ready
to help, but we do not look up to him nor do we follow
his instructions. Help comes and will come from within,
but one must turn that way. The first step is to be firm in
your bhajan and simran, especially simran or the repetition of the five Holy Names. If you find it very difficult,

begin with half an hour every day and go on increasing
the period every week until the minimum amount of two
and a half hours daily is reached. Then continue for at
least two and a half hours regularly every day. Pray to the
Master to help you.

* * *

358.   As to your own wish to be of similar help to
others, the first step is to devote the required time (and
more if possible) *regularly* to bhajan and simran with a
feeling of faith and devotion, which will ultimately lead to
Love. The effect of such daily practice reflects itself in our
daily conduct and manner of dealing with our fellowmen.
Then one automatically becomes really helpful to others
also.

* * *

359.   As for what you have read in Radha Soami books
and literature about the advantages of being in the personal presence of the Master, that is correct. But the
Great Master, in his mercy and grace, has definitely said
more than once, and has written it many times also, that
space and distance are no bar to spiritual progress. If one
is devoted and lovingly thinks of the Master, and does his
bhajan and simran according to instructions, he suffers no
disadvantage. Whether people are in the physical presence of the Master or far away from him, whatever they
are to gain will be gained by following instructions and
going in. And for this, faith and love alone are required.

It is true that some Americans are here and have been
here, but this does not mean that it is absolutely necessary for all of you to be at the Dera. You can do your
bhajan and simran with faith and love quite as effectively
in your own home, for the Master is within and you have

only to go in to contact him. You will also realize that the
Dera is open to all satsangis, and if anyone wishes to
come he is very welcome. We do not encourage or advise
people to come here for the sake of bhajan and simran,
but if they are so minded and want to come here for that
purpose, we also do not discourage them.

You should think of the Master who initiated you. I
hope this clears the position.

* * *

360.   We have no symbols and no formalities. It would
be perfectly all right for you to address followers of other
mystic brotherhoods simply as "brother" or travelers on
the path. The Surat Shabd Yoga, or the discipline of attaching the surat (soul or spirit) to the Divine Sound within, is the highest mystic training and takes you beyond
the reach of mind and maya.

* * *

361.   The aura is a sort of indicator of the mental and
spiritual development of a person, and his moods as well
as his character are suitably reflected therein. A skilled
person can read both the temporary changes as well as
the permanent traits which are automatically reflected.
The aura reflects the inner spiritual condition in fine
astral-spiritual matters outside.

It is not the person acting on the Master's behalf who
initiates, but the Master himself does the initiating in the
Shabd form. As the initiating power is Shabd, the character and habits of the person initiating by proxy do not
affect the initiate unless he develops close personal association or relation, which is a different matter altogether.

Each soul has to follow its individual goal, whether
through community living or individual living. The Power

that governs the world and world conditions determines what is best for them through well-defined laws. Even in this world, less highly evolved souls accept natural leaders, and men put their faith and trust in and obey their political leaders.

The laws of evolution are but imperfectly known in this world and are being modified from time to time. When the full story is known, such an idea would not be found to be in conflict with the purpose of evolution. The scientists, by the very nature and scope of their work, do not discuss soul and take no account of such possibilities. Neither does this conflict with the laws of karma. A proper and careful understanding of the laws of karma would show that there is nothing fortuitous in this world of cause and effect. What has been said about this in the Radha Soami literature is correct, and we had confirmatory accounts from the lips of the Great Master himself. Such Saints, however, are rare.

When we say that we should let the Master live in the heart, it means that we should be thinking of the Master consciously and subconsciously. As for the eye center, you need not attempt to make the Master live in the third eye. He is already very close to it.

Yes, you are permitted to defend the lives of your family and yourself, but you must not be the aggressor.

Yes, it is necessary for two people who wish to live as man and wife to go through a ceremony of marriage. They should conform to the marriage laws and customs of the country in which they live.

Definitely *no* intoxicating liquor is to be taken, as it retards spiritual progress. Smoking is not forbidden but it is not good for the health and might become a nervous habit which cannot easily be broken; hence it may enslave one. There is no spiritual objection to smoking if it is moderate and can be discontinued at will. Most sat-sangis do not smoke, and the few who do are expected to abstain from it at the Dera.

There are various methods of concentration for reaching the eye center. After that there is only *one royal road.* Whatever is necessary will always be made available to the disciple by the Satguru, who watches his interests and guides his progress.

* * *

362. I am highly pleased to hear of your inner experiences. It is really very creditable that you have accomplished so much in such a short time. Please be assured that you are going in the right direction.

After seeing the two eyes, that will merge into one eye, which is known as tisra til or third eye, our attention should be thoroughly concentrated in the very center of that eye or opening, and then we will pass through that very eye. The Sound which you hear is also right. Pay no attention to what you hear from the left ear. Really the Sound does not come from either ear but only seems that way in the beginning. This Sound is to pull us up, but it will do so only when we are absolutely concentrated.

Please do not give your attention to scenery, clouds and other things, but try to concentrate on that third eye.

Yes, when we meditate properly and are sufficiently concentrated, it seems as though someone else is doing the repeating and we are only listening.

* * *

363. The attention should not go towards the ear but should be kept in the center. In this way you will hear the Sound better. Please ignore the sound from the left side altogether and pay absolutely no attention to it. Attend

only to the Sound coming from the right side and keep
your attention fixed in the center. When the attention is
well fixed and the internal Sound is clear, you will not
hear the outside noise. It is only in the beginning that it is
disturbing. Please attend to your meditations regularly
and punctually, and you will get better results.

* * *

364. The five Names which have been given to you are,
as you must have been told, the names of the Lords of the
five spiritual regions inside. They are also names of Power, and if any difficulty is encountered or fear is felt at the
time of meditation or any other time, the Names should
be repeated confidently with the feeling of love and devotion, and whatever difficulty or danger there may be will
immediately disappear. You may feel free to write to me
anytime. I shall always be glad to help you.

* * *

365. Yes, you are right. Long listening to the bell
sound takes your attention to the inner center and develops your understanding. Intellect and understanding
become clearer. When you see explanations, that is, the
inner and true explanations of causes and conditions of
present life, you should feel thankful for things thus revealed to you, but should not dwell much upon them because the real object is detachment from everything else
and attachment to Shabd. Karma is indeed all-powerful,
but the grace of the Master and the power of Nam can
erase karmic writings.

As for things that you hear during bhajan, you can
take brief notes on coming out and check them afterwards. Sometimes useful and important information may
be given to you. At other times the information may be

misleading and a trick of the negative power. The best way to guard against this is to think of the Master and internally repeat the five Names. The repetition may be subconscious but will eliminate anything from a questionable source. Anything that is revealed to you whilst you are hearing the bell sound from the right or center, or while you are having darshan of the Guru inside, is above suspicion.

* * *

366. A disciple who devotedly practices the Shabd abhyas benefits not only himself but also those connected with him and those who love him.

* * *

367. Interpretations are meant to lead us on to devotion to Nam, and whatever helps us in that direction or takes us in that direction is the correct interpretation, though there can be slight individual differences.

The idea of unconditional surrender is correct and is in fact the basis of the entire system. When that surrender has been accomplished, little remains to be done—for the individual will is replaced by the will of the Satguru, and whatever is necessary follows as a matter of course. But this unconditional surrender is not an intellectual or reasoning exercise. It is an inner, spiritual fact, and only by constant devotion to Shabd does it come.

We ought to take reasonable care of the body, using it as a vehicle for higher and better things. We should neither pamper it too much nor should we starve it and subject it to ascetic practices.

Real peace is in the mind. If one is engaged in bhajan and simran regularly and lovingly, one finds as much peace even while living in the world as one does in a

monastery or in solitude. Both the body and the mind
must be kept busy.

As you put your attention steadily in bhajan and simran and contact the Shabd, your doubts and difficulties
will automatically resolve themselves. Then you will have
a feeling of peace and good-will beyond all measure towards everyone with whom you come in contact, and the
mind will be filled with true humility.

The holder of this office has been called "Maharaj Ji"
by tradition, therefore people here address me as such.
Those who come from abroad follow the example and do
the same. You may address me as you like.

The only thing which can drive out Kal is devotion to
Nam and Shabd. Mere words, this or that, can neither invite nor repel Kal.

There is no such thing as a pronunciation key to
Indian words as related to our sounds. It is the teachings
which matter. *Sar Bachan* is pronounced, first *a* long, and
the *ch* is the same as the *ch* in *church*; but it does not matter much how you pronounce it if you try to follow what is
written inside the book.

* * *

368.   The conception is not correct. In Sat Desh there
were no covers. It is not possible to comprehend these
mysteries of creation till we have crossed the frontiers of
mind and maya, and one should leave them alone.

Yes, souls who are permanent denizens of those regions sometimes incarnate themselves in this world in accordance with the scheme of creation and, after doing
their work, go back to their place. Other souls also, who
for one reason or another are staying in these regions, do
from time to time incarnate here primarily for speeding
their progress or seeking higher initiations in order to

reach Sat Desh. Progress is much quicker here than in upper regions.

There is a difference between mind and the mental apparatus. Mind is not to be judged quantitatively. Accumulated knowledge or tendencies in previous lives come to a head and make a man a genius. Those who have come up from lower lives and have accumulated lower tendencies inherit inferior mental apparatus and become idiots. The background in both cases is that of karmas.

If one member of a family suffers from mental illness, whether other members of the family are to any extent responsible for that condition or whether that ill individual regains his mental health in his next incarnation, all depends on individual cases. No hard and fast rule can be laid down.

Members of a family are grouped according to their karmas and previous relations. A number of people with different backgrounds and different temperaments live together in the same hotel or home. They have their lodging and boarding in common but not necessarily their aims and outlook in common.

The nature of the suffering of those in the "regions of correction" in the higher heavenly spheres is the deprivation of the presence of Sat Purush, which is punishment enough for them.

Yes, great Saints (*Param Sants*) like Swami Ji or Kabir know from early childhood of their high spiritual standing. The veil of maya, though not very dense in their case, has still to be pierced to be fully illumined. The lamp, the oil and the wick are there, but a spark is still needed.

Only those who understand *bani* (the teachings of the Gurus) correctly and understand that Nam and Shabd are identical, recognize the necessity of a living Master and accept him. Their number is limited.

Real love is engendered and fostered only when you go in, come in contact with Shabd and have a glimpse of the Master inside. In addition to bhajan and simran, the best way to engender this love is to read Sant Mat literature, associate with devoted satsangis who go in and are in touch with Shabd, render selfless service to satsang (that is, without any desire or expectation), have the company of and association with a living Master whenever possible, and last but not least, do intensive simran— repetition of the five Holy Names.

We should not waste time in speculation, but devote every available minute to simran and bhajan. Then we shall prove for ourselves the truths of Sant Mat.

* * *

369. Our birthdays serve only to remind us that time is passing and so much precious valuable time has gone. If it has been devoted to bhajan and simran then it has been properly utilized; otherwise it has just been wasted. Therefore, a birthday is a good time to take stock of oneself and make a renewed and determined effort to devote more time to bhajan and simran, thus utilizing the time to best advantage. Unless we do this, the whole life is wasted because the very purpose of life in the human form is to attain God-realization. This cannot be done without love and devotion coupled with his grace, which in turn is the result of *regular* bhajan and simran.

* * *

370. You will be pleased to know that we have been able to register a Society under the Religious and Charitable Act. A copy of the rules and regulations is enclosed.

I have transferred all the funds and the property to the Society. Mentally I feel very light, though I know this will not relieve me of much responsibility. I shall have to work the same way and keep an eye on their activities, but still I am glad that some leading satsangis have been made responsible for their property, which was held by me and by my predecessors in the past.

* * *

371.   As mentioned in my other letter to you today, all satsang property and all satsang funds have been trans-ferred by me to the registered Society consisting of old and reliable satsangis. The idea has been in mind for a number of years but could not be given final shape on account of legal complications and other difficulties which you can well understand. I have received valuable help from R. S. Munshi Ram and several other satsangis in this connection, and it is with their help and assistance that it has at last taken shape. I have written to you about this separately, and with that letter I am sending you a copy of the rules and regulations of the association.

* * *

372.   A living Master is very essential for contacting the Inner Sound. We are so engrossed in the love of worldly pursuits that it becomes difficult for us to detach our-selves from the affection of those things unless we have some other and better object or being to love. And what could be a more suitable object in this world than a liv-ing Master? For his real form is not body, but Shabd.

Our object is to be absorbed in Shabd. We must have someone to love. In order to give up our attachment for people and things of this world, we must have something higher and better to cling to. The Master has already traveled the path, and if we attach ourselves to him with love and devotion, he will lead us back to our True Home.

There are so many problems and obstacles on the way that we need the assistance of a living Master, who has traversed the path, to help us on the way. The Master really does not need our love, but it is to our advantage to surrender ourselves to him and concentrate on him. He transfers this love, and that aids us in withdrawing our attention and affections from worldly objects and people. Of course we are to love our fellow creatures, but in a detached manner of selfless service in his name, and without passion or the idea of possession.

Sant Mat does not believe in forcing anyone. The object of satsang for non-initiates is only to lay our cards on the table, so to speak, and let them decide for themselves. It is our duty to help the sincere seekers and give them all available information on the subject. Those who are destined to do so will automatically accept the Master's teachings.

Regarding the so-called innocent pleasures, the more we indulge in them, the more we scatter our mind in these worldly things. Our object is to *concentrate the mind*. The very fact that we long for these pleasures is proof that we have not sufficiently withdrawn to enjoy the real Bliss inside.

Even these so-called innocent pleasures are not only short-lived, but they also have their negative reactions. However, concentration at the eye center results in lasting benefits to the soul. Besides, whatever instructions the Master has laid out for us are for the good of our own souls, and we should never even think of evading or trespassing them. We should be disciplined soldiers and obey our General. He knows best what is good for us, and we should always try to remain within his orders. Whatever things have been specifically forbidden to us, whether they are good or bad, it is for our own good.

Our aim is to be in touch with the Sound Current, and in order to attain that, we have to abstain from worldly pleasures. But that does *not* mean that we are to enjoy these worldly pleasures if we have not yet had the good fortune to contact the Sound Current. We must work up to it and avoid these worldly pleasures while doing so; for the one leads up and the other leads us down, and it is impossible to go up and down at the same time.

When we contact the Shabd inside, the great internal Bliss will automatically withdraw our attention from all outside or worldly pleasures. But of course we have to work for it. And during the period of training we have to exercise some self-control and observe discipline. It may appear to be difficult, but this is only because the mind is scattered not only throughout the body but also in various interests in this world. And this little sacrifice is nothing in view of the great Goal which we have before us and which will relieve us of all karmic bonds and free us from the cycle of births and deaths.

The best way to draw the Master's help at the time of meeting and answering questions is for you to sit in bhajan for at least one hour before attending the meetings.

* * *

GLOSSARY

ABHYAS—Spiritual practice, spiritual exercise.

ABHYASI—One who performs abhyas.

AHANKAR—Egotism or egoism; pride, haughtiness, conceit.

AKASH—Sky, heavens; matter that surrounds the earth beyond the air ('ether', for want of a better word).

AKASH BANI—Sound from the sky, heavenly melody, voice or teachings from heaven; esoterically, the Voice of God, Shabd, Word, Logos, Sound Current.

ANAHAD SHABD—Unstruck Sound, Unstruck Music; the Word or the spiritual Sound which is present in everyone, and can be heard under proper conditions.

ANAMI—The Nameless; the Absolute; the ruler of the eighth and highest spiritual region.

ARJUN DEV, GURU—The fifth Guru in the line of Guru Nanak.

ASANAS—Postures; usually yogic postures.

ATMA—Soul; spirit.

AWAGAWAN—Coming and going; cycle of birth and death.

BANG-I-ASMANI—The Muslim name for Akash Bani.

BANI—Teachings, particularly of the Saints, whether oral or written; esoterically, the inner Sound or Shabd.

BHAJAN—A form of spiritual practice; constant dwelling on the Lord; applying the spirit to the internal Word or Shabd, also called Surat Shabd Yoga.

BHAKTI—Devotion; worship.

BHANDARA—Religious feast; large-scale feeding of people; esoterically, the internal spiritual feast.

BHILNI—The feminine of *bhil*, a tribe of low-class untouchables of dark color, living in the central hills of India.

BIREH, VIREH or BIRHA—The pain of separation, intense longing; pain of one who has been separated from the beloved.

BRAHMAN—The priestly class; the first and the highest of the four castes into which Hindu society was divided, the other three being: Kshatriya—the regal and warrior class; Vaisya—trading and agricultural classes; Sudra—menial and unskilled labor.

BRAHMAND—Literally, the egg of Brahm; the entire universe over which Brahm has jurisdiction.

CHAKRA—'Wheel'; the six energy centers in the body.

CHATRAK or PAPIHA—Rainbird; so called because it will drink no water other than fresh rain water; it will die of thirst rather than drink anything else.

CHAURASI—Literally means eighty-four, hence 'the wheel of eighty-four'; the name indicates the eighty-four lakh species or eight million four hundred thousand species into which the soul may have to incarnate; the whirlpool or wheel of transmigration.

DADU—Sixteenth-century Saint of Rajputana, well known for his bold utterances in beautiful poetry.

DARSHAN—Implies looking intently at the Master with one-pointed attention.

DAYA—Mercy, grace.

DERA—'Tent, camp'; here refers to Dera Baba Jaimal Singh, the Radha Soami Colony near Beas.

DHARAM RAI—The 'King Judge', who administers reward or punishment after death, according to the karmas of the souls. However, the initiated soul is not under his jurisdiction because the Master himself takes care of the soul, and he tempers justice with mercy.

DHUNATMAK NAM—Inexpressible, primal Sound, which cannot be spoken or written, nor can it be heard with the physical ears; another name for Shabd. *See also* NAM.

DHYAN—Contemplation; a form of spiritual practice; esoterically, beholding the form of the Master within.

GHAZEE—Any Muslim who has taken a vow to kill kafirs.

GUNAS—The three attributes or qualities: *sattva* (pleasure, light), *rajas* (action, delusion) and *tamas* (inertia, pain, darkness).

GURBANI—Literally, teachings of the Guru; esoterically, Nam, Shabd or Word.

GURDWARA—Name used by the Sikhs for their house of worship.

GURMUKH—Literally, one whose face is turned towards the Guru; one who has completely surrendered himself to the Guru; one who is guided by the Guru. A highly advanced soul.

GURMUKHTA—The quality of being a Gurmukh; devotion and surrender to the Guru; obedience.

GURU BHAKTI—Devotion to Guru.

GYAN—Knowledge; true knowledge; spiritual knowledge; spiritual wisdom; spiritual enlightenment.

HAR MANDIR—God's temple; esoterically, the human body as the temple of the Living God.

HAR RAS—Literally, God's nectar or elixir; hence God's love.

HOMEN—Egotism, egoism, I-ness, ego-consciousness; separateness.

HUKAM—Order, command; esoterically, Shabd, Nam or Word.

HUZUR MAHARAJ JI—In this book refers to Maharaj Baba Sawan Singh Ji.

ISME-I-AZIM—'The greatest name'; Shabd, Sound, Word.

JAP or JAPA—Recitation; prayer; mental repetition of the Name of God.

JIVA—Living being; the individual or unliberated soul.

JIVATMA—Individual soul; spirit embodied in the physical form.

JOT—Light, flame; esoterically, the light of the first spiritual region, Sahansdal Kanwal.

KA'ABA—A place of Muslim pilgrimage in Mecca.

KABIR SAHIB—A well-known Saint who lived in Benares (Kashi), and preached and practiced Surat Shabd Yoga. He condemned the follies and the external observances of Hindus and Muslims alike.

KALAM-I-ILLAHI—Voice of God; Shabd, Word, Sound Current.

KALMA—Arabic for Bani.

KAM—Lust; desire, sensory tendencies; any outward tendencies of the mind.

KARMA—Action and reaction; the law of action and reaction; the fruit or result of past thoughts, words and deeds. There are three types of karma:

1. *Prarabdh* or *Pralabdh*–That portion of our karma which is allotted to this life and is responsible for our present existence; also called fate or destiny.

2. *Kriyaman*–The result or fruit of new actions performed during the present life.

3. *Sanchit* or *Sinchit*–Those karmas which still remain to be taken out of our own stored-up lot and are to be worked off or to bear fruit in future incarnations.

KARM KAND or KARAM—Rituals and rites, ceremonies and outward observances of the various religions.

KRIYAMAN—*See* KARMA.

KUN—Muslim name for God, meaning Allah the High, the All-in-All; also means Shabd or Word.

MAHABHARAT—The great epic poem of the Hindus, the main subject of which is the war between the Pandavas and the Kauravas.

MANMUKH—Literally, facing the mind; that is, he who obeys the dictates of the mind; a devotee of the mind and of the ways of the world.

MAUJ—Wave; will; especially the will or pleasure of the Satguru or of the Supreme Being.

MAYA—Illusion or delusion, deception, unreality; phenomenal universe; all that which is not eternal, is not real or true, is called 'maya'; it appears but is not; it conceals the vision of God from our sight.

MEHR—Grace, love, kindness, friendship, mercy.

MUKTI—Liberation; salvation; redemption; emancipation.

MUNI—Holy man, sage, devotee; literally, he who hears or experiences.

NAD—Sound, Shabd; Word; inner Music.

NAM—Name; the same as Shabd, Word or Logos; the Immortal Creator. Nam is of two kinds; *varnatmak* (that which can be expressed or uttered) and *dhunatmak* (that which can be heard only within as Nad or Shabd). *Varnatmak nam* acts as a pointer and leads to the real or *dhunatmak Nam* within, which is not really a word but a Power that emanates from the Supreme Being.

NAM BHAKTI—Devotion to Nam.

NAMDEV—Fourteenth-century Saint, born in Maharashtra; he spent the last 18 years of his life in the village of Ghuman, Punjab.

NAM RAS—The elixir of Nam. The soul drinks that heavenly nectar within and enjoys supreme bliss.

NANAK, GURU—Well-known Saint, born in Punjab, who traveled widely, spreading the message of Nam. His compositions were preserved by his successors and form the basis of the Adi Granth.

NAR NARAYAN or NAR NARAYANI DEH—'Human body divine', the life or form in which the soul can realize God.

NIRAT—The soul's power of seeing.

NIRVAN—The state of complete absorption in meditation.

OMKAR—Brahm; esoterically, Lord of the second spiritual region.

PALTU SAHIB—A Hindu Saint noted for his bold utterances and out-spoken description of the mystic path.

PANDAVAS—The five sons of Pandu, the brother of Dhritarashtra, king of Hastina-pura. The Pandavas were deprived of their rightful inheritance, which was the cause of the great war between the Pandavas and the Kauravas, known as the *Mahabharat*.

PARMATMA—Literally, supreme soul; God.

PARAM SANT—Supreme Saint; a Saint who has reached the highest stage.

PAR BRAHMAND—Spiritual region beyond Brahmand.

PIND—The physical body; the physical and material universe; region of lower mind and matter.

PRALABDH—*See* KARMA.

PRAN or PRANA—Vital force; vital air, the control and regulation of which is the basis of the system known as Pranayam; essence.

PREM—Love.

PUNYA—Religious or spiritual merit; charity.

RAIDAS or RAVIDAS—Well-known Saint of northern India; a con-temporary of Kabir.

RAM DAS JI—The fourth Guru in the line of Guru Nanak.

RAM NAM—Same as Nam.

RISHI—A sage; literally, one who sees.

SACHI BANI—True teachings, true Word; the same as Gurbani.

SACH KHAND, SAT DESH, SAT LOK or NIJ DHAM—Literally, the true or imperishable region; esoterically, the fifth spiritual region, presided over by Sat Purush.

SADH or SADHU—Holy man, following a path of spiritual discipline; sometimes the name is applied to an Adept or true Saint; esoterically, a devotee who has reached the third spiritual stage and thus has crossed the region of mind and matter.

SADHAN—Spiritual discipline, practice; mode of worship.

SAHAJ or SEHJ—Easy, natural, real; esoterically, the transition from the state of 'becoming' into that of 'being' one with the Su-preme Lord.

SAHANSDAL KANWAL—Thousand-petalled lotus; appellation of the first spiritual region.

SAKAT—Irreligious; manmukh; one who seeks power.

SAMADHI or SMADHI—A state of deep concentration in which all consciousness of the outer world is transcended.

SANGAT—Congregation.

SANSKARAS—Impressions, both good and bad; spiritual outlook and spiritual fitness; spiritual bent of mind; tendencies due to impressions from past lives.

SANT SATGURU—A Saint who is also a spiritual teacher. Everyone who has reached the fifth spiritual region is a Saint, but not all Saints accept followers or are designated to teach. Hence every true Master or Satguru is a Saint, but not all Saints are Satgurus.

SAT—True; actual; right; fit; essence; existence; permanent; abiding; eternal.

SAT DESH—The same as Sach Khand.

SATGURU—A Master or spiritual teacher who has access to the fifth spiritual region.

SAT LOK—Same as Sach Khand.

SAT PURUSH—God; True Lord.

SEVA—Service.

SHABD—Word, Sound; spiritual Sound, Audible Life Stream, Sound Current. The same as the Word in the Bible; *Kalma, Isme-i-Azim, Bang-i-Asmani* or *Kalam-i-Illahi* in the Koran; the *Nad* or *Udgit* in the Vedas; and *Nam, Ram Nam, Hari Nam, Gurbani, Bani, Ajapajap, Akathkatha, Har Ras, Har Jas, Har Simran* and *Dhun* in the Adi Granth.

SHAH RAG or SHAH RUG—Literally, royal vein, but this does not refer to a vein in the physical body. It is the central current or canal in the finer body, which is located and traversed by means of spiritual practice according to the instructions of a true Master. It is also called Sushmana or Sushumna.

SHAR‘A or SHAR’IAT—Muslim religious law; Quranic law and ritual.

SHUDRAS—The fourth or lowest order of Hindu society; the menials and laborers.

SIMRAN—‘Repetition’; repetition of the five Holy Names according to the instructions of a perfect Master.

SINCHIT—*See* KARMA.

SUNN—Void, emptiness, vacuum; name of the third spiritual region.

SURAT—Soul; consciousness; inner attention.

SUSHMANA or SUSHUMNA—Same as Shah Rug.

TAP—The practice of austerities; penance.

TATTWA—'Element'. The entire universe is made up of five tattwas: earth (*prithvi*), water (*jal*), air (*vayu*), fire (*agni*) and ether (*akash*).

TISRA TIL—Third eye; the seat or headquarters of the mind and the soul in the human body, situated between the two eyebrows; since the nine doors of the body (eyes, ears, nose, mouth, etc.) lead outward, this is also called the Tenth Door or Tenth Gate, and is the only one which leads within, to the spiritual regions.

TRIKUTI—Three Prominences; appellation of the second spiritual region; also called Musallasi by the Muslim Saints, as it means three-cornered; Gagan is the sky of Trikuti.

TULSI SAHIB—Nineteenth-century Saint who settled in Hathras, near Agra; exponent of Sant Mat and author of *Ghat Ramayan*. Swami Ji came in contact with him.

VAH GURU or WAH-I-GURU—Name for God, the Supreme Lord.

VAIRAGYA—Detachment from the world and its pleasures; renunciation; asceticism.

VARNATMAK NAM—Expressible, spoken or written names. There are two forms of Nam or Shabd—one is varnatmak and the other is dhunatmak. *See also* NAM.

YAGYA—Sacrifice; a ritual or religious ceremony, which in ancient times often included the sacrifice of an animal.

YAMA—God of death; lord of the nether regions.

YUG or YUGA—Age or cycle of time. Hindu tradition divides time into four yugas; we are now passing through the fourth, Kali Yuga (the Dark or Iron Age).

INDEX

⎡ **P** denotes page numbers; ⎤
⎣ **L** denotes letter numbers ⎦

⎡ **P** denotes page numbers; ⎤
⎣ **L** denotes letter numbers ⎦

$$\begin{bmatrix} \text{P} & \text{denotes page numbers;} \\ \text{L} & \text{denotes letter numbers} \end{bmatrix}$$

⎡ P denotes page numbers; ⎤
⎣ L denotes letter numbers ⎦

⎡P denotes page numbers;⎤
⎣L denotes letter numbers⎦

INFORMATION AND BOOKS
ARE AVAILABLE FROM:

The Secretary
Radha Soami Satsang Beas
P.O. Dera Baba Jaimal Singh 143204
District Amritsar, Punjab, India

Radha Soami Book Dept.
P.O. Box 242
Gardena, CA 90247 USA
Phone 213-329-5635

CANADA

Dr. J. Khanna, 5550 McMaster Road, Vancouver V6T 1J8, B.C.

Mr. Reginald S. Davis, R.R. 1 Crapaud, Prince Edward Island, COA 1JO

U.S.A.

Mr. Roland G. deVries, 10901 Mill Spring Drive, Nevada City, California 95959

Col. E. R. Berg, U.S. Air Force (Ret'd.), 4001 Mavelle Drive, Minneapolis, Minn. 55435

Mr. Roy E. Ricks, 651 Davis Street, Melrose Park, Ill. 60160

Mr. Henry F. Weekley, 2121 No. Ocean Blvd., Apt. 1108E, Boca Raton, Fla. 33431

MEXICO

Mr. Jorge Angel Santana, Cameta 2821, Jardines Del Bosque, Guadalajara, Jalisco

SOUTH AMERICA

Dr. Gonzalo Vargas N., P.O. Box 2666, Quito, Ecuador

Mr. Leopoldo Luks, Ave. Maracay, Urb. Las Palmas, Qta. Luksenburg, Caracas, Venezuela

Mrs. Rajni B. Manglani, c/o Bhagwan's Store, 18 Water St., Georgetown, Guyana

WEST INDIES

Mr. Thakurdas Chatlani, 2A Gittins Avenue, Maraval, Trinidad

Mr. Sean Finnegan, P.O. Box 2314, Port-au-Prince, Haiti

Mr. Bhagwandas Kessaram, c/o Kiddies Corner, Swant Street, Bridgetown, Barbados

ENGLAND
Mrs. F. E. Wood, c/o Lloyd's Bank, 20 North Street, Leatherhead, Surrey

SWEDEN
Mr. T. Gunther, Skakeltorp 6018, 441 00 Alingsas

DENMARK
Ms. Inge Gregersen, Askevenget–15, 2830 Virum

HOLLAND
Mr. Jacob Hofstra, Geulwijk 6, 3831 LM Leusden

WEST GERMANY
Mr. Rudolf Walberg, Falkenstr. 18, D–6232 Bad Soden/Taunus

AUSTRIA
Mr. Hansjorg Hammerer, Sezenweingasse 10, A–5020, Salzburg

SWITZERLAND
Mr. Olivier de Coulon, Route de Lully, 1111 Tolochenaz

FRANCE
Count Pierre de Proyart, 7 Quai Voltaire, 75007 Paris

SPAIN
Mr. H. W. Balani, Balani's International, P.O. Box 486, Malaga

PORTUGAL
Mr. Alberto C. Ferreira, R. Machado dos Santos 20, 2775 Parede

GIBRALTAR
Mr. Arjan M. Thadani, Radha Soami Satsang Beas, P.O. Box 283

ITALY
Mr. Ted Goodman, Via Garigliano 27, Rome 00198

GREECE
Dr. Constantine Siopoulos, Thrakis 7, 145 61 Kifissia

CYPRUS
Mr. Hercules Achilleos, Kyriakou Matsi 18,
    Pallouriotissa—T.K. 9077, Nicosia

WEST AFRICA
Mr. Krishin Vaswani, Vaan-Ahn Enterprise Ltd., P.O.Box No. 507, Monrovia, Liberia

Mr. Nanik N. Balani, Kewalram (Nig.) Ltd., P.O. Box No. 320, Lagos, Nigeria

EAST AFRICA
Mr. Sylvester Kakooza, P.O. Box 31381, Kampala, Uganda

Mr. Sohan Singh Bharj, P.O. Box 47036, Nairobi, Kenya

Mr. D. N. Pandit, United Timber Traders Ltd., P.O. Box No. 1963, Dar-es-Salaam, Tanzania

Mr. David Bowskill, P.O. Box 11012, Chingola, Zambia

Mr. Vernon Lowrie, P.O. Box 690, Harare City, Zimbabwe

SOUTH AFRICA
Mr. Sam Busa, P.O. Box 41355, Craighall, Transvaal 2024

Mr. R. Attwell, P.O. Box 5702, Durban 4000

MASCARENE ISLANDS
Mr. D. S. Sumboo, Harbour View I, Flat Cardinal No. 15, Justice Street, Port Louis, Mauritius

ISRAEL
Mrs. H. Mandelbaum, P.O. Box 2815, Tel Aviv–61000

U.A.E.
Mr. Jiwatram Lakhiani, P.O. Box 1449, Dubai

KUWAIT
Mr. & Mrs. Ghassan Alghanem, P.O. Box No. 25549, Safat, Kuwait

AFGHANISTAN
Mr. Manak Singh, c/o Manaco, P.O. Box 3163, Kabul

SRI LANKA
Mr. D. H. Jiwat, Geekay Ltd., 33 Bankshall Street, Colombo–11

NEW ZEALAND
Mr. Tony Waddicor, P.O. Box 5331, Wellesley St. P.O., Auckland 1

AUSTRALIA

Dr. John Potter, Long Wood Road, Heathfield, South Australia 5153

Mr. A. J. Walker, 8/445, Canning Highway, Melville,
Western Australia 6156

INDONESIA

Mr. G. L. Nanwani, Yayasan, Radhasoami Satsang Beas,
JL. Kelinci Raya No. 32A, Jakarta Pusat

Mr. Odharmal Chotrani, 51 Djl. Bubutan, P.O. Box 144, Surabaya

SINGAPORE

Mr. Bhagwan Asnani, 1806 King's Mansion, Singapore–1543

MALAYSIA

Mr. N. Pal, c/o Muhibbah Travels Agency, Sdn. Bhd.,
46 Jalan Tanku Abdul Rahman, Kuala Lumpur 01–07

THAILAND

Mr. Harmohinder Singh Sethi, Sawan Textiles, 154 Serm Sin Kha,
Sampheng Street, Bangkok–2

HONG KONG

Mrs. Cami Moss, Hongkong Hilton, G.P.O. Box No. 42

Mr. Gobind Sabnani, G.P.O. Box 3906

PHILIPPINES

Mr. Kay Sham, P.O. Box 2346 MCC, Makati, Metro Manila

JAPAN

Mr. L. H. Parwani, Radha Soami Satsang Beas, 2–18 Nakajimadori
1–Chome, Aotani, Fukiai-ku, Kobe–651

*   *   *   *   *   *   *   *

FOR OTHER FOREIGN ORDERS WRITE TO:

Mr. Krishin Babani, Buona Casa Bldg., 2nd Floor, Sir P.M. Road,
Fort Bombay–400 001, India

Addresses changed since this book was printed:

BOOKS ON THIS SCIENCE

Swami Ji Maharaj
1. *Sar Bachan*

Baba Jaimal Singh
2. *Spiritual Letters* (to Huzur Maharaj Sawan Singh: 1896–1903)

Huzur Maharaj Sawan Singh
3. *Discourses on Sant Mat*
4. *Philosophy of the Masters* (*Gurmat Sidhant*), 5 vols. (an encyclopedia on the teachings of the Saints)
5. *My Submission* (introduction to *Philosophy of the Masters*)
6. *Philosophy of the Masters* (abridged)
7. *Tales of the Mystic East* (as narrated in satsangs)
8. *Spiritual Gems* (letters: 1919–1948)
9. *The Dawn of Light* (letters: 1911–1934)

Sardar Bahadur Jagat Singh Maharaj
10. *The Science of the Soul* (discourses and letters: 1948–1951)

Maharaj Charan Singh
11. *Die to Live* (answers to questions on meditation)
12. *Divine Light* (discourses and letters: 1959–1964)
13. *The Path* (first part of *Divine Light*)
14. *Light on Saint Matthew*
15. *Light on Sant Mat* (discourses and letters: 1952–1958)
16. *Quest for Light* (letters: 1965–1971)
17. *Light on Saint John*
18. *Spiritual Discourses*
19. *Spiritual Heritage* (from tape-recorded talks)
20. *The Master Answers* (to audiences in America: 1964)
21. *Thus Saith the Master* (to audiences in America: 1970)
22. *Truth Eternal* (a discourse)

Books about these Masters

1. *Call of the Great Master*—Diwan Daryai Lal Kapur
2. *The Living Master*—Katherine Wason
3. *With a Great Master in India*—Dr. Julian P. Johnson
4. *With the Three Masters*, 3 vols.—from the diary of
    Rai Sahib Munshi Ram

Books on Sant Mat in general

1. *A Soul's Safari*—Netta Pfeifer
2. *In Search of the Way*—Flora E. Wood
3. *Kabir, the Great Mystic*—Isaac A. Ezekiel
4. *Liberation of the Soul*—J. Stanley White, Ph.D.
5. *Message Divine*—Shanti Sethi
6. *Mystic Bible*—Dr. Randolph Stone
7. *Mysticism, the Spiritual Path*, 2 vols.—Prof. Lekh Raj Puri
8. *Radha Soami Teachings*—Prof. Lekh Raj Puri
9. *Ringing Radiance*—Sir Colin Garbett
10. *Sant Mat and the Bible*—Narain Das
11. *Sarmad, Jewish Saint of India*—Isaac A. Ezekiel
12. *Teachings of the Gurus*—Prof. Lekh Raj Puri
13. *The Inner Voice*—Colonel C.W. Sanders
14. *The Mystic Philosophy of Sant Mat*—Peter Fripp
15. *The Path of the Masters*—Dr. Julian P. Johnson
16. *Yoga and the Bible*—Joseph Leeming

Mystics of the East Series

1. *Saint Paltu*—Isaac A. Ezekiel
2. *Saint Namdev, His Life and Teachings*—J. R. Puri and
    V. K. Sethi
3. *Tulsi Sahib, Saint of Hathras*—J. R. Puri and V. K. Sethi
4. *Tukaram, Saint of Maharashtra*—C. Rajwade
5. *Dadu, the Compassionate Mystic*—K. N. Upadhyaya, Ph.D.
6. *Mira, the Divine Lover*—V. K. Sethi
7. *Guru Ravidas, Life and Teachings*—K. N. Upadhyaya, Ph.D.
8. *Guru Nanak, His Mystic Teachings*—J. R. Puri
9. *Kabir, the Weaver of God's Name*—V. K. Sethi